THE CONTINUOUS PATH

AMERIND STUDIES IN ANTHROPOLOGY
Series Editor **Christine R. Szuter**

THE CONTINUOUS PATH

PUEBLO MOVEMENT AND THE ARCHAEOLOGY OF BECOMING

EDITED BY
Samuel Duwe and Robert W. Preucel

THE UNIVERSITY OF ARIZONA PRESS
TUCSON

The University of Arizona Press
www.uapress.arizona.edu

We respectfully acknowledge the University of Arizona is on the land and territories of Indigenous peoples. Today, Arizona is home to twenty-two federally recognized tribes, with Tucson being home to the O'odham and the Yaqui. Committed to diversity and inclusion, the University strives to build sustainable relationships with sovereign Native Nations and Indigenous communities through education offerings, partnerships, and community service.

© 2019 by The Arizona Board of Regents
All rights reserved. Published 2019
First paperback edition 2024

ISBN-13: 978-0-8165-3928-4 (cloth)
ISBN-13: 978-0-8165-5500-0 (paper)
ISBN-13: 978-0-8165-3992-5 (ebook)

Cover design by Sara Thaxton
Cover art: *Green Mobile* © Victor Masayesva Jr. "Placing the green automobile (and the wreck in the yard) below the ancestral ruins at Kawestima asserts that we still live here at Kawestima. The seemingly empty, uninhabited ruins are in fact anticipating our return. They are waiting for us when we return by foot, car, wind, cloud, rain, or memory. This is my tribute to the ancestors who have gone before and who await us, looking for the swirling dust that signifies our transport-time" (Victor Masayesva Jr., *Husk of Time: The Photographs of Victor Masayesva*, 91).

Publication of this book is made possible in part by a subsidy from Brown University.

Library of Congress Cataloging-in-Publication Data
Names: Duwe, Samuel, editor. | Preucel, Robert W., editor.
Title: The continuous path : Pueblo movement and the archaeology of becoming / edited by Samuel Duwe and Robert W. Preucel.
Other titles: Amerind studies in anthropology.
Description: Tucson : The University of Arizona Press, 2019. | Series: Amerind studies in anthropology | Includes bibliographical references and index.
Identifiers: LCCN 2018040713 | ISBN 9780816539284 (cloth : alk. paper)
Subjects: LCSH: Pueblo Indians—History. | Pueblo philosophy.
Classification: LCC E99.P9 C728 2019 | DDC 978.9004/974—dc23 LC record available at https://lccn.loc.gov/2018040713

Printed in the United States of America
♾ This paper meets the requirements of ANSI/NISO Z39.48-1992 (Permanence of Paper).

In memory of Damian Garcia and Saul Hedquist

Sadly, shortly before publication we received word of the untimely passing of two of this volume's contributors, Damian Garcia and Saul Hedquist, due to wholly unrelated circumstances.

Damian, whose work and love for the history and culture of his community is illustrated in chapter 1, was the Pueblo of Acoma's inaugural tribal historic preservation officer. During his all too brief tenure, Damian was an advocate of an engaged cultural resource management approach, which respects his Pueblo's traditional values and views archaeology as a tool with which Acoma can fulfill its sacred obligation to be a steward of its homeland and a trustee of its cultural inheritance.

Saul's work, reflected in his contribution to chapter 5, embodies the best of contemporary archaeology: solid empirical research framed through a lens of collaboration and respect. He embraced a holistic approach to anthropology that included conducting ethnography for and with the Hopi and other tribes and employing cutting-edge archaeological science, the latter of which was informed by his deep appreciation for the landscapes and histories of the Pueblo people.

These fine men will be dearly missed by their many friends and colleagues. It is with deep respect and fondness for Saul and Damian that we dedicate this book to their memory.

There is a song which goes like this:

> Let us go again, brother; let us go for the shiwana.
> Let us make our prayer songs.
> We will go now. Now we are going.
> We will bring back the shiwana.
> They are coming now. Now, they are coming.
> It is flowing. The plants are growing.
> Let us go again, brother; let us go for the shiwana.

A man makes his prayers; he sings his songs. He considers all that is important and special to him, his home, children, his language, the self that he is. He must make spiritual and physical preparation before anything else. Only then does anything begin.

A man leaves, he encounters all manners of things. He has adventures, meets people, acquires knowledge, goes different places; he is always looking. Sometimes the traveling is hazardous; sometimes he finds meaning and sometimes he is destitute. But he continues; he must. His traveling is a prayer as well, and he must keep on.

A man returns, and even the returning has moments of despair and tragedy. But there is beauty and there is joy. At times he is confused, and at times he sees with utter clarity. It is all part of the traveling that is a prayer. There are things he must go through before he can bring back what he seeks, before he can return to himself.

The man comes and falls. The shiwana have heeded the man, and they have come. The man has brought back the rain. It falls, and it is nourishing. The man returns to the strength that his selfhood is, his home, people, his language, the knowledge of who he is. The cycle has been traveled; life has beauty and meaning, and it will continue because life has no end.

—Simon J. Ortiz, "Prologue"

CONTENTS

Preface — xi

Introduction: Engaging with Pueblo Movement — 1
Robert W. Preucel and Samuel Duwe

Part I. On Becoming

1. Movement as an Acoma Way of Life — 37
   Damian Garcia and Kurt F. Anschuetz

2. Movement Encased in Tradition and Stone: Hemish Migration, Land Use, and Identity — 60
   Paul Tosa, Matthew J. Liebmann, T. J. Ferguson, and John R. Welch

3. Anshe K'yan'a and Zuni Traditions of Movement — 78
   Maren P. Hopkins, Octavius Seowtewa, Graydon Lennis Berlin, Jacob Campbell, Chip Colwell, and T. J. Ferguson

4. Tewa Origins and Middle Places — 96
   Samuel Duwe and Patrick J. Cruz

5. To and From Hopi: Negotiating Identity Through Migration, Coalescence, and Closure at the Homol'ovi Settlement Cluster — 124
   Samantha G. Fladd, Claire S. Barker, E. Charles Adams, Dwight C. Honyouti, and Saul L. Hedquist

Part II. Always Becoming

6. Seeking Strength and Protection: Tewa Mobility During the Pueblo Revolt Period — 149
   Joseph Aguilar and Robert W. Preucel

7. Apache, Tiwa, and Back Again: Ethnic Shifting
   in the American Southwest   166
   Severin Fowles and B. Sunday Eiselt

8. Moving Ideas, Staying at Home: Change and
   Continuity in Mid-Eighteenth-Century Tewa Pottery   195
   Bruce Bernstein, Erik Fender, and Russell Sanchez

9. Toward the Center: Movement and Becoming
   at the Pueblo of Pojoaque   222
   Samuel Villarreal Catanach and Mark R. Agostini

10. Getting Accustomed to the Light   242
    Joseph H. Suina

    Commentary: Pueblo Perspectives on
    Movement and Becoming   254
    Paul Tosa and Octavius Seowtewa

    Contributors   261
    Index   271

PREFACE

This book is the result of our desire to rethink aspects of southwestern archaeology by taking Pueblo conceptions of history and philosophy seriously. With this goal in mind, we invited Native and non-Native scholars and community members who are leaders in collaborative archaeologies to join us in a session titled "Pueblo Movement and the Archaeology of Becoming" at the 82nd Annual Meeting (2017) of the Society for American Archaeology (SAA) in Vancouver, British Columbia. Our aim was to present a series of collaborative papers of wide geographical breadth (from Hopi to Taos) that explored Pueblo movement and history and that emphasized continuities from ancient times to the present day. We are particularly indebted to T. J. Ferguson, who graciously helped to shape the session, particularly in connecting us with new colleagues (and new friends) and in assisting Paul Tosa and Octavius Seowtewa in preparing their comments. We also thank Tobi Brimsek, the former executive director of the SAA, who reduced the costs of attending the meeting for our non-archaeologist Pueblo colleagues. The original session included most of the authors in this volume, as well as a wonderful paper by Porter Swentzell, who unfortunately had obligations that precluded him from being included here. However, anyone who was in the room that Thursday morning will never forget his telling of the story of Turkey Girl and its connection to the importance of Tewa places.

We were delighted with the vigorous discussions that began at the SAA session (both during the question-answer portion and afterward) and were thrilled to be invited to continue these at an SAA Amerind Seminar. The resulting workshop, held over four days in September 2017 at the Amerind Foundation in in Dragoon, Arizona, was among the most intellectually and emotionally satisfying experience of our academic careers. The participants were both Pueblo and non-Pueblo, and although we had different backgrounds and life experience, all were passionate about Pueblo history. Our dialogue, steeped in archaeological language, was guided by the interests and concerns of our Pueblo colleagues. In particular, Paul Tosa and Octavius Seowtewa played an integral role in highlighting the essential conceptual elements of this project. Their experience as participants in the seminar is recounted in the final chapter, which can also be read as an alternative introduction to this volume. We wish to thank Christine Szuter, the director of the Amerind Foundation, for providing a supportive environment and being one of the biggest champions of this project.

We wish to thank two Pueblo artists whose creative practices continue to inspire us. First, we thank Victor Masayesva Jr. for the image we have used on the cover of the book. This image appears in his book of photography *Husk of Time: The Photographs of Victor Masayesva*. We were drawn to this image because of the way it juxtaposes senses of time, space, and technology. This image happens to be a favorite of Sev Fowles and, indeed, he brought it to our attention. Second, we thank Simon Ortiz for allowing us to publish his poem "Prologue" from his amazing book *Woven Stone*. This poem beautifully expresses the idea of movement as a prayer, linking lives, *shiwana*, clouds, rain, and growth in the endless cycle of Pueblo life.

The process of transforming our thoughtful discussions into the book you are holding now required an enormous effort by a large number of people. First and foremost, we wish to thank our contributors, who were asked to write (and revise multiple times) complex and collaborative papers. Each chapter stands alone as an important contribution, and we are honored that they chose to be a part of this project. The Amerind Foundation secured funding and support for the seminar series and this publication. Allyson Carter, Scott De Herrera, and the staff at the University of Arizona Press gently but firmly encouraged us to submit our manuscript on an expedited schedule, and through kindness they helped push us across the finish line. This process was aided by two anonymous reviewers, who provided thoughtful and timely critiques and suggestions on the chapters and the volume as a whole.

Finally, we would like to express our deepest gratitude to our families. Sam would like to thank Kate Newton, his wife, and his son, Benjamin, for their patience and understanding as he spent far too much time in front of his computer. Bob would like to thank his wife, Leslie Atik, for her longstanding support and partnership that began on the Pajarito Plateau over thirty years ago!

While we are proud of this finished volume, we are most excited by the unfinished and ongoing discussions between the archaeologists, anthropologists, and tribal scholars and community members brought together over the course of this project. We hope that our friendships will continue to result in scholarship based on mutual respect and will inspire others to do the same.

Samuel Duwe
Robert W. Preucel

Introduction
Engaging with Pueblo Movement

Robert W. Preucel and Samuel Duwe

For the Pueblo Indian people of the North American Southwest, movement is enshrined in tradition and marked by pathways, sacred places, and ancestral villages. Movement figures prominently in their origin traditions: complex accounts of groups of people coming together and moving apart as each people sought and found their "middle place" and in the process established unique relationships with each other and the land. Although movement was sharply constrained during the Spanish colonial period, the Pueblos strategically employed mobility as acts of cultural survival and revitalization. And this use of mobility continued throughout the Mexican and American occupations of their ancestral landscapes. Thus, the process of movement is ongoing and never complete, for today, as in the past, Pueblo people move frequently between their villages for feast days, marriage ceremonies, jobs, and socializing. They also temporarily leave their communities to attend university, serve in the military, and hold jobs in major cities. Yet all the while, the people are intimately tethered to the traditional homelands defined by their villages, sacred peaks, and life-sustaining rivers.

The dominant image of Pueblo people, for both anthropologists and the public alike, is that of sedentary village farmers. Places like Acoma's Sky City and Taos Pueblo evoke a timeless permanence that is well founded: many villages have been lived in for over seven centuries. Anthropologists have therefore struggled with reconciling the paradoxical nature of Pueblo life—perpetual movement and village-centered life—a sentiment embodied in Robin Fox's (1967:24) description of the Pueblos as "urbanized nomads." Archaeologists, in particular, have periodically embraced and rejected the dynamism of Pueblo movement in interpreting the Pueblo past over the last century. However, in recent decades southwestern archaeology, spurred by collaboration with the Pueblos and theoretical changes in the field, has begun to acknowledge that movement was (and is) a central component of Pueblo history (Lyons 2003; Nelson and Strawhacker 2011; Ortman 2012). Movement shaped the identities and worlds of the historic and modern Pueblo people. According to Severin Fowles (2013:258), "Migrations make history; new landscapes constitute new futures."

As the chapters in this volume detail, movement must be seen as more than an economic opportunity or a response to social conflict. Rather, it is constituent of the Pueblo way of being. Tessie Naranjo (1995), from Santa Clara Pueblo, states that movement is one of the "big ideological concepts" of Pueblo thought because it is necessary for the perpetuation of life. The people, as one with the larger cosmos that includes clouds, wind, spirits, blessings, and animals, are in a state of "constant re-creation and transformation" (Swentzell 1993:141). Finding harmony and balance in a dynamic world of tensions and oppositions, a process the Tewa call "seeking life," requires embracing movement and change. Movement is seen as a never-ending and directed journey toward an ideal existence and a continuous path of becoming. This path began as the Pueblo people emerged from the underworld and sought their middle places, and it continues today and into the future at multiple scales integrating the people, the village, and the individual. The quote at the beginning by the Acoma author Simon J. Ortiz (1992) eloquently exemplifies this point. Written as the prologue to his book of poetry *Woven Stone*, it is a kind of origin story—one that speaks indirectly of his own movements through time and space as a veteran, a poet, a storyteller, a father, and, most of all, a member of Acoma Pueblo. He speaks of a man's travels as a way of gaining knowledge and the return home to a place where that knowledge can be realized and enjoyed. The blessings are flowing, and the rain has come.

The goal of this book is to challenge southwestern archaeologists to take Pueblo concepts of movement as seriously as Pueblo people themselves do. The following chapters—collaborative essays written by archaeologists, anthropologists, and tribal community members—each weave multiple perspectives together to write partial histories of particular Pueblo peoples (figure I.1). Within these histories are stories of movements of people, materials, and ideas and the interconnectedness of all as the Pueblo people find, leave, and return to their middle places. These contributions also take the next critical step, one unusual in an

Introduction

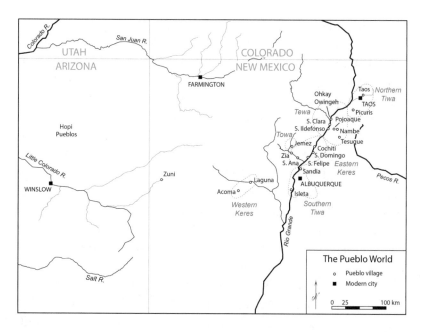

Figure I.1 The location of the modern Pueblos.

archaeological volume: each privileges Pueblo concepts of being and becoming in the interpretation of anthropological data. What results is an emphasis on historical continuities and the understanding that the same concepts of movement that guided the actions of Pueblo people in the past continue into the present, and the future. That is to say, this book is as much about contemporary Pueblo worlds as it is about Pueblo history. Taking them together, we hope to begin to explore what the Tewa call *nah poeh meng*, "the continuous path" of the Pueblo people from the time of emergence to the twenty-first century.

PUEBLO MIGRATIONS AND MOVEMENTS

Southwestern archaeologists have a long history of studying Pueblo Indian migrations and population movements. They have struggled with incorporating movement into explanatory narratives and culture history interpretations and have often made the assumption that movement was an anomalous disruption of "normal" village life (Fowles 2011). Instances of movement have often been regarded as adaptive responses to environmental and social stress, and abandoned villages were understood as parts of failed cultural systems. The concept of movement as a catalyst for culture change has alternatively been embraced and dismissed, a result of larger paradigm shifts in the discipline and a sign of the changing relationships between archaeologists and Pueblo people.

The earliest anthropological studies typically combined ethnography, linguistics, and archaeology to address questions of cultural similarity and difference (Fowler 2000). Scholars such as Frank Hamilton Cushing (1890) and Jesse Walter Fewkes (1900), while primarily interested in the contemporary beliefs and practices of Zuni and Hopi, respectively, spent considerable time trekking into the hills surrounding modern villages to visit ancient sites with their consultants to inquire about the people's histories. Cushing and his contemporaries, including Victor and Cosmos Mindeleff (Mindeleff 1900; Mindeleff 1891), believed that Pueblo oral tradition has a historical basis and hence stories of great migrations and finding middle places could be linked to the archaeological record (Fowler 2000:18). These traditions could also be used to understand the development of modern Pueblo societies at multiple scales from the village to individual clans and societies (Cushing 1890). For example, after gathering clan migration stories from Hopi elders on First Mesa, Fewkes (1904) conducted both survey and excavation in central Arizona to verify these traditions of movement. For these archaeologists, movement was seen as a fundamental concept in Pueblo history, just as it was to the people they studied. This premise stemmed from the close working relationships between archaeologists and Pueblo people and their belief in the unbroken (but evolving) continuity between the present and the past.

The movement of Pueblo people continued to be a significant focus of southwestern archaeology during its maturation in the first half of the twentieth century. Beginning with Clark Wissler's (1917) rejection of the continuity between ethnography and the past, however, archaeologists began to divorce themselves from the work of ethnologists and the voices of Pueblo people. The new archaeology of A. V. Kidder (1924), Nels Nelson (1916), and others defined culture history frameworks independently of ethnographic analogy and relied on newly devised chronological methods and large-scale survey and excavation data. Movement, as the migration of people and the diffusion of ideas, was an important explanatory factor in interpreting this history. For example, Erik Reed (1949) hypothesized a migration of people from the Mesa Verde region to the Rio Grande valley that catalyzed the development of the modern Rio Grande Pueblos, and Emil Haury (1958) examined migrations from the Kayenta-Hopi region to east-central Arizona. Tracking these movements, and the identities of groups of people across the landscape in time, established the baseline for the culture history of the Pueblo world. However, the processes of how and why these movements occurred, and how these shaped the people, remained poorly understood. So, too, were the implications of this movement for contemporary Pueblo people.

In the 1960s, movement, and particularly migration, fell out of favor as an explanatory concept due to the influence of processual archaeology (Anthony 1990). Lewis Binford (1962:218) roundly critiqued what he called "historical explanations," of which migration was an example, as analytically inadequate to account for culture process. As he put it, if migration can be shown to have taken place, then it presents an explanatory problem: what adaptive circumstances, or evolutionary process, induced the migration? He held that archaeologists need to seek explanations of historical events in systemic terms in order to contribute to the further advancement of anthropological theory. Closely related to this was his critique of ethnographic analogy. Binford (1967) famously argued that ethnographic analogy was not a viable interpretive method in and of itself, but rather was a way of proposing testable hypotheses. Some scholars took this as a license to reject any use of ethnographic analogy (Wylie 1985). Steadman Upham (1987), for example, critically reviewed analogy in southwestern archaeology and concluded that the magnitude of the changes during the Spanish contact period were so great as to invalidate its use in prehistoric contexts.

On the strength of these critiques, southwestern archaeologists shifted their emphasis to questions of abandonment and systemic collapse (Cameron and Tomka 1996; Tainter 1988). And yet migration, along with other forms of movement, was difficult to avoid. Linda Cordell (1984:87) observed that since whole regions were abandoned in different time periods, the inhabitants must have gone somewhere and migration into other areas is a logical supposition. An increased interest in the process of aggregation—or the construction of fewer but larger villages—began to drive questions of how people move together to create village life (Adler

1996; Rautman 2000; Spielmann 1998). Scholars began to explore other types and scales of movement related to agriculture and ritual practice, including short-term and seasonal mobility (Nelson and LeBlanc 1986; Powell 1983; Preucel 1991), feasting (Mills 2004, 2007), and pilgrimage (Judge 1989; Malville and Malville 2001). And as sophisticated archaeometric techniques became more common, archaeologists started to acknowledge the large-scale flow of material (namely pottery and obsidian) across the landscape, indicating additional forms of movement involved in trade and exchange. In many cases this movement was viewed through an economic or ecological lens. For example, the migration from Mesa Verde to the Rio Grande relied on push/pull factors relating to available (or lack of) moisture (Ahlstrom et al. 1995), and aggregation was seen as an adaptive measure in an increasingly competitive landscape (Adler et al. 1996).

In the last two decades, southwestern archaeologists have revisited the importance of movement in the Pueblo past (Cabana and Clark 2011; Lyons 2003; Nelson and Strawhacker 2011; Ortman 2012). The results have yielded more sophisticated investigations of different kinds of migration (Ortman and Cameron 2011), the exploration of the social consequences of aggregation (Varien and Potter 2008), the examination of cultural landscapes and memory (Ferguson and Colwell-Chanthaphonh 2006), and an appreciation for large-scale and sophisticated social networks (Mills et al. 2013), among others. Archaeologists working in the historic era have also focused on the ways that the Pueblo people responded to effects of Spanish, Mexican, and American colonialism and enslavement, and particularly how the imposition of heavy-handed policies and the restriction of movement led to cultural reorganization and revitalization (Cameron 2016; Liebmann 2012a; Preucel 2006; Spielmann 2017). Movement is now back on the table.

We attribute this change to three factors. The first of these is the expanding set of theoretical perspectives born from the postprocessualism of the 1980s and 1990s. This includes postcolonial narratives (Liebmann and Rizvi 2010) and Indigenous archaeologies (Smith and Wobst 2005; Watkins 2000) that critique the imposition of Western frameworks on non-Western people. The second factor is the outcome of legislation. Beginning with federally mandated consultation stemming from the Native American Graves Protection and Repatriation Act (NAGPRA), archaeologists and Pueblo people have created institutions and research programs centered on collaboration and addressing questions relevant to multiple parties (Ferguson et al. 1996). Indeed, NAGPRA is challenging archaeologists to reconsider archaeological cultures in social terms (Cameron and Ortman 2017). The third and most important factor is the agency of Native American scholars who are both knowledgeable about and critical of the academy. Rina Swentzell from Santa Clara Pueblo, for example, implored archaeologists to take seriously the knowings of the Pueblo people, for whom movement was a primary concern. She writes, "The Pueblo culture, obviously, cannot be directly transposed on the old Anasazi culture, because cultures transform through time. But, because of the persistence of traditional stories, languages, and lifestyles in the Pueblo communities, it cannot be denied that modern Pueblo people are closer to the sensibilities of the Anasazi world than are the Western-European archaeologists" (Swentzell 1991:1980).

COLLABORATION AND THE CO-PRODUCTION OF KNOWLEDGE

Southwestern archaeology is being transformed by collaborative practices of knowledge production (Colwell 2016). The current focus can be traced back to a particular moment in the human sciences. In the 1980s and 1990s anthropology, and other cultural fields, experienced what is sometimes called the "crisis of representation." This refers to a skepticism of the authority of "grand theory" and a growing appreciation of contextual issues, particularly the meanings of social lives held by the actors themselves (Marcus and Fisher 1986:8). In many ways this movement was foreshadowed by Clifford Geertz (1973, 1980), who pioneered a cultural hermeneutics based upon an insider's view of culture and grounded in his method of "thick description." Significantly, this crisis, which might be considered the first ontological turn, had ethical and practical implications for ethnography.

The most important of these implications centered on temporality. As Johnannes Fabian (1983:31) notes, anthropologists tended to consider the people they were studying as occupying a time frame different from that of the fieldworker. He critiqued this assumption on the grounds that communication is fundamentally about creating shared time. In this sense, coevalness is to be understood as a condition for the production of ethical knowledge. In other words, it is a temporal relationship that "must be created or at least approached" (Fabian 1983:34), such that "the anthropologist and his interlocutor only 'know' when they meet each other in one and the same contemporality" (Fabian 1983:164). From this point of view, ethnographic knowledge production is made possible through a series of exchanges between anthropologists and their co-subjects in shared time and space. Knowledge is both intersubjective and co-produced.

The field of anthropology has been wholly transformed by this insight. Instead of treating people as research objects who occupy radically different worlds and from whom information is to be gathered and re-represented as knowledge, scholars are now engaging with Native peoples on equal terms in a common world, as co-subjects who productively design and shape the scope of research. This is one of the key arguments of Indigenous Studies, and it underlies Linda Tuhiwai Smith's influential critique of anthropological research. Smith (1999), a Maori professor of education, holds that Western science is inextricably linked to European imperialism and that decolonizing methodologies are necessary to provide knowledge for community benefit. These methodologies include empowering Indigenous people and communities to conduct research on their own terms and for their own purposes.

Southwestern archaeologists have played a leading role in advancing collaboration as an ethical epistemology. This is an outcome of the archaeologists working with and sometimes for the Apache tribes (Eiselt 2012; Welch et al. 2005), the Hopi Tribe (Dongoske et al. 1993; Ferguson et al. 1995), the Navajo Nation (Klesert and Downer 1990), the Tohono O'odham (Darling 2009; Darling et al. 2015; Ravesloot 1990), and the Zuni Tribe (Ferguson and Anyon 2001). In 2008 Chip Colwell-Chanthaphonh and T. J. Ferguson edited an important volume entitled *Collaboration in Archaeological Practice: Engaging Descendant Communities*. Here they define collaborative research as research that takes community interests and perspectives into account as a way of making science more inclusive. They note that archaeological research is implicated in multiple relationships, including those with research institutions, granting agencies, and employees. However, they identify local descendant communities as the key "stakeholders" in archaeological research because they have more compelling interests than those of the other communities, including the archaeological community itself (Colwell-Chanthaphonh and Ferguson 2008). Collaborative research typically involves forming a group of co-researchers, establishing the conditions for group learning, addressing the research question, and producing group knowledge. In practice, collaborative research is fluid and flexible and, indeed, there is a collaborative continuum of different strategies for working productively with different stakeholders.

Collaboration is also central to the new international movement known as Indigenous archaeology (Smith and Wobst 2005). Indigenous archaeologies currently comprise a broad set of theories, methods, and strategies for the study of the human past for the benefit of contemporary Indigenous peoples, as well as the scientific community. Significantly, these approaches are informed by Indigenous values, concerns, and goals (Nicholas 2008; Watkins 2000). Indigenous archaeologies are particularly active in the debates regarding repatriation and sacred sites. They engage with heritage management, museum studies, collaborative research practices, and the sociopolitics of archaeology (Smith and Wobst 2005). Current research focuses on differences between Indigenous and Western epistemologies, on inequalities in representation and decision-making, and on challenges relating to sovereignty (Atalay 2012; Wilcox 2009).

This volume is the outcome of a series of collaborative partnerships between archaeologists, cultural anthropologists, and tribal historic preservation officers with Pueblo and Apache tribes. Some of these projects are long term, such as the relationships that E. Charles Adams and his Homol'ovi team have built up with the Hopi Tribe and that T. J. Ferguson has established with the Hopi and Zuni Tribes. Others are relatively new, such as Kurt Anschuetz and Damian Garcia's work for the Pueblo of Acoma and Bruce Bernstein's work at the Pueblo of Pojoaque. But all are built upon notions of mutual respect and a concern for the health and well-being of the tribal communities involved. They are grounded in the idea that knowledge production is fundamentally an ethical activity and that writing of Pueblo histories is an inclusive project, one that must acknowledge the sovereignty of Pueblo people as a first principle. Our goal then is to investigate how Indigenous concepts can be joined with archaeology to provide intercultural modes of understanding. We are convinced that this approach not only produces a richer account of past people's lives, but also that it makes the necessary connections to living peoples and their futures.

One of the most important insights emerging from our work is the idea that not all knowledge is to be publicly shared. In Western society, knowledge is regarded as a public good to be freely exchanged for the benefit of all, the Googlization of information, if you will. Early southwestern anthropologists justified the documentation of Pueblo culture as a way to record human cultural variation, believing that the Pueblo peoples were assimilating and abandoning their traditions. In Pueblo society, however, knowledge is associated with ritual power and social responsibility. Pueblo people learn about ritual practices and secrecy as children, and this knowledge grows as they take on different offices and roles within the community. This secrecy is sometimes interpreted as a historical legacy of the practical need to shield Pueblo religion from Spanish missionizing practices (Sando 1979) or as a way of preserving the political power of specific religious sodalities within a village (Brandt 1980). As Joseph Suina (1992) notes in his chapter, secrecy continues to be an important way of protecting Pueblo communities from the prying eyes of anthropologists. Today, it is quite clear that the assimilationist view was profoundly misguided. Pueblo culture has been (and still is) changing, but it remains Pueblo nonetheless. In respecting Pueblo survivance, we and our collaborators seek to discuss those aspects of movement that can be publicly shared and used to promote cross-cultural understanding. This is one reason why the migration stories shared here are partial and incomplete.

Another insight is that archaeologists and Pueblo people have tended to understand Pueblo history in radically different ways. Swentzell (1991:177) saw these differences as evidence that these groups are, philosophically speaking, "from distinct worlds." She argued that archaeologists often focus on the details and differences between Pueblo people in both space (e.g., Hopi and Taos) and time (e.g., ancestral and modern Pueblos). This serves to divorce contemporary people from their ancestors and the shared experiences of the Pueblo people from one another. The Pueblo people, conversely, focus on larger wholes rather than the parts. Everything and everybody have a context within which they belong, and the focus is on connections and relationships through time and space. The primary question is not "Why are people different?" but rather "How does one, or one's group, activity, or place, fit into the larger whole?" (Swentzell 1991:177). This idea of a larger whole emphasizing interrelationships between communities offers valuable new insights for the interpretation of archaeological sites.

CONTINUITY AND CHANGE

In 1927 A. V. Kidder invited the leading southwestern archaeologists to an impromptu conference at Pecos Pueblo to share information about the state of research in the American Southwest. The most important outcome of the meeting was a chronological sequence known as the Pecos Classification (Woodbury 1993). This classification organized Pueblo (then called Anasazi) culture into a series of time periods (Pueblo I–Pueblo V), each of which was characterized by a list of specific cultural traits. For example, Pueblo III (AD 1100–1350), or the Great Pueblo period, was characterized by cliff dwellings and multistoried pueblos, black-on-white ceramics, and extended burials (Kidder 1927).

The Pecos Conference continues to the present day, and southwestern archaeologists continue to use versions of this classification system (indeed, we rely upon it here). However, we should recall that there are no "natural chronologies," and, in fact, the different chronologies we use each serve specific purposes. If we consider the assumptions underlying the Pecos Classification, we can see that it privileges cultural transformations at the expense of cultural continuities. This insight reveals that southwestern archaeology has prioritized theories of cultural evolution at the expense of the histories and cultural heritage of living peoples. When this perspective is combined with the study of sacred sites and burial grounds, it should not be surprising that many Pueblo people have a negative view of archaeology.

Matthew J. Liebmann (2012b) makes this same point in his critique of southwestern archaeology. He suggests the field has done a disservice to Pueblo people in its single-minded focus on the prehistoric period. This emphasis has quite literally bracketed off the historic period with the implication that nothing of anthropological interest happened after Spanish contact. As Stephen Lekson (2009:247) writes, "After 1600, the Southwest was no longer native, no longer aboriginal, no longer 'ancient.'" Indeed, archaeologists tended to treat the historic period as one of cultural degradation or "devolution" due to the practices of assimilation and acculturation. Because of this, southwestern archaeologists have failed to investigate important events within the historic period, for example the Pueblo responses to Spanish, Mexican, and Anglo authority. They have also ignored the important interactions that occurred within and between Pueblo communities and between Pueblo and other Native American tribes (but see Eiselt 2012; Fowles et al. 2017). This stance has the overall effect of denying Pueblo people's agency in successfully responding to a series of ongoing social and political challenges and making their own futures.

Similarly, Bruce Bernstein and colleagues (this volume) critique the standard art historical studies of Pueblo pottery and note that they are typically based upon Western aesthetics and ideas about stylistic change. That is to say, they assume a linear evolutionary sequence and shared practice of pottery making, and they neglect idiosyncratic differences that are the result of individual preference, skill, and age. It is remarkable that the meanings of pottery for contemporary Pueblo people have yet to be fully incorporated into archaeological studies. For example, archaeologists have documented that prehistoric pottery in the Lower Rio Puerco region is characterized by potsherd temper (Eckert 2008). Scholars of Pueblo pottery have documented how this technique has been used by contemporary Acoma and Zuni potters (Harlow 1973). However, few studies have investigated the meaning and cultural significance of the continuities in this cultural practice (see Christenson 2010).

We wish to build upon Liebmann's and Bernstein's insights and suggest that cultural continuities should be positioned at the center of our research agenda. It is, after all, these continuities that Pueblo people themselves feature in their oral histories. This refocusing is not a denial of cultural differences or cultural change but rather a statement of the ethical and moral responsibilities of our field to the peoples with whom we work. Pueblo people live in a world that was made possible by a series of decisions, large and small, taken by their ancestors. It is this survivance that must be acknowledged. Paul Tosa and Octavius Seowtewa (this volume) from Jemez and Zuni, respectively, explain, "While our clothing and pottery have changed over time, our culture remains the same." The upshot is that there is no endpoint in our discussion of Pueblo history. The same principles that guided the people during their great migration continue to direct their actions today. The Pueblos are always in a state of becoming.

ON BEING AND BECOMING

Our collaborative projects have foregrounded the centrality of ideas of being and becoming to Pueblo world views. To be a Pueblo person is to have experienced a series of stages of physical and social growth, much like the stages of the growth of a corn plant. Among the Tewa, children are initiated into societies and given detailed instructions as to their roles (Ortiz 1972). For many Pueblo people, the developmental stage of corn plants is associated with the growth states of children, and indeed, at Hopi the same words are used to describe both (Black 1984:280). As they mature in age and experience, children with particular promise are selected to take on new roles and may apprentice with ritual leaders. These roles typically include the cacique, war chiefs, and society leaders (both male and female). With the advent of Spanish governance, new positions were created such as the governor, lieutenant governor, major *fiscale*, lieutenant fiscale, and various minor officials. To be a "finished" person means that one has taken on these responsibilities for the benefit of the entire community. There is thus a process of growth or movement from "unripe" to "ripe," and this corn lifeway is central to the Pueblo "way of being" (Sekaquaptewa and Washburn 2015).

The preeminent accounts of being and becoming are origin stories. Upon emergence the people were considered not yet fully formed or "unripe," a sentiment expressed at Acoma (Garcia and Anschuetz, this volume) and Zuni (Hopkins et al., this volume), among other places (Ortiz 1969:16–17). These early ancestors, while unfinished, nevertheless had distinct cultural identities. The people were then tasked by their spiritual leaders to find the center, and the location of their eventual homes, described variously as Zuni's "middle place" (Hopkins et al., this volume), Acoma's "place prepared" (Garcia and Anschuetz, this volume), and Jemez's place of a sacred eagle (Tosa et al., this volume). The commencement of great migrations to the south and east—and many other places throughout the greater Southwest—began the process of becoming. By overcoming adversity, suffering loss and gaining knowledge, and meeting others, the Pueblo people moved along a directed and prophesized path that recounts their many histories and their cultural and spiritual development. Even though the Pueblos view their tenure in the Southwest as extending to time immemorial, they also acknowledge that the people changed during this journey. According to Swentzell (quoted in Naranjo 2009:4), "As clouds shift and seasons change, so do human thoughts and human-made processes."

For Pueblo people there is an intimate association between being and place. In fact, the history of the people is primarily understood in relation to space rather than linear time, and "some realities, most notably the sacred, have little meaning except in the context of their spatial referents" (Ortiz 1977:17). That is to say, the place or location of a happening is often more important than the precise date of an event. Alfonso Ortiz explains further,

> The Tewa know not when the journey southward began or when it ended, but we do know where it began, how it proceeded, and where it ended. We are unconcerned about time in its historical dimension, but we will recall in endless detail the features of the twelve places our ancestors stopped. We point to these places to show that the journey did indeed take place. This is the only proof a Tewa requires. And each time a Tewa recalls a place where they paused, for whatever length of time, every feature of the earth and sky comes vividly to life, and the journey itself lives again [Ortiz 1991:7].

T. J. Ferguson and Chip Colwell-Chanthaphonh (2006) have elaborated upon this insight and documented how history literally "resides in the land" in their multivocal ethnographies of the San Pedro Valley of southern Arizona. They document how Native people reconnect with their ancestors and gather knowledge to be used in educating younger generations of Pueblo people by visiting archaeological sites and sacred places, many of which are on traditional lands outside the boundaries of their reservations. Kurt F. Anschuetz and Richard Wilshusen (2011) have taken these ideas further with their concept of "ensouled places," which refers to the metaphysical flow of life energies between living people residing in communities at their landscape's center and supernatural beings residing beyond the edge. The ebb and flow of people moving among the landscape's many centers and edges were constant, constantly transforming, and forever renewing (Anschuetz and Wilshusen 2011:327).

For Pueblo people, the idea of being and becoming is linked to the idea of good stewardship—the moral responsibility of taking care of the land for the benefit of future generations. This idea is expressed by the covenant between the creator and the Pueblo people. For example, the Hopi people entered into a covenant with the deity Ma'saw for the stewardship of the earth (Ferguson et al. 1995). The ceremonies, pilgrimages, and rituals that sustain the Hopi religion are inextricably tied to shrines that were established in ancient times at specific springs, mountain peaks, and other sacred areas. These shrines were created in accordance with divine instructions as permanent physical testaments to the covenant. Each shrine and sacred place contains an irreplaceable life essence that prohibits any relocation or alteration of the shrine. This view underlies the recent collaborative video *Then, Now, and Forever: Zuni in the Grand Canyon (La Sap Da Ya Kya, La' Gi, E Sha Maldeh: A:shiwi Lak Chimikyanakyadaya:ah)* created by the Zuni Tribe and the U.S. Bureau of Reclamation. It shows Zuni ritual leaders making a pilgrimage to their traditional salt-gathering sites located near the place where they emerged from the underworld.

These insights offer new ways of thinking about the so-called ontological turn in cultural anthropology. This turn is often seen as a response to the global ecological crisis and as a critical interrogation of the ways in which humans and nonhumans are entangled in their engagements with the world (Kohn 2015). In archaeology, it is represented by symmetrical archaeology and arguments for the recuperation of the material (Alberti 2016). The ontological turn offers a critique of the symbolic meaning of things in favor of their emergent qualities. Pueblo perspectives, however, cause us to question the very assumptions of this theoretical framing—the distinction between ontology and epistemology is, after all, a product of Western philosophy. Just as anthropology is now critical of the Cartesian mind/body opposition, so, too, must it reconsider the philosophical distinction that artificially separates being from knowing. As John Dewey put it, the "knowns are always and everywhere inseparable from the knowings" (Boydston 1989:85). Pueblo perspectives reveal that how we know what we know about the world is inseparable from our lived experiences of the world. The moral responsibilities established through covenants with supernatural beings give direction and purpose to social groups. Indeed, it is precisely the reciprocal relationships between people, spirits, places, and living things (plants, animals, clouds, rain) that constitute the moral universe.

The American Southwest is a difficult place to be a successful farmer, a point of pride for the Hopi (Hays-Gilpin 2010) and other Pueblo people. Therefore, maintaining balance and harmony in both social and natural contexts "is the greatest aim and desire of traditional Pueblo people" (Naranjo and Swentzell 1989:258). Because the world is in a state of "constant re-creation and transformation," the "achievement of harmony is transitory" (Swentzell 1993:141). The dualities that permeate and structure the Pueblo world—summer and winter, pumpkin and turquoise, hunting and farming, female and male, life and death—are simultaneously complementary and in tension. The constant process of searching for harmony and balance between these opposites, known as "seeking life," is therefore the most basic concept of Pueblo thinking (Laski 1959; Naranjo and Swentzell 1989; Sweet 2004). To find balance among dialectic forces is to acknowledge that these dichotomies complement each other as part of larger wholes, as do the seasons or the sexes. To seek life is to avoid stasis and to embrace movement and the transformation of life that results from mediating the tension of opposites (Swentzell 1993:45). Movement is therefore crucial to the health, healing, being, and becoming of the Pueblo people (Naranjo and Swentzell 1989).

METAPHORS OF MOVEMENT

A crucial principle that unifies the Pueblos past and present, and serves as the thread running through each chapter, is embodied in the metaphor *life as movement*. Regardless of philosophical differences, archaeologists and Pueblo people are deeply concerned with histories of movement in the Pueblo world and seek out evidence of ancestors traveling through and shaping the landscape of the American Southwest. For archaeologists, this evidence takes the form of the movement of people, things, and ideas, as observable in the material culture left behind. For the Pueblos, the movements and deeds of ancestors are memorialized at ancient villages, shrines, and other remembered places, and these histories are passed down through story and song (Malotki 1993; Sekaquaptewa and

Washburn 2004). Movement is not just something that people did in the past. Instead, it embodies the correct way of being in the world and is conducive to becoming, to achieving balance and harmony in the present and future (Naranjo and Swentzell 1989).

For many Pueblo people, life is conceptualized as movement along a path or roadway. This concept features prominently in every Pueblo origin tradition that describes the emergence of the people into this world. These paths and the connections between current villages and ancestral places are often viewed as "umbilical cords," for "the connection between mother and child is like the connection between our shrines and us" (Tosa and Seowtewa, this volume). To visit these places and then return to the village—such as the Zuni pilgrimaging to the place of emergence in the Grand Canyon (Hopkins et al., this volume) and the Acoma offering prayers of renewal on Mount Taylor (Garcia and Anschuetz, this volume)—is to reexperience the ancestors' histories of movement and to reaffirm the people's connections in the larger world. Because in the Pueblo world space and time are inversely linked and the edges of the world are timeless (Ortiz 1977), these pilgrimages across the landscape are akin to traveling through time. While the effects of colonization have sometimes limited movement (Bernstein et al., Hopkins et al., and Suina, this volume), pilgrimage remains a central component to maintaining Pueblo identity in the modern world.

The concept of the pathway is also extended to the lives and histories of peoples and individuals who are in a constant process of becoming. As Ortiz (1972) explains for the Tewa, at the beginning of life there is a single path for all people. This changes with the initiation ceremony, when the child embarks upon one of two parallel paths associated with the Summer and Winter People (the two "moieties" that govern life in Tewa villages). Upon death, the two paths come together and become one in the afterlife. The central importance of this idea is commemorated by the name of the Poeh Cultural Center at Pojoaque Pueblo and is the reason why the museum's first exhibit was titled *Nah po'eh meng*, or *The Continuous Path*. This notion of a path implies an individual's purposeful, directed movement and, at the same time, acknowledges responsibility and commitment to the community. The late Esther Martinez, an elder at Ohkay Owingeh (San Juan Pueblo) who was famous for her work on language teaching (as recognized by the Esther Martinez Native

American Languages Preservation Act of 2006), described the core of her community life as sharing knowledge with the younger generation. She wrote, "People still come to my house wanting help with information for their college paper or wanting a storyteller. Young folks from the village, who were once my students in bilingual classes, will stop by for advice in traditional values or wanting me to give Indian names to their kids or grandkids.... This is my *po'eh* (my path). I am still traveling" (Jacobs et al. 2004:9–10).

Along the path, the Pueblo people left evidence of their journeys so that future generations could remember and find their way. These include ancestral villages, shrines, petroglyphs, and objects—material evidence of movement that archaeologists call "sites." For the Hopi these places are called *itaakuku*, "footprints," and are associated with clan migrations from the place of emergence to the Hopi Mesas (Ferguson and Colwell-Chanthaphonh 2006:95; Fladd et al., this volume). One of the instructions that Màasaw gave the people was *ang kuktota*, literally, "along there, make footprints" (Kuwanwisiwma and Ferguson 2002). Garcia and Anschuetz (this volume) describe this same metaphor at Acoma, along with fingerprints, impressions, and imprints that convey the lessons of "living, sacrifice, and history" that the people of Acoma learn as their cultural heritage and that they intend to pass on to their following generations. Zuni similarly views material culture, such as pottery and groundstone, as "memory pieces": a way in which the ancestors memorialized their history (Ferguson and Colwell-Chanthaphonh 2006:162). We find that these metaphors of movement and place convey a deeper understanding of how the Pueblo people conceptualize their identity. They can also serve as a middle ground for productive collaborative research between archaeologists and the Pueblos.

Oral traditions about movement and migration, and knowledge of the precise geographic locations where events took place, are not only historical accounts of what happened in the past. They are also resources for transmitting an entire culture with proven strategies for survival (Silko 1996:158). Similar to the Western Apache's notion of wisdom sitting in places (Basso 1996), stories about these places are also tools that can be used as examples of morally appropriate behavior. Movement in this sense is much greater than the histories of people. It also includes attempts to achieve a precarious balance in an interconnected cosmos

Introduction

that includes plants, animals, deities, clouds, water, and wind. Pueblo philosophy is therefore concerned with the processes and energies in the universe, viewed as the interrelationships between all living things (human, natural, and spiritual), and how they can be applied to the life of the community (Cajete 2000). These other "actors" guide the people, for "movement, clouds, wind, and rain are one" and "movement must be emulated by the people" (Naranjo 1995:248).

ORGANIZATION OF THE VOLUME

The goal of this volume is to encourage Native community members and scholars, archaeologists, and cultural anthropologists to explore Pueblo history together through the principles of movement and becoming. To this end, the contributors offer ten case studies from across the Pueblo world addressing the Hopi Pueblos, Zuni, Acoma, Jemez, Cochiti, Pojoaque, San Ildefonso, Ohkay Owingeh, Taos, and Picuris. This geographic breadth is coupled with substantial temporal diversity, and discussions range from histories of emergence and migration to the social and economic challenges of the twentieth century. The key argument here is that these time periods are not to be thought of as separate temporal phases, but as intimately interconnected.

While all chapters are thematically linked by Pueblo ontological concepts, we have separated this book into two parts. The first part, "On Becoming," surveys histories of emergence and migration as Pueblo people sought their middle places and developed their own unique identities and cultures. The authors strive to incorporate both oral tradition and archaeological evidence to understand the creation and reorganization of the Pueblo world. Equally important, each chapter is firmly rooted in the present and explores the importance of historic movements to the Pueblo people today. The second part, "Always Becoming," addresses the continual becoming and ongoing movement of the Pueblo people as they faced (and continue to face) the challenges of colonialism, including leaving and finding again their middle places. These chapters demonstrate how the same principles that guided the people in the pre-Hispanic past operate in the historical and modern eras.

In part 1, Damian Garcia and Kurt Anschuetz offer a deeply thoughtful investigation of the ideology of movement in the context of Acoma history and identity. They develop Gregory Cajete's idea of *spiritual ecology*, which they define as "the traditional relationship and participation of indigenous people with place that includes not only the land itself, but also the way people perceive the reality of their worlds and themselves." This is based in a covenant that the First Acoma People made with spiritual beings at Shipap'u at the time of emergence in exchange for the promise of Haak'u at the end of migration. Movement is thus a form of perception and a way of both becoming and being Acoma. They go on to discuss some of the metaphors that Acoma people use in talking about archaeological sites. As "footprints," archaeological sites show Acoma's people (and the rest of us) where their ancestors lived and traveled. As "fingerprints," archaeological sites show what these people did during their lives. As "impressions" and "imprints," archaeological sites convey the lessons of "living, sacrifice, and history" that the people of Acoma have inherited and that they intend to pass onto following generations. Being an Acoma person requires continual movement across the landscape, from the center to distant peripheries, to fulfill sacred stewardship obligations and reaffirm culture, history, and identity.

Paul Tosa and his colleagues provide an equally ambitious discussion of Hemish (Jemez) history and show how migration, travel, and landscape are key elements in Hemish identity. Their discussion is centered on Wâavêmâ, which refers to both the sacred peak that looms over the village of Walatowa and the mountains that ring the Valles Caldera. Beginning with a detailed history of the people's migration to Walatowa, the authors describe how the Hemish people, once emerged, received a prophesy that a sacred eagle would reveal their new homeland. Taking many paths and making many stops across the greater Southwest, the people eventually reached the base of Wâavêmâ, where, looking up, they saw the silhouette of an eagle etched in the side of the peak among the rocks and pines: they had found their home. Hemish identity is therefore inscribed in the land by an ancestral geography, one that includes thousands of place-names, including Wâavêmâ. Many of these same places are associated with contemporary and historic religious pilgrimages, hunting, collecting, and other land uses, and therefore the continued movement of the Hemish people across their landscape supports tribal sovereignty and cultural revitalization. The authors demonstrate the antiquity and scope of this movement through an innovative obsidian provenance study that tracks the continued movement of the Hemish people between Walatowa and the Valles Caldera over the past seven centuries.

The focus on movement and place is continued in the chapter by Maren Hopkins and her colleagues, who state that both the concept and the act of movement are part of remembering, retaining, and transmitting Zuni culture; they are part of being Zuni. They focus on Anshe K'yan'a, "Bear Springs," also the area of Fort Wingate Depot Activity. This sacred place is recalled in the prayers of Zuni medicine society leaders that recount the migrations of Zuni ancestors from the Grand Canyon to the middle place of Zuni Pueblo. It has complex associations with the medicine societies that use the bear, the Bear Clan, and the War God. The water located within springs of Anshe K'yan'a was first consecrated by the medicine societies when they migrated to the middle place, and it continues to be used today by ritual leaders to reconnect with their ancestors. The authors detail a collaborative project between anthropologists and the Zuni to document these places of traditional history held in collective memory that were inaccessible to the Zuni for over a generation. By navigating both metaphorical and real (unexploded ordinance!) hurdles of colonialism, the Zuni have remembered these places and are reconsecrating them through acts of being and becoming.

Samuel Duwe and Patrick Cruz reexamine the history of the Tewa Pueblos, whose origins (as migrants or locally) have spurred a century of debate among southwestern archaeologists. They reframe the messy and contradictory archaeological evidence in light of the Tewa people's own view of history that allows for manifold truths and multiple middle places. The authors propose that Tewa history is hardly monolithic. By synthesizing both oral tradition and archaeological data, they examine the individual histories of two areas of the Tewa homeland, the middle northern Rio Grande and the Rio Chama valley, and suggest different scenarios for the coalescence of both Indigenous and migrant groups. While the six modern Tewa villages share the common experience of distantly related people (Summer and Winter People) coming together, the way each village did so is unique and historically contingent. For the Tewa, becoming was a process rather than an event, and therefore archaeologists must be open to contradictory ideas, multiple middle places, and shifting and complex histories.

Samantha Fladd and her colleagues similarly explore the nuances of Hopi history, a complexly woven story of individual clans traveling across the greater Southwest and eventually gathering on the Hopi Mesas. Along the way people came together and moved apart, accumulating individual and group identities through shared experiences and relationships with the landscape. The authors focus on an important stop on this journey—the Homol'ovi Settlement Cluster—where immigrants from diverse backgrounds founded large villages and negotiated new community identities on their way to becoming Hopi. Drawing on over three decades of archaeological research, they examine the founding of these villages, the reorganization of people through intra-village movement, and the eventual closure of these places and emigration to the Hopi Mesas. This chapter highlights the importance of alternative forms of movement, including aggregation, small-scale moves, and depopulation. Importantly, the authors also explain the importance of Homol'ovi today as an integral part of the Hopi cultural landscape and one that is returned to and continues to constitute Hopi memory in the twenty-first century.

While emergence, migration, and finding the middle place are foundational to all Pueblo histories, the process of becoming is ongoing and never complete. With the arrival of the Spaniards in the sixteenth century, the Pueblos faced new and different challenges but continued to seek balance and harmony through movement. In part 2, Joseph Aguilar and Robert Preucel examine mobility as a strategy of survivance during the Pueblo Revolt period. They focus on the settlements built and occupied in the highlands and mesas during the tumultuous and violent reconquest of New Mexico by Diego de Vargas between 1694 and 1696. Previous studies have emphasized these villages as places of defense and refuge and have highlighted their military significance. The authors go beyond these interpretations by adopting a Tewa perspective to argue that these mesa tops and upland areas were also the locations where ancestors lived and that the people deliberately moved to these areas to draw spiritual strength from the power of place. Focusing on San Ildefonso and ancestral villages on Tunyo and the Pajarito Plateau, they demonstrate that mobility was (and is) multifaceted and incorporated spiritual, symbolic, and strategic considerations.

The Pueblos, of course, are not the only Native people who lived in the pre-Hispanic Southwest, and with the coming of the Spanish the region increasingly became a complex cultural landscape of competition and alliances (Ford 1972). Severin Fowles and Sunday Eiselt examine the intimate relationships between Taos and Picuris Pueblos and the Jicarilla Apache. In this case, mobility was both physical (movement between the Pueblos and the plains) and ethnic shifting (in which Pueblos fluidly became Apache and vice versa). The authors document a deep history of interethnic exchange and collaboration between the Pueblos and the Apache and argue that, in fact, these groups can be best understood as a single people. Historical contingencies, both before and after European colonization, helped dictate where and how these people lived. The chapter highlights the importance of these ethnic crossovers and how the process of "becoming other" is a significant and often overlooked tradition of indigenous mobility in the Southwest.

With the introduction of foreign Spanish, Mexican, and Anglo governments, whole Pueblos were no longer able to move. What circulated in these contexts were ideas, technologies, materials, and commodities. Bruce Bernstein and his colleagues discuss movement from the point of view of staying in place. They critically examine the role of wheat in the Tewa world and note that as a foreign crop it occupied a liminal space, on the one hand a valued foodstuff but on the other a crop without a ceremonial role. Yet it took on political connotations. The growing of wheat demonstrated the willingness of Tewa communities to embrace change and even become "Hispanicized." Here, adopting wheat helped people stay in place and thus preserve Tewa cultural continuity. The authors' argument is supported by an examination of Ogapoge Polychrome, a new type of pottery and a crucial part of the technology of wheat production. This specialized pottery both imbued the foreign wheat with Tewa meaning and kept it separate from the sacredness of Tewa plant-life ideologies, thus demonstrating the Tewa people's resourcefulness and resiliency in a restrictive colonial landscape.

In the spirit of "always becoming," Samuel Villarreal Catanach and Mark Agostini discuss the Pueblo of Pojoaque's continuous and unbroken attempt to return to the middle place. Pojoaque was severely impacted by Spanish colonization and missionization beginning in the sixteenth century. This coincided with the settlement of ethnically mixed people in the Pojoaque Valley after the reconquest. Using historical records, the authors demonstrate how the coming together of these disparate people (Tewas and Hispanic settlers) resulted in the emergence and development of a new kind of civic-based identity status called *vecino* in the eighteenth and early nineteenth centuries. At Pojoaque the resulting identities had strains of both Hispanic and Tewa practice and social identification. The authors argue that these vecino identities preserved and encapsulated Pueblo concepts of movement and becoming and contributed to the reestablishment and revitalization of Pojoaque as a Tewa village in the 1930s. The Pueblo of Pojoaque is a community of mixed cultural and historical backgrounds that are embraced by its people, but it is their shared Pojoaque and Tewa identity, with its fluid and dynamic flexibility, that sustains them.

In the penultimate chapter, Joseph Suina provides a contemporary discussion of both the challenges and opportunities facing the Pueblos. He notes that Pueblos have successfully managed their social and environmental situations for thousands of years by moving villages. In times of severe drought or when resources were no longer enough to support the group, they found a more suitable location. After the Spanish invasion and the Anglo imposition, however, the Pueblos were no longer as free to move. They have had to engage with foreign ideas and technologies at their home villages, in some cases very rapidly. Suina discusses the processes by which electricity was adopted at his home village in the 1950s and notes that it was initially seen as useful, providing light for evening activities and energy for televisions and refrigerators. But it also came at a cost, introducing Pueblo people to the ills of American capitalism and threatening the ties of community solidarity. He discusses how his village has begun to overcome these challenges by actively engaging in the contemporary world of education and politics, and he offers a contemporary perspective on the relation between movement and social change.

We reserve the last words for our colleagues Paul Tosa and Octavius Seowtewa. Tosa and Seowtewa were inspirational participants in both our SAA session and our Amerind Foundation workshop. They acted as "gentle teachers" (a term offered by Tosa, which he associated with one of his most revered Hemish teachers) and shared personal information about their lives and communities, much of which is not appropriate to include here. Their purpose in doing this was to establish relationships of trust between the participants and to impress upon all of us the responsibilities and obligations that come with different kinds of information. In their commentary, assisted by T. J. Ferguson, they offer their reflections on our session, the Continuous Path project, and the relationship of southwestern archaeology to contemporary Pueblo lives.

CONCLUSIONS

We regard the idea of the Continuous Path as a commitment to using Pueblo concepts to help rethink southwestern archaeology. We have chosen to highlight the importance of movement as a central organizing concept—considered from multiple scales and perspectives—in much the same manner that Pueblo people do. This means appreciating that individual sites are linked into a larger narrative about origins, movement, and the search for the middle place. Although we focus primarily on Pueblo communities, we feel this movement-based, collaborative approach is applicable to other Indigenous communities in the Southwest and beyond.

We seek to reorient southwestern archaeology toward a consideration of continuity. Our profession's tendency to privilege change over continuity in pursuit of theories of cultural evolution has had the unacknowledged consequence of separating Pueblo people from their cultural heritage. It has complicated their testimony in land claims and water rights cases in the court of law (Ebright et al. 2014). The very real changes that have taken place in Pueblo culture are sometimes used to deny Pueblo connections to ancestral lands and traditional-use areas. A focus on being and becoming helps us appreciate continuities and survivance and allows us to bridge epistemological gaps between anthropological and Indigenous knowledge, thereby contributing to larger theoretical discussions regarding ontology, representational practices, and sovereignty.

We also seek to highlight the value of collaborative methodologies as a way of producing new knowledge that respects similarities and differences in Western and Pueblo ways of knowing. Our collaborations vary from case to case—as the "collaborative continuum" model recognizes (Colwell-Chanthaphonh and Ferguson 2008)—but they all share a commitment to the co-production of knowledge for the benefit of Pueblo communities. This perspective has encouraged us to highlight the metaphors of movement as conceptual resources for cultural survival and reproduction. These metaphors challenge archaeologists to take a holistic view of Pueblo history that incorporates both the present and the past, to focus on continuities and relationships, and to acknowledge how the Pueblos view their own history when writing historical narratives.

We, as Native and non-Native archaeologists, anthropologists, and elders, need to work together to facilitate Pueblo access to ancestral places. It is this connection between people and place, so well documented in the recent collaborative video *Then, Now, and Forever: Zuni in the Grand Canyon*, that demonstrates the cultural practices necessary for the reproduction of Zuni culture. Related to this, we should assist in the education of Pueblo youth by developing educational programs, internships, and workshops to enhance their appreciation of their deep land-based histories. Preserving the vital interconnections between the past and present ensures the survivance of their remarkable cultures into the future.

Most importantly, we hope that this volume will be useful to Pueblo tribes as they develop their own cultural resource management programs and tribal historic preservation offices, educate new generations of community leaders, and share aspects of their cultures with the wider public.

REFERENCES

Adler, Michael A. (editor). 1996. *The Prehistoric Pueblo World, AD 1150–1350*. University of Arizona Press, Tucson.

Adler, Michael A., Todd Van Pool, and Robert Leonard. 1996. Ancestral Pueblo Population Aggregation and Abandonment in the North American Southwest. *Journal of World Prehistory* 10(3):375–438.

Ahlstrom, Richard V. N., Carla R. Van West, and Jeffrey Dean. 1995. Environmental and Chronological Factors in the Mesa Verde–Northern Rio Grande Migration. *Journal of Anthropological Archaeology* 14(2):125–142.

Alberti, Benjamin. 2016. Archaeologies of Ontology. *Annual Review of Anthropology* 45:163–179.

Anschuetz, Kurt F., and Richard H. Wilshusen. 2011. Ensouled Places: Ethnogenesis and the Making of the Dinétah and Tewa Basin Landscapes. In *Movement, Connectivity and Landscape Change in the Ancient Southwest*, edited by Margaret C. Nelson and Colleen Strawhacker, pp. 321–344. University Press of Colorado, Boulder.

Anthony, David W. 1990. Migration in Archaeology: The Baby and the Bathwater. *American Anthropologist* 92(4):895–914.

Atalay, Sonya. 2012. *Community-Based Archaeology: Research with, by, and for Indigenous and Local Communities*. University of California Press, Berkeley.

Basso, Keith H. 1996. *Wisdom Sits in Places: Landscape and Language Among the Western Apache*. University of New Mexico Press, Albuquerque.

Binford, Lewis R. 1962. Archaeology as Anthropology. *American Antiquity* 28(2): 217–225.

Binford, Lewis R. 1967. Smudge Pits and Hide Smoking: The Use of Analogy in Archaeological Reasoning. *American Antiquity* 32(1):1–12.

Black, Mary E. 1984. Maidens and Mothers: An Analysis of Hopi Corn Metaphors. *Ethnology* 23(4):279–288.

Boydston, Jo Ann. 1989. *John Dewey: The Later Works, 1925–1953. Volume 16: 1948–1952*. Southern Illinois University, Carbondale.

Brandt, Elizabeth. 1980. On Secrecy and the Control of Knowledge: Taos Pueblo. In *Secrecy: A Cross-Cultural Perspective*, edited by Stanton K. Tefft, pp. 123–146. Human Sciences, New York.

Cabana, Graciela S., and Jeffery J. Clark (editors). 2011. *Rethinking Anthropological Perspectives on Migration*. University Press of Florida, Gainesville.

Cajete, Gregory. 2000. *Native Science: Natural Laws of Interdependence*. Clear Light Press, Santa Fe, New Mexico.

Cameron, Catherine M. 2016. *Captives: How Stolen People Changed the World*. University of Nebraska Press, Lincoln.

Cameron, Catherine M., and Scott G. Ortman. 2017. Movement and Migration. In *The Oxford Handbook of Southwestern Archaeology*, edited by Barbara J. Mills and Severin Fowles, pp. 715–728. Oxford University Press, Oxford.

Cameron, Catherine M., and Steve A. Tomka (editors). 1996. *The Abandonment of Settlements and Regions: Ethnoarchaeological and Archaeological Approaches*. Cambridge University Press, Cambridge.

Christenson, Andrew L. 2010. On the Reincorporation of Sherds into Pots. *Pottery Southwest* 28(4):2–14.

Colwell, Chip. 2016. Collaborative Archaeologies and Descendant Communities. *Annual Review of Anthropology* 45:113–127.

Colwell-Chanthaphonh, Chip, and T. J. Ferguson (editors). 2008. *Collaboration in Archaeological Practice: Engaging Descendant Communities*. AltaMira Press, Lanham, Maryland.

Cordell, Linda. 1984. *Prehistory of the Southwest*. Academic Press, New York.

Cushing, Frank Hamilton. 1890. Preliminary Notes on the Origin, Working Hypothesis, and Primary Research of the Hemenway Southwestern Archaeological Expedition. *Compte-Rendu de la Septieme Session, Congres International de Americanistes, Berlin 1888*:152–194.

Darling, J. Andrew. 2009. O'odham Trails and the Archaeology of Space. In *Landscapes of Movement: Trails, Paths, and Roads in Anthropological Perspective*, edited by James E. Snead, Clark L. Erickson, and J. Andrew Darling, pp. 61–83. University of Pennsylvania Museum of Archaeology and Anthropology, Philadelphia.

Darling, J. Andrew, Barnaby V. Lewis, Robert Valencia, and B. Sunday Eiselt. 2015. Archaeology in the Service of the Tribe: Three Episodes in Twenty-First-Century Tribal Archaeology in the US-Mexico Borderlands. *Kiva* 81(1–2):62–79.

Dongoske, Kurt, Leigh Jenkins, and T. J. Ferguson. 1993. Understanding the Past Through Hopi Oral History. *Native Peoples* 6(2):24–31.

Ebright, Malcolm, Rick Hendricks, and Richard W. Hughes. 2014. *Four Square Leagues: Pueblo Indian Land in New Mexico*. University of New Mexico Press, Albuquerque.

Eckert, Suzanne L. 2008. *Pottery and Practice: The Expression of Identity at Pottery Mound and Hummingbird Pueblo*. University of New Mexico Press, Albuquerque.

Eiselt, B. Sunday. 2012. *Becoming White Clay: A History and Archaeology of Jicarilla Apache Enclavement*. University of Utah Press, Salt Lake City.

Fabian, Johannes. 1983. *Time and the Other: How Anthropology Makes Its Object*. Columbia University Press, New York.

Ferguson, T. J., and Roger Anyon. 2001. Hopi and Zuni Cultural Landscapes: Implications of History and Scale for Cultural Resources Management. In *Native Peoples of the Southwest: Negotiating Land, Water, and Ethnicities*, edited by Laurie Weinstein, pp. 99–122. Bergin and Garvey, Westport, Connecticut.

Ferguson, T. J., Roger Anyon, and Edmund J. Ladd. 1996. Repatriation at the Pueblo of Zuni: Diverse Solution to Complex Problems. *American Indian Quarterly* 20(2):251–273.

Ferguson, T. J., and Chip Colwell-Chanthaphonh. 2006. *History Is in the Land: Multivocal Tribal Traditions in Arizona's San Pedro Valley*. University of Arizona Press, Tucson.

Ferguson, T. J., Leigh Jenkins, and Kurt Dongoske. 1995. Managing Hopi Sacred Sites to Protect Religious Freedom. *Cultural Survival Quarterly* 19(4):36–39.

Fewkes, Jesse W. 1900. Tusayan Migration Traditions. *19th Annual Report of the Bureau of American Ethnology of the Years 1897–1898*, Pt. 2, pp. 573–634. Government Printing Office, Washington, D.C.

Fewkes, Jesse W. 1904. Two Summers' Work in Pueblo Ruins. *22nd Annual Report of the Bureau of American Ethnology, 1903–4*, pp. 3–220. Washington, D.C.

Ford, Richard I. 1972. Barter, Gift, or Violence: An Analysis of Tewa Intertribal Exchange. In *Social Exchange and Interaction*, edited by Edwin N. Wilmsen, pp. 21–45. Anthropological Papers 46. Museum of Anthropology, University of Michigan, Ann Arbor.

Fowler, Don D. 2000. *A Laboratory for Anthropology: Science and Romanticism in the American Southwest, 1846–1930*. University of New Mexico Press, Albuquerque.

Fowles, Severin. 2011. Movement and the Unsettling of the Pueblos. In *Rethinking Anthropological Perspectives on Migration*, edited by Graciela S. Cabana and Jeffery J. Clark, pp. 45–67. University Press of Florida, Gainesville.

Fowles, Severin. 2013. *An Archaeology of Doings: Secularism and the Study of Pueblo Religion*. School for Advanced Research Press, Santa Fe, New Mexico.

Fowles, Severin, Jimmy Arterberry, Lindsay Montgomery, and Heather Atherton. 2017. Comanche New Mexico: The Eighteenth Century. In *New Mexico and the Pimería Alta: The Colonial Period in the American Southwest*, edited by John G. Douglass and William M. Graves, pp. 157–186. University Press of Colorado, Boulder.

Fox, Robin. 1967. *The Keresan Bridge: A Problem in Pueblo Ethnology*. Monographs on Social Anthropology 35. London School of Economics, London.

Geertz, Clifford. 1973. *The Interpretation of Culture*. Basic Books, New York.

Geertz, Clifford. 1980. Blurred Genres: The Refiguration of Social Thought. *American Scholar* 49(2):165–179.

Harlow, Francis H. 1973. *Matte-Paint Pottery of the Tewa, Keres and Zuni Pueblos*. Museum of New Mexico Press, Santa Fe.

Haury, Emil. 1958. Evidence at Point of Pines for a Prehistoric Migration from Northern Arizona. In *Migrations in New World Culture History*, edited by Raymond H. Thompson, pp. 1–7. University of Arizona Press, Tucson.

Hays-Gilpin, Kelley A. 2010. Behold the Brightly Shimmering Land: An Introduction. In *Painting the Cosmos: Metaphor and Worldview in Images from the Southwest Pueblos and Mexico*, edited by Kelley A. Hays-Gilpin and Polly Schaafsma, pp. 1–18. Museum of Northern Arizona Bulletin 67. Museum of Northern Arizona, Flagstaff.

Jacobs, Sue-Ellen, and Josephine Binford (editors), with M. Ellien Carroll, Henrietta M. Smith, and Tilar Mazzeo. 2004. *My Life in San Juan Pueblo: Stories of Esther Martinez*. University of Illinois Press, Urbana.

Judge, W. James. 1989. Chaco Canyon—San Juan Basin. In *Dynamics of Southwest Prehistory*, edited by Linda S. Cordell and George J. Gumerman, pp. 209–261. Smithsonian Institution, Washington, D.C.

Kidder, Alfred V. 1924. *An Introduction to the Study of Southwestern Archaeology with a Preliminary Account of the Excavations at Pecos*. Yale University Press, New Haven, Connecticut.

Kidder, Alfred V. 1927. Southwest Archaeological Conference. *Science* 68:489–491.

Klesert, Anthony L., and Alan S. Downer (editors). 1990. *Preservation on the Reservation: Native Americans, Native American Lands, and Archaeology*. Navajo Nation Papers in Anthropology No. 26. Navajo Nation Archaeology Dept., Navajo Nation Historic Preservation Dept., Window Rock, Arizona.

Kohn, Eduardo. 2015. Anthropology of Ontologies. *Annual Review of Anthropology* 44:311–327.

Kuwanwisiwma, Leigh J., and T. J. Ferguson. 2002. Ang Kukota. *Expedition* 46(2):24–29.

Laski, Vera. 1959. *Seeking Life*. Memoirs of the American Folklore Society 50. American Folklore Society, Philadelphia.

Lekson, Stephen H. 2009. *A History of the Ancient Southwest*. School for Advanced Research Press, Santa Fe, New Mexico.

Liebmann, Matthew J. 2012a. *Revolt: An Archaeological History of Pueblo Resistance and Revitalization in the 17th Century, New Mexico*. University of Arizona Press, Tucson.

Liebmann, Matthew J. 2012b. The Rest Is History: Devaluing the Recent Past in the Archaeology of the Pueblo Southwest. In *Decolonizing Indigenous Histories: Exploring Prehistoric/Colonial Transitions in Archaeology*, edited by Maxine Oland, Siobhan M. Hart, and Liam Frink, pp. 19–44. University of Arizona Press, Tucson.

Liebmann, Matthew J., and Uzma Z. Rizvi (editors). 2010. *Archaeology and the Postcolonial Critique*. AltaMira Press, Lanham, Maryland.

Lyons, Patrick D. 2003. *Ancestral Hopi Migrations*. Anthropological Papers of the University of Arizona No. 68. University of Arizona Press, Tucson.

Malotki, Ekkehart (editor). 1993. *Hopi Ruin Legends: Kiqotutuwtutsi*. University of Nebraska Press, Lincoln.

Malville, J. M., and N. J. Malville. 2001. Pilgrimage and Periodic Festivals as Process of Social Integration in Chaco Canyon. *Kiva* 66:329–344.

Marcus, George E., and Michael M. J. Fischer. 1986. *Anthropology as Cultural Critique: An Experimental Moment in the Human Sciences*. University of Chicago Press, Chicago.

Mills, Barbara J. (editor). 2004. *Identity, Feasting, and the Archaeology of the Greater Southwest*. University Press of Colorado, Boulder.

Mills, Barbara J. 2007. Performing the Feast: Visual Display and Suprahousehold Commensalism in the Pueblo Southwest. *American Antiquity* 72(2):201–239.

Mills, Barbara J., Jeffery J. Clark, Matthew A. Peeples, W. R. Haas Jr., John M. Roberts Jr., J. Brett Hill, Deborah L. Huntley, Lewis Borck, Ronald L. Breiger, Aaron Clauset, and M. Steven Shackley. 2013. Transformation of Social Networks in the Late Pre-Hispanic US Southwest. *PNAS* 110(15):5785–5790.

Mindeleff, Victor. 1891. *A Study of Pueblo Architecture: Tusayan and Cibola*. Annual Report of the Bureau of American Ethnology No. 8. Smithsonian Institution, Government Printing Office, Washington, D.C.

Mindeleff, Cosmos. 1900. *Localization of Tusayan Clans*. Annual Report of the Bureau of American Ethnology No. 19. Smithsonian Institution, Government Printing Office, Washington, D.C.

Naranjo, Tessie. 1995. Thoughts on Migration by Santa Clara Pueblo. *Journal of Anthropological Archaeology* 14:247–250.

Naranjo, Tessie. 2009. Some Recent Thoughts about Tewa Ancestral Movement. Paper presented at the New Mexico Archaeological Council Fall Conference, November 14, Albuquerque.

Naranjo, Tito, and Rina Swentzell. 1989. Healing Spaces in the Pueblo World. *American Indian Culture and Research Journal* 13(3–4):257–265.

Nelson, Ben A., and Steven A. LeBlanc. 1986. *Short-Term Sedentism in the American Southwest: The Mimbres Valley Salado.* University of New Mexico Press, Albuquerque.

Nelson, Margaret C., and Colleen Strawhacker (editors). 2011. *Movement, Connectivity and Landscape Change in the Ancient Southwest.* University Press of Colorado, Boulder.

Nelson, Nels. 1916. Chronology of the Tano Ruins, New Mexico. *American Anthropologist* 18(2):159–180.

Nicholas, George P. 2008. Native Peoples and Archaeology. *Encyclopedia of Archaeology,* edited by Deborah M. Pearsall, pp. 1660–1669. Academic Press, New York.

Ortiz, Alfonso. 1969. *The Tewa World: Space, Time, Being and Becoming in a Pueblo Society.* University of Chicago Press, Chicago.

Ortiz, Alfonso. 1972. Ritual Drama and the Pueblo World View. In *New Perspectives on the Pueblos,* edited by Alfonso Ortiz, pp. 135–161. University of New Mexico Press, Albuquerque.

Ortiz, Alfonso. 1977. Some Concerns Central to the Writing of "Indian" History. *Indian Historian* 10(1):17–22.

Ortiz, Alfonso. 1991. Through Tewa Eyes: Origins. *National Geographic* 180(4):6–13.

Ortiz, Simon. 1992. *Woven Stone.* University of Arizona Press, Tucson.

Ortman, Scott G. 2012. *Winds from the North: Tewa Origins and Historical Anthropology.* University of Utah Press, Salt Lake City.

Ortman, Scott G., and Catherine M. Cameron. 2011. A Framework for Controlled Comparisons of Ancient Southwestern Movement. In *Movement, Connectivity, and Landscape Change in the Ancient Southwest,* edited by Margaret C. Nelson and Colleen Strawhacker, pp. 233–252. University Press of Colorado, Boulder.

Powell, Shirley. 1983. *Mobility and Adaptation: The Anasazi of Black Mesa, Arizona.* Southern Illinois University Press, Carbondale.

Preucel, Robert W. 1991. *Seasonal Agricultural Circulation and Residential Mobility: A Prehistoric Example from the Pajarito Plateau, New Mexico.* Garland Press, New York.

Preucel, Robert W. 2006. *Archaeological Semiotics.* Blackwell Press, Oxford.

Rautman, Alison. 2000. Population Aggregation, Community Organization, and Plaza-Oriented Pueblos in the American Southwest. *Journal of Field Archaeology* 27(3):271–283.

Ravesloot, John. 1990. On the Treatment and Reburial of Human Remains: The San Xavier Bridge Project, Tucson, Arizona. *American Indian Quarterly* 14(1):35–50.

Reed, Erik. 1949. Sources of Upper Rio Grande Pueblo Culture and Population. *El Palacio* 56(6):163–184.

Sando, Joe S. 1979. The Pueblo Revolt. In *Southwest*, edited by Alfonso Ortiz, pp. 194–197. Handbook of North American Indians, Vol. 9. Smithsonian Institution Press, Washington, D.C.

Sekaquaptewa, Emory, and Dorothy Washburn. 2004. They Go Along Singing: Reconstructing the Hopi Past from Ritual Metaphors in Song and Image. *American Antiquity* 69(3):457–486.

Sekaquaptewa, Emory, and Dorothy Washburn. 2015. *Hopi Katsina Songs*. University of Nebraska Press, Lincoln.

Silko, Leslie Marmon. 1995. Interior and Exterior Landscapes: The Pueblo Migration Stories. In *Landscape in America*, edited by George F. Thompson, pp. 155–169. University of Texas Press, Austin.

Smith, Claire, and H. Martin Wobst (editors). 2005. *Indigenous Archaeologies: Decolonizing Theory and Practice*. Routledge, London.

Smith, Linda Tuhiwai. 1999. *Decolonization Methodologies: Research and Indigenous Peoples*. Zed Books, London.

Spielmann, Katherine A. (editor). 1998. *Migration and Reorganization: The Pueblo IV Period in the American Southwest*. Arizona State University Anthropological Research Papers No. 51. Arizona Board of Regents, Tempe.

Spielmann, Katherine A. (editor). 2017. *Landscapes of Social Transformation in the Salinas Province and the Eastern Pueblo World*. University of Arizona Press, Tucson.

Suina, Joseph. 1992. Pueblo Secrecy: Result of Intrusion. *New Mexico Magazine* 70(1):60–63.

Sweet, Jill. 2004. *Dances of the Tewa Pueblo Indians: Expressions of New Life*. 2nd ed. School of American Research Press, Santa Fe, New Mexico.

Swentzell, Rina. 1991. Levels of Truth: Southwest Archaeologists and Anasazi/Pueblo People. In *Puebloan Past and Present: Papers in Honor of Stewart Peckham*, pp. 177–181. Archaeological Society of New Mexico, Albuquerque.

Swentzell, Rina. 1993. Mountain Form, Village Form: Unity in the Pueblo World. In *Ancient Land, Ancestral Places: Paul Logsdon in the Pueblo Southwest*, by Stephen H. Lekson and Rina Swentzell. pp. 139–147. Museum of New Mexico Press, Santa Fe.

Tainter, Joseph A. 1988. *The Collapse of Complex Societies*. Cambridge University Press, Cambridge.

Upham, Steadman. 1987. The Tyranny of Ethnographic Analogy in Southwestern Archaeology. In *Coasts, Plains and Deserts: Essays in Honor of Reynold J. Ruppé*, edited by Sylvia Gaines and G. A. Clark, pp. 265–279. Anthropological Research Paper No. 38. Arizona State University, Tempe.

Varien, Mark D., and James M. Potter (editors). 2008. *The Social Construction of Communities: Agency, Structure, and Identity in the Prehispanic Southwest*. AltaMira Press, Lanham, Maryland.

Watkins, Joe. 2000. *Indigenous Archaeology: American Indian Values and Scientific Practice*. AltaMira Press, Lanham, Maryland.

Welch, John R., Chip Colwell-Chanthaphonh, and Mark Altaha. 2005. Retracing the Battle of Cibecue: Western Apache, Documentary, and Archaeological Interpretations. *Kiva* 71(2):133–163.

Wilcox, Michael V. 2009. *The Pueblo Revolt and the Mythology of Conquest: An Indigenous Archaeology of Contact*. University of California Press, Berkeley.

Wissler, Clark. 1917. *The American Indian: An Introduction to the Anthropology of the New World*. Douglas C. McMurtrie, New York.

Woodbury, Richard. 1993. *60 Years of Southwestern Archaeology: A History of the Pecos Conference*. University of New Mexico Pres, Albuquerque.

Wylie, Alison. 1985. The Reaction Against Analogy. *Advances in Archaeological Method and Theory* 8:63–111.

Plate 1 An Acoma Tribal Historic Preservation Office Advisory Board member inspects an inward-circling spiral petroglyph in the Jesus Valley on the northwest side of Kaweshtima Kuutyu (Mount Taylor). *Photograph by Kurt F. Anschuetz*

Plate 2 Jemez cultural resource coordinator Chris Toya (*left*) discusses the Wâavêmâ landscape with Pat Waquie (*right*), leader of the Jemez Eagle Society. *Photograph by Matthew Liebmann*

Plate 3 Clayton Panteah (*left*) and Octavius Seowtewa (*right*) measure a historic wagon road on the Fort Wingate Depot Activity during Zuni ethnographic fieldwork. *Photograph by Jacob Campbell*

Plate 4 Looking northwest toward the place of emergence from Tsip-in'owingeh on the edge of the Tewa world. *Photograph by Samuel Duwe*

Plate 5 An aerial view of Chevelon Canyon. Dense concentrations of petroglyphs and cultural material demonstrate use of the area for thousands of years. Along with the rest of the Homol'ovi region, it remains an important location for the Hopi people. *Photograph by Henry D. Wallace*

Plate 6 Archaeologist Chet Walker prepares a drone to fly over Tunyo near San Ildefonso Pueblo. *Photograph courtesy of Archaeo-Geophysical Associates, LLC*

Plate 7 Erik Fender examines Ogapoge pottery at the School for Advanced Research, June 2017. *Photograph by Bruce Bernstein*

Plate 8 Members of the Pueblo of Pojoaque Youth Hoop Dancers perform in front of the Pueblo of Pojoaque Feliciana Tapia Viarrial Dream Chapel during the community gathering T'owa vi Thaa (Peoples' Day) in October 2013. *Photograph by Shirley Catanach*

PART I
ON BECOMING

Movement as an Acoma Way of Life

Damian Garcia and Kurt F. Anschuetz

> Mythic roads lead us beyond ourselves.
> It doesn't matter where they lead.
> We are there on them heading beyond.
> They could be returning or leaving.
> We could be leaving or returning.
>
> —Simon J. Ortiz, "Epic"

Movement Is Life is a prevalent metaphor in Pueblo culture, and researchers have examined its possible meanings through a variety of anthropological approaches. For example, one of us, after investigating this metaphor through a cultural-ecological perspective in a study of pre-Hispanic Pueblo agricultural practice, suggested that old fieldworks can, under circumstances where sustainable land-use practices were sustained for generations, be a material manifestation of a people's commitment to place over a long-term cycle of ecological renewal (Anschuetz 2001:52). As each of the chapters in this volume demonstrates, however, movement in Pueblo culture entails much more activity and meaning than a materialist-economic strategy for sustainable crop production.

The charge of the present contribution is to consider how movement traditionally has been—and continues to be—an all-encompassing way of life at the Pueblo of Acoma. We organize our remarks in two principal sections.

Our discussion begins at the beginning to show the essential place that movement occupies in Acoma Pueblo's cultural-historical account of its *becoming* from the time of Emergence. Although the Natural World and the People were not fully formed—Acoma traditions characterize the First People as being *unripe*—they are said to have been self-aware and conscious of their distinct cultural identity. We continue our examination of the formative process of the First Acoma People's epic Migration in their search for Haak'u, the home prepared especially for them in exchange for their commitment to serve as caretakers of the

Natural World for eternity. During their journey, the First Acoma People constructed a knowable world out of sometimes capricious, often dangerous, and ever-changing surroundings. In this process, they were creative agents in *ripening* their Natural World—and *preparing* (i.e., *ripening*) themselves. We next turn our attention to a consideration of how Acoma's traditional principles of stewardship are founded in the lessons that the First Acoma People learned during their Migration. They not only learned how they needed to interact with the land, water, soils, plants, and animals to sustain their families and Pueblo, they constructed and refined a cultural landscape that informs the People's understandings of place, time, community, and identity. We continue with a deliberation on the special and spiritual qualities of the material traces, many (although certainly not all) of which archaeologists readily recognize as cultural resources, that Acoma's ancestors left behind while they were on the move.

In the second part of our discussion, we explore the Pueblo's essential, traditional ethic: that *being* Acoma requires their continued movement. Upon their arrival at Haak'u, their promised home, the First Acoma People realized that their continuing journey of becoming required them, in fulfillment of their sacred stewardship obligations, to cover their cultural landscape in a continuous ebb and flow of movement between the center and the distant peripheries to maintain balance and unity in the Natural World. We consider how Acoma members maintain their occupation of their homeland through diverse economic and ritual movements. While many of these passages leave observable traces, other kinds of movements, such as thoughts, stories, songs, dances, and prayers, which are integral to good stewardship, do not. We also acknowledge the variance inherent in the temporal rhythms of these movements, with some occurring continuously and others periodically. We find that each movement, regardless of its length or patterns of temporality, renews the Pueblo's cherished stories and reaffirms Acoma's culture, history, inheritance, and identity.

FIRST STEPS: EMERGENCE

Since the time of Creation, the Pueblo of Acoma has been a community on the move. Acoma elders hold a core belief that the details of Creation and Emergence are not for outsiders to know. We respect their opinion and guidance on these matters and remain mindful of our responsibilities

Movement as an Acoma Way of Life

to protect privileged information. While we will be careful not to dwell on these topics in ways that violate trust, we are compelled to share several generalized observations about Creation and Emergence. We do so because Creation and Emergence effectively establish cultural contexts for understanding what Acoma elders have shared with us about the record of the people's movement, beginning with Acoma's Migration from Shipap'u, the "Place of Emergence," and search for Haak'u, the "Place Prepared." The idea of Haak'u represents more than the preordained and prepared end point of Acoma's Migration. One individual explained that depending on the context in which it is used, the word *Haak'u* can also refer to the road that Salt Woman prepared for the First Acoma People to follow while on their journey.

For our present purposes, it is sufficient to say that among the oral traditions held by the Pueblos, including those cherished at Acoma, there is a common understanding that the First People, Spiritual Beings, animals, and plants all lived together in the Underworld and that death was unknown (Ortiz 1969:13). Yet realizing that they were still "soft and pliable, and unripe or unfinished" (Williamson 1984:62; see also Ortiz 1969:16–17), the First People emerged onto the surface of the Natural World, much like the plants that they were later to sow and depend upon. They carried with them the geographic features and resources found in the Natural World today (Parsons 1996:102–103). Even then, the Natural World, the First People, and the ways that humans lived were incomplete and lacked many of the defining characteristics and qualities known today.

Emergence marks the beginning of the interdependent relationship between the First People and the Natural World in a never-ending cultural-historical process of *becoming* (Ortiz 1969:1), which, in Pueblo philosophy, refers both to the malleability of the people and the ideas that they pass on to subsequent generations as their inheritance (after Cajete 1994). Nevertheless, "the Emergence was an emergence into a precise cultural identity" (Silko 1995:162). That is, in Pueblo oral traditions, Emergence marks the time when the people "became aware of themselves as they are even now" (Silko 1995:162). Pueblo oral traditions maintain further that the ancestors of Acoma (and every other Pueblo) not only possessed self-awareness upon Emergence, they were conscious of their cultural distinctiveness and identity—that which sets each Pueblo apart from all others.

Figure 1.1 A petroglyph of an inward circling, counterclockwise spiral. Photograph by Kurt F. Anschuetz.

To fulfill their destiny to *become*, the First Acoma People and all of the other First Peoples set forth from Shipap'u to cover the world in search of their promised homes, each through their own unique and epic Migration. The First Acoma People alone followed Salt Woman's guidance. She said to them, "I shall travel anti-clockwise around the earth, circling inward (spiral fashion [from north to west, to south, to east, and so on]) to its center. Follow after me. Tell your children and your children's children that they will meet me again at a place called Acoma [Haak'u], in the middle of the world" (Benedict 1930:59; figure 1.1, plate 1).

MIGRATION

BECOMING THROUGH MOVEMENT

Acoma oral traditions record how the First Acoma People constructed social order among themselves during their Migration from Shipap'u in search of Haak'u. They also recognized interdependent environmental orders through their experiences, which instructed them about the dynamic complexities inherent in their relationships with the natural and supernatural realms of the cosmos. Through recognition, understanding, and purposeful deeds, the First Acoma People were actors in their own culturally and historically contingent process of becoming in which they and their landscape ripened and assumed an increasingly solid form in unison.

Underscored by characteristics of value, persistence, and continuity, the First Acoma People established their most treasured traditions, which generally relate to people's understandings of "how they became who they are" (Peckham 1990:2) and persist to this day. Although they are dynamic and subject to change over time given the latitude in their form and practice, traditions allow for persistence and continuity of the essential culturally informed principles (after Peckham 1990:2–5).

Salt Woman's characterization of the Migration from Shipap'u to Haak'u as an inward circling, counterclockwise spiral (Benedict 1930:59; see also Roberts 1932:151; see figure 1.1) offers insights into the traditions informing how Acoma people today conceptualize their cultural landscape and understand the archaeological traces and other cultural resources within their homeland's embrace. The winding path, which the First Acoma People followed in Salt Woman's footsteps, implicates the vast geographic breadth of their cultural-historical experience across the northern Southwest (figure 1.2). Because the First Acoma People set out from Shipap'u at the same time as other First Peoples began their own journeys, it is clear that Acoma's forebears interacted with other human communities along their way. Additionally, the specification of a counterclockwise pathway that looped in ever-tightening circles from north to west, to south, and to east established a framework from which the people learned to define their sense of *rightful orientation* (Cajete 1994:37; see also Tyler 1964:171): how to live life appropriately within the Natural World. This fundamental lesson—which Gregory Cajete (1994:49) observes "is more than physical context and placement. . . . It is about how the human spirit understands itself"—prepared the people to recognize when they had, at long last, arrived at Haak'u.

Through the association of cardinal directions with particular natural and cultural phenomena that they experienced in their landscape, the First Acoma People built mental orders, or "maps in the mind" (Basso

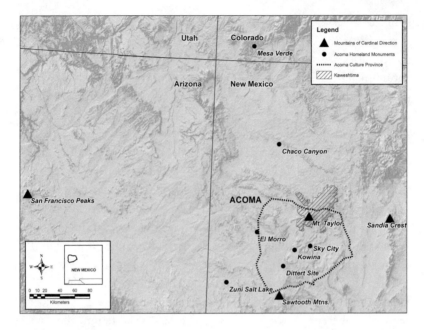

Figure 1.2 The location of the Acoma Culture Province (a.k.a., the Western Keres Culture Province) in its regional context, with selected landscape features important to the Pueblo of Acoma.

1996:43), which seem "less to control the environment than to control the world within" (Johnson 1995:200). By defining direction and placement, Acoma's ancestors imposed cultural order in a world that was otherwise chaotic, even perilous, in its raw state of existence. Through this process, they effectively ripened their Natural World—and themselves—through movement.

PRINCIPLES OF STEWARDSHIP FOUNDED IN MOVEMENT

We would be remiss not to briefly mention the covenant that the First Acoma People made with Spiritual Beings at Shipap'u at the time of Emergence in exchange for the promise of Haak'u at the end of Migration. This covenant helps us understand Acoma's sense of *spiritual ecology*, which is "the traditional relationship and participation of indigenous people with place that includes not only the land itself, but also the way people perceive the reality of their worlds and themselves" (Anschuetz 2007:132; after Cajete 1994:43–44). It also provides valuable context for comprehending the values that Acoma members continue to place on the cultural resources that Acoma's ancestors created and left behind during their Migration in search of Haak'u.

The pact between Spiritual Beings and the First Acoma People specifies the Pueblo's eternal obligation to serve as the stewards of the Natural World in exchange for the privilege of receiving Haak'u (Duff et al. 2008:10). The many places where the First Acoma People stayed during their journey, including White House, Mesa Verde, Chaco Canyon, and Kowina, represent a record of the pragmatic lessons through which Acoma's ancestors learned how to interact with the land, water, soils, plants, animals, and one another to sustain their families and community into the future.

Laguna Pueblo author Leslie Marmon Silko offers a relevant observation:

> The land, the sky, and all that is within them—the landscape—includes human beings. Interrelationships in the Pueblo landscape are complex and fragile. The unpredictability of the weather, the aridity and harshness of much of the terrain in the high plateau country explain in large part the relentless attention the ancient Pueblo people gave to the sky and the earth around them. Survival depended upon harmony and cooperation not only among human beings, but also among all things—the animate and the less animate [Silko 1995:157].

The First Acoma People also learned to remember that if they lived well and fulfilled their solemn responsibilities as stewards of the Natural World, then the land and its resources would always be there for them—and for all other people—during times of need. Under the watch of ever-present Guardians, who stood as sentinels to protect them during their journey of discovery during Migration, the First Acoma People drew upon their keen observations and the accumulation of experience to construct and refine a cultural landscape that simultaneously documents and informs the people's understandings of place, time, community, and identity.

The First Acoma People, just like so many other Indigenous communities of the northern Southwest (e.g., Basso 1996; Kelley and Francis 1996; Linford 2000), recorded place-names that identify physiographic features and resource locations through descriptions of their ecological characteristics or by recounting their actions and those of ancestors or Spiritual Beings. Descriptive names not only tell what may be found at a location, they refer to revered stewardship principles embedded in instructive backstories.

The latter class of place-names comprises the building blocks of *landscapes as memory* (Küchler 1993), through which "the present is not so much produced by the past but reproduces itself in the form of the past" (Morphy 1993:239–240). These complementary classes of place-names bridge the difference between small places on the landscape used for particular purposes and general stories that outline culture history and evaluate change (Anschuetz 2002:2.8). Whether invoking stewardship obligations or reliving history in "the active present tense" (Basso 1996:33), place-names additionally orient people within their physical environment. Silko (1995:158) writes, "Through the stories we hear who we are." In other words, the *storied landscape* (Kelley and Frances 1996) informs people of their identity.

The values and emotions that traditional stories convey serve as the moral compasses (after Ferguson 2002:4.6; Young 1987:4–9) within the Pueblo's cultural inheritance that continue to guide Acoma's stewardship of the land and its natural and cultural resources. Silko (1995:162–163) explains further that in delineating "the complexities of the relationship that human beings must maintain with the surrounding world if they hope to survive," the "prominent geographic features and landmarks that are mentioned in the narratives exist for ritual purposes."

CREATED BY A PEOPLE ON THE MOVE, CULTURAL RESOURCES ARE ALIVE

Among the people of Acoma (AHPO Advisory Board Members 2012), as well as among the other Pueblos generally (Anschuetz 2002:3.33), the artifacts, ash, and features observed at archaeological sites represent more than just the material residues of their ancestors' activities during their journey from Shipap'u to Haak'u. These, and other cultural resources that lack recognizable archaeological signatures, serve as reference points within Acoma's storied landscape. Moreover, they are invested with the energy of life itself.

Acoma members also share the widely held Pueblo belief that the spirits of their ancestors continue to live at the places where they lived during their natural lives (Krall and Andreani 2007:9). One elder has observed that Acoma's ancestral sites serve as a reminder that "we were here" and that "we are still here" (Charlie et al. 2001). Another elder has explained, "The oral histories say that, as people got old during the migrations, some couldn't travel. So they made a site and they were like, 'I want to die here' . . . the elders would say, 'they were left behind not to be left behind, but because they could not travel anymore,' and that is why these sites will always be alive" (Duff et al. 2008:10).

The artifacts, ash, and features that Acoma members see at archaeological sites do not continue to live lives without meaning. Even the smallest, seemingly most mundane trace of human activity relates both to the landscape of which Acoma's members are a part and their cultural construction of identity. Archaeological artifacts, features, and sites are cherished because these resources describe how the ancestors engaged in the greatest event imaginable on the most holy of all stages: the *becoming* of the Acoma Pueblo within its cultural landscape. These traces are the "footprints," "fingerprints," and other lasting "impressions" and "imprints" of the First Acoma People's presence (AHPO Advisory Board Members 2012; Charlie et al. 2002; Concho et al. 2001).

Talking further about the footprints, fingerprints, and impressions and imprints of their ancestors, Acoma elders have said that these traces are "good signs of where we come from" (Charlie et al. 2002). Moreover, the goodness that their ancestors left at their sites is available to sustain the contemporary world. In fact, each of these cultural properties has a teaching purpose through its beauty, structure, and role in Acoma's history of becoming (Charlie et al. 2001).

At one level, specific knowledge of particular archaeological sites is not a prerequisite; general knowledge that the footprints, fingerprints, and impressions and imprints exist within Acoma's landscape is sufficient, given the cultural-historical contexts that people learn as members of their Pueblo, to comprehend the information that these living traces convey about the people who invested their natural lives there

(Anschuetz 2012:33). Material "evidence," so prized by archaeologists, is less important than the context in which the archaeological traces reside for Acoma elders to glean information about the ancestors. Knowledgeable Acoma members explain:

> As "footprints," archaeological sites show Acoma's people (and the rest of us) the locations of where their ancestors lived and traveled.
> As "fingerprints," archaeological sites show what the People did during their lives.
> As "impressions" and "imprints," archaeological sites convey the lessons of "living, sacrifice, and history" (AHPO Advisory Board Members 2012) that the people of Acoma have inherited as their cultural heritage and that they intend to pass on to their following generations.

One elder, as he examined traces left by the First Acoma People in the northern San Juan Basin, expressed the sentiment, "They [Acoma's ancestors] made it possible for us." Another elder, reflecting on the love and faith that his Pueblo's ancestors held for their families and community, including the generations to come, quietly observed, "How hard would it have been for them to leave what they knew—and had experienced—for a promise of what still awaited them?"

MOVING IN AND OUT OF THE CENTER TO SUSTAIN THE WHOLE

When the First Acoma People climbed a high mountain that many of us know today as Mount Taylor, they realized that they had reached Kaweshtima Kuutyu. Climbing to the summit, the people unfurled a blanket. The textile opened as it rolled down the mountain's slope and spread out onto the plains, mesas, and canyons to the west, south, and east. The people understood that these lands were part of Kaweshtima Kuutyu. They rejoiced knowing that they were close to Haak'u.

Arriving at the base of a striking mesa, the First Acoma People called out "Haak'u" in each of the four cardinal directions, north, west, south, and east, just as the Spiritual Beings at Shipap'u had instructed. When they heard their calls echo back to them from these same four directions, and in the same counterclockwise order, the people were happy with the knowledge that they had arrived at Haak'u and that their Migration had concluded. They built their home, which is known as Sky City and continues to be occupied, on top of the mesa.

Drawing from what the First Acoma People learned during their spiraling journey across the geographic expanse of the northern Southwest, both near and far, they constructed a cultural landscape that established the Pueblo of Acoma's sense of rightful orientation in the Natural World, as well as within the greater cosmos. Cardinal directions figure prominently in the Keres conceptualization of a square, flat Natural World (figure 1.3). Places near the corners of the Natural World, where powerful Spiritual Beings reside, are also important in this construction. Through the association of colors, plants, and animals with the cardinal directions, the First Acoma People imposed further organization on the wealth of observation and experience that they compiled during Migration. They recognized mountains, including their beloved Kaweshtima Kuutyu, which towers above all others as a conspicuous reminder of the prominence of north in the Pueblo's Emergence and Migration traditions. The First Acoma People also identified springs and other features associated with Spiritual Beings and places of blessing in their "maps in the mind" (after Basso 1996:43). They further understood that these meaningful features and places are markers along pathways that, literally and figuratively, unite Haak'u with the ends of the Natural World.

Even though they had arrived at Haak'u, the First Acoma People's travels throughout their cultural landscape were only just beginning. Their calls of Haak'u to the cardinal directions, which had echoed back and forth between the edges of the Natural World that they had traversed and the center where they now stood, informed the First Acoma People of what their next steps needed to be in their continuing journey of becoming.

Just as Haak'u was the "Place Prepared" to receive them, the First Acoma People were themselves prepared through their experience of Migration to accept the privilege and responsibility of receiving Haak'u. The meaning inherent in Acoma's cultural landscape–based construction of relationship and connectivity, founded on Emergence and Migration and actualized in the echo of the ritualized chant at the base of Haak'u,

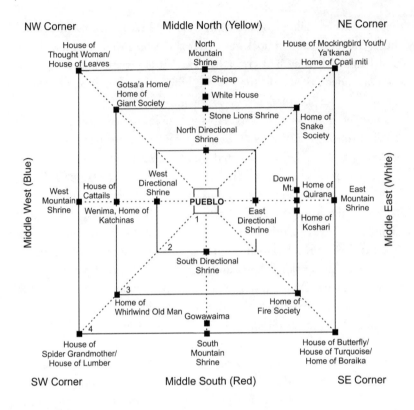

Figure 1.3 A composite depiction of the Keres world. Adapted from Duwe 2011:Figure 2.5; Snead and Preucel 1999:Figure 8.1.

is clear. The First Acoma People comprehended that their sacred trust as the land's stewards required them to return to the distant areas of their homeland in which their forebears lived during their Migration from Shipap'u not only in their thoughts, prayers, songs, and stories, but also in pilgrimages.

The "mythic roads," to which Simon Ortiz (2002) refers in his poetry and which are depicted graphically in constructions of the Keres world (see figure 1.3), unify Haak'u with the ends of Acoma's cultural landscape and must be followed still. Silko (1995:162) explains that the "continued use of [those routes] creates a unique relationship between the ritual-mythical world and the actual, everyday world." The dictate to use the mythic roads to sustain relationships between the natural and supernatural worlds applies even if most of Acoma's members never experience either the physical reality of standing on the edge of their community's landscape or the metaphysical reality of knowing the Pueblo's most privileged traditions about where the places with greatest spiritual power lie.

As a community of disparate social parts, the Pueblo of Acoma comprises an assembly of clans, each of which has its own cultural-historical experience. Community members also have differential access to privileged cultural information based on their social positions and affiliations within the Pueblo. It is unsurprising, therefore, that there exists considerable variability in how people talk about their relationships with particular areas of their Pueblo's aboriginal stewardship area. (For this reason, it is unlikely that any individual would recognize all of the elements depicted in figure 1.3, which is a composite depiction of the Keres world.)

While there are differences in accounts among Acoma members regarding the identification, organization, and meaning of features in the Pueblo's cultural landscape, two indispensable principles unite these many remembrances and points of view. The first is that the people of Acoma possess an expansive homeland (see figure 1.2), which they have occupied since time immemorial. The second is that the Pueblo's members continue to occupy their homeland to this day, and they strive to do so into the future. They maintain these relationships through varied secular and ritual actions that celebrate and maintain Acoma's cultural and historical identity as a distinct community within its landscape.

Secular activities involving the movement of Acoma's people into the landscape include farming, plant gathering, hunting, mineral collecting, trading, sheepherding, and cattle ranching. These actions, although certainly including requests for assistance and gratitude for the blessings received, focus on tangible production, processing, and consumption to fulfill the physical needs of the people and their community. The spatial and temporal organization and structure of such outwardly mundane, economic undertakings, however, are not simply defined by objective and measureable variables, such as distance, natural environmental characteristics, and proximity to other human communities. Acoma's organization of the geographic space upon which the people depend for their material well-being and the structure of their activities is further conditioned by the Pueblo's traditions of movement within and beyond an area bounded by a multitude of blessing features and other cultural markers, including Guardians, that define the core of Acoma's aboriginal homeland. This area is known to anthropologists as either the Acoma Culture Province (Dittert 1959, 1998; Ruppé 1990) or the Western Keres Culture Province (Marshall 1990), and Acoma members rely on oral traditions naming these landscape features to commemorate the becoming of their Pueblo and to know who they are as a people. Importantly, these diverse landscape features do not denote a tangible border limiting movement and land use. Instead, they symbolically demarcate the transition between Acoma's landscape of everyday living and the broad geographic expanse of the Pueblo's greater aboriginal homeland through which the First Acoma People traversed during Migration. For the people of the Pueblo, the core homeland is *Acoma*, while the distant areas in which their forebears resided over the countless generations of their Migration are all part of the ancestral homeland.

Archaeologists have discussed the seasonal, annual, and intergenerational movements of Acoma people back and forth across the breadth of the Acoma core homeland from Sky City. They describe a pattern of movement, which they term "seasonal agricultural dispersion," in which small groups of people (the size of a family or smaller) would leave their permanent village to farm in remote settings and return to their residential pueblo in the fall with the fruits of their labor (e.g., Anschuetz 2009; Dittert 1959, 1998). Initially, archaeologists viewed seasonal agricultural dispersion as a way to reduce the potential for competition over limited arable lands in response to increasing population densities experienced throughout the Acoma Culture Province during the eleventh century. Archaeologists further cast this economic strategy as a defining organizational principle of Acoma settlement system at around AD 1100 in response to the combined factors of continuing population growth and the patchy distribution of arable lands. With the shift from summer-dominated to winter-dominated precipitation at around the end of the thirteenth century, the organization of Acoma's seasonal agricultural dispersion strategy underwent a transformation as centers of year-round residence increasingly focused on a few well-watered locations. Rather than abandoning vast tracts within the province, people reorganized their land-use practices in a way that maintained a high degree of cultural continuity in the geographic reach of their occupation within established traditional frameworks. Areas that formerly had been loci of dense year-round settlement, such as the Cebolleta Mesa and North Plains districts, became important locations for seasonal agricultural season dispersion (Dittert 1959, 1998). The people periodically returned to the settings of their former homes to farm when local temperature and precipitation patterns were favorable.

Archaeologists apply materialist frameworks to describe how ancestral Acoma populations maintained access to the broad expanse of the Acoma Culture Province to buffer the threat of agricultural crop failures at varying spatial and temporal scales (Anschuetz 2009). They even characterize settlement systems based on frequent residential movements as the practice of short-term sedentism (Anschuetz 2009, citing Nelson and LeBlanc 1986). Acoma elders, however, view these seemingly secular movements as the practice of the Pueblo's established, sacred stewardship traditions.

Acoma traditions broadly conform with those of other Pueblos (Anschuetz 2005, 2007, 2017) by referring to the ideas of *rest*, *renewal*, and *reuse* (after Louie Hena, personal communication 1999) in discussions of the movements of their ancestors in and out of old settlements over time, sustainable agricultural land use, and managed foraging and collecting areas (e.g., Duff et al. 2008:1). They also generally agree with a sentiment shared by Tessie Naranjo (personal communication 1995), a Santa Clara Tewa scholar, who has examined movement within her community's traditions: "The ground has to rest, the ground has to breathe."

Notions of rest, renewal, and breath coincide neatly with the concept of fallow cycles for hunting and gathering territories, as well as agricultural land, sometimes employed by archaeologists (e.g., Anschuetz 2005). The idea that the Pueblos would leave a locality to allow it to "rest and renew" (its fertility) implies that the People will return to this location in the future. These principles, in turn, challenge the uncritical application of the archaeological concept of abandonment to describe settlement pattern changes. Instead, the three R's of Pueblo life are guiding principles (after Louie Hena, personal communication 1999) within a world of frequent residential movement.

These principles similarly inform the traditional practice of recycling cultural resources left by Acoma's ancestors in the landscape. Based on attitudes, perceptions, and values that cultural resource managers find challenging, Acoma elders have expressed a firm, unified opinion that, in an ideal world, the material remains of the living footprints, fingerprints, and other lasting impressions and imprints should be repatriated to the Pueblo faced with destruction during proposed development. This action would assist their forebears in finally completing their journey to Haak'u. Once home, these traces would also receive appropriate treatment, which potentially includes renewal and reuse, in accord with Acoma's cultural values. For example, fragments of pottery made by the ancestors are prized in the preparation of temper needed for contemporary ceramics. This interaction of the ancestors and the present-day generation of Acoma, in turn, reproduces the present through a material use of the past to sustain living traditions into the future.

As a storied landscape, Acoma's outlying homeland expanse, which represents a geographic space similarly shared by other Pueblo communities for their own purposes, is imbued with values and meanings beyond the domain of everyday secular concerns. Traditionally, Pueblos did not reside in their outlying homeland for extended periods after the First Acoma People reached Haak'u. Despite this lack of permanent residential use, the Pueblo of Acoma has continued to occupy the entirety of its cultural landscape through focused thought and action.

The people commemorate the love and sacrifices of the ancestors. Liturgical rites observed at Haak'u include the retelling of privileged oral traditions, prayers, songs, dances, and so forth and may relate to the Emergence of Acoma's people, their subsequent Migration, and their becoming. Complexly nested metaphors reassert and confirm the multiplicity of culturally and historically contingent meanings inherent in the seemingly facile idea that movement is life. However, metaphors of movement in ritual, whether expressed in discourse, performance, or material culture, are neither held nor expressed among Acoma's members homogeneously. Additionally, many of these constructs likely "reflect longstanding ontological beliefs that structure thought and action below the level of conscious awareness" (Ortman 2009:4; see his discussion for a cogent examination of the nature of metaphor in Pueblo thought).

Blessings emanating from rituals observed in Sky City, atop Haak'u, spread out across Acoma and the greater ancestral homeland following pathways (and Ortiz's [2002] "mythic roads") that intersect a multitude of Holy Places in the landscape. Other rituals involve pilgrimages by elders, who possess the privileged training and experience needed to interact with great power, to Holy Places in the Pueblo's hinterlands. Pilgrims deliver blessings upon their arrival at destinations, which usually only few Acoma people are privileged to know, under the protective watch of Guardians. They relive the traditions of Emergence, Migration, and becoming during their return home to Haak'u. Certain pilgrimages cover great distances and extend well north of the Four Corners. The pathways of such far-reaching journeys may pass by landscape markers that are considered "doors," which demarcate the pilgrims' movement in the objective realm of the Natural World from a realm of increasingly mythical space and time.

With complementary outward and inward foci, these contrasting forms of traditional activity involve physical and metaphysical forms of ritual movement. Through their actions, and the thoughts that inform their deeds, Acoma's members demonstrate their continuing fulfillment of their Pueblo's sacrosanct stewardship pledge and petition Spiritual Beings for assistance to benefit the whole of humanity. Equally important, the people also rededicate themselves to the goodness of—and their attendant responsibility for—Acoma's cultural-historical inheritance.

CONCLUSIONS

Two decades ago, Linda S. Cordell (1998:64) observed that archaeologists were beginning to comprehend Pueblo population movement as "something to have been embraced rather than resisted." We agree with Cordell in a general sense that archaeologists have been expanding their comprehension of why population movement was embraced within the materialist perspective of scientific archaeology. Nonetheless, archaeologists still have much work to do to incorporate the ideational aspects of Pueblo choreographies of movement into their interpretive constructs and efforts to evaluate the significance of cultural resources.

Renowned Santa Clara Pueblo members and scholars Tito Naranjo and Rina Swentzell (1989:261) write, "Movement is the revered element of life." Tessie Naranjo (1995:248) adds, "Movement, clouds, wind and rain are one. Movement must be emulated by the people."

This chapter demonstrates that for the people of Acoma, movement is not just something to be revered and emulated, it truly is a way of life. Referents to movement permeate traditional thought to organize and structure action.

From the perspective of cultural landscapes, movement provides an ideational cohesiveness through which a "web of memories and ideas that create an identity [and] is a part of oneself" is created and sustained (Silko 1995:167). Places on the landscape, which the First Acoma People moved through and came to know as part of both the Pueblo and themselves, are now the places that their descendants, including today's generations, commemorate through movement. The people move across their inner and outer landscapes for many purposes, including secular, ritual, and spiritual needs. This movement can occur in a myriad of guises, including economic and ritual activity. Movements in the form of gathering, hunting, farming, ranching, fuelwood cutting, clay and mineral collecting, piñon-nut gathering, and pilgrimages to Holy Places near and far most readily come to mind because they are tangible activities and sometimes leave material traces that demonstrate Acoma's continuing occupation. Other movements by Acoma members across their landscape can be invisible and leave no mark. These movements may include thoughts, stories, songs, dances, and prayers, whose blessings travel like the wind along "mythic roads" depicted in Ortiz's (2002) poetry and in illustrations of the Keres world (see figure 1.3), as well as Holy Places in communication with Spiritual Beings residing in the supernatural realm of the cosmos. Lastly, Acoma's varying movements follow a wide range of choreographies, many with unique temporal rhythms. Some movements, such as personal prayer, occur on a daily basis, while others, such as dances and certain pilgrimages, comply with calendrical events traced with precision by traditional practitioners entrusted with privileged cultural knowledge over the course of the annual cycle. Some regular journeys even occur on interannual or intergenerational cycles whose periodicity, again, is known only to a few members of the Pueblo.

While movements back into the distant hinterlands where the First Acoma People lived during their epic Migration are sporadic and often occasioned in response to fortuitous circumstances, such as some federal undertaking requiring Section 106 consultation, the landscape—the homeland in which the ancestors lived on their journey to become who they are today—has never been forgotten. Each movement, regardless of its length or periodicity, renews the Pueblo's cherished stories and reaffirms Acoma's culture, history, inheritance, and identity. The meanings intrinsic to these narratives, in turn, follow their own paths through the art of oral literature. Silko (1996:48–49) observes that the movement and meaning inherent in "Pueblo expression resembles something like a spider's web—with many little threads radiating from the center, crisscrossing one another. As with the web, the structure emerges as it is made, and you must simply listen and trust, as Pueblo people do, that meaning will be made."

Like *becoming* Acoma, *being Acoma* requires a mix of continuous and periodic movements throughout the core of the Acoma traditional homeland surrounding Haak'u and usually in view of Kaweshtima Kuutyu, as well as at great distances where the First Acoma People traveled and lived during their Migration. Even though time moves on, through enduring acts of movement Acoma Pueblo's past, present, and future *become* as one.

ACKNOWLEDGMENTS

We wish to thank the members of the Pueblo of Acoma Historic Preservation Office Advisory Board for offering us their patience and guidance.

REFERENCES

AHPO Advisory Board Members. 2012. Ethnographic Study and Traditional Cultural Properties Consultation for the Proposed Roca Honda Uranium Mine, April 11 to June 8, 2012, at Pueblo of Acoma Historic Preservation Office, Acoma Pueblo, NM. Pasqual Concho, Ernest M. Vallo Sr., and Everett J. Vallo. Notes on file, Rio del Oso Anthropological Services, LLC, Albuquerque, New Mexico.

Anschuetz, Kurt F. 2001. Soaking It All In: Northern New Mexican Pueblo Lessons of Water Management and Landscape Ecology. In *Native Peoples of the Southwest: Negotiating Land, Water, and Ethnicities*, edited by Laurie Weinstein, pp. 49–78. Greenwood Publishing Group, Westport, Connecticut.

Anschuetz, Kurt F. 2002. A Healing Place: Rio Grande Cultural Landscapes and the Petroglyph National Monument. In *"That Place People Talk About": The Petroglyph National Monument Ethnographic Landscape Report*, by Kurt F. Anschuetz, T. J. Ferguson, Harris Francis, Klara B. Kelley, and Cherie L. Scheick, pp. 3.1–3.47. Community and Cultural Landscape Contribution VIII.

Prepared for USDI National Park Service, Petroglyph National Monument, Albuquerque, New Mexico. NPS Contract No. 1443ICX712098003 (RGF 109B). Rio Grande Foundation for Communities and Cultural Landscapes, Santa Fe, New Mexico.

Anschuetz, Kurt F. 2005. Landscapes as Memory: Archaeological History to Learn From and to Live By. In *Engaged Anthropology: Research Essays on North American Archaeology, Ethnobotany, and Museology, Papers in Honor of Richard I. Ford*, edited by Michelle Hegmon and B. Sunday Eiselt, pp. 52–72. Anthropological Papers No. 94. Museum of Anthropology, University of Michigan, Ann Arbor.

Anschuetz, Kurt F. 2007. The Valles Caldera National Preserve as a Multi-Layered Ethnographic Landscape. In *More Than a Scenic Mountain Landscape: Valles Caldera National Preserve Land Use History*, by Kurt F. Anschuetz and Thomas Merlan, pp. 129–162. General Technical Report RMRS-GTR-196. USDA Forest Service, Rocky Mountain Research Station, Fort Collins, Colorado.

Anschuetz, Kurt F. 2009. Pueblo of Acoma Significance Statement. In Continuation Sheet, Section 12, by the Pueblo of Acoma, Hopi Tribe, Pueblo of Laguna, Navajo Nation, and Pueblo of Zuni, pp. 5–36. Application for Registration, New Mexico State Register of Cultural Properties: Mount Taylor Cultural Property. Submitted to the New Mexico Cultural Properties Review Committee for Listing on the State Register of Cultural Properties on June 5, 2009, by Chestnut Law Offices, Albuquerque, New Mexico. Manuscript on file, Historic Preservation Division, Department of Cultural Affairs, Santa Fe, New Mexico.

Anschuetz, Kurt F. 2012. The Pueblo of Acoma Ethnographic Study and Traditional Cultural Properties Consultation for the Proposed Roca Honda Uranium Mine at the Foot of Kaweshtima Kuutyu in the San Mateo Valley, New Mexico, by Kurt F. Anschuetz, with Theresa Pasqual, Pasqual Concho, Ernest M. Vallo Sr., and Everett J. Vallo. Prepared for the Pueblo of Acoma for submission to the Cibola National Forest, USDA Forest Service, Albuquerque, New Mexico. Document on file, Acoma Historic Preservation Office, Pueblo of Acoma, New Mexico.

Anschuetz, Kurt F. 2017. Perspectives on Managing Multi-Cultural Landscapes: Use, Access, and Fire-Fuels Management Attitudes and Preferences of User Groups Concerning the Valles Caldera National Preserve (VCNP) and Adjacent Areas. Revised for publication. Prepared for USDA Forest Service Rocky Mountain Research Station, Fort Collins, Colorado, and Valles Caldera Trust, Valles Caldera National Preserve, Jemez Springs, New Mexico. USDA Forest Service Joint Venture Agreement No. 07-JV-11221602. Manuscript on file, USDA Forest Service Rocky Mountain Research Station, Fort Collins, Colorado.

Basso, Keith. 1996. *Wisdom Sits in Places: Landscape and Language Among the Western Apache*. University of New Mexico Press, Albuquerque.

Benedict, Ruth. 1930. Eight Stories from Acoma. *American Folklore Society* 43(167):59–87.

Cajete, Gregory. 1994. *Look to the Mountain: An Ecology of Indigenous Education*. Kivakí Press, Durango, Colorado.

Charlie, Ron, Steven Concho, Damian Garcia, Juanico Sanchez, and Ernest Vallo Sr. 2001. Group interview by Angie Krall, November 16, 2001, Pueblo of Acoma Historic Preservation Office, Acoma, New Mexico. Notes on file, Anthropological Research, Tucson, Arizona.

Charlie, Ron, Steven Concho, Damian Garcia, Juanico Sanchez, and Ernest Vallo Sr. 2002. Group review session with Angie Krall, January 22, 2002, Pueblo of Acoma Historic Preservation Office, Acoma, New Mexico. Notes on file, Anthropological Research, Tucson, Arizona.

Concho, Steven, Damian Garcia, Juanico Sanchez, and Ernest Vallo Sr. 2001. Group interview by Angie Krall during fieldwork, November 7 and 8, 2001, El Segundo archaeological sites and Chaco Culture National Historical Park, New Mexico. Notes on file, Anthropological Research, Tucson, Arizona.

Cordell, Linda S. 1998. *Before Pecos: Settlement Aggregation at Rowe, New Mexico*. Anthropological Papers, No. 6. Maxwell Museum of Anthropology, University of New Mexico, Albuquerque.

Dittert, Alfred E., Jr. 1959. Culture Change in the Cebolleta Mesa Region, Central Western New Mexico. PhD dissertation, Department of Anthropology, University of Arizona, Tucson.

Dittert, Alfred E., Jr. 1998. The Acoma Culture Province During the Period A.D. 1275–1500: Cultural Disruption and Reorganization. In *Migration and Reorganization: The Pueblo IV Period in the American Southwest*, edited by Katherine A. Spielmann, pp. 81–88. Anthropological Research Papers No. 51. Arizona State University, Tempe.

Duff, Andrew I., T. J. Ferguson, Susan Bruning, and Peter Whiteley. 2008. Collaborative Research in Living Landscape: Pueblo Land, Culture, and History in West-Central New Mexico. *Archaeology Southwest* 22(1):1–22.

Duwe, Samuel G. 2011. The Prehispanic Tewa World: Space, Time, and Becoming in the Pueblo Southwest. PhD dissertation, School of Anthropology, University of Arizona, Tucson.

Ferguson, T. J. 2002. Western Pueblos and the Petroglyph National Monument: A Preliminary Assessment of the Cultural Landscapes of Acoma, Laguna, Zuni, and Hopi. In *"That Place People Talk About": The Petroglyph National Monument Ethnographic Landscape Report*, by Kurt F. Anschuetz, T. J. Ferguson, Harris Francis, Klara B. Kelley, and Cherie L. Scheick, pp. 4.1–4.24. Community and Cultural Landscape Contribution VIII. Prepared for National Park Service, Petroglyph National Monument, Albuquerque, New Mexico.

NPS Contract No. 14431CX712098003 (RGF 109B). Rio Grande Foundation for Communities and Cultural Landscapes, Santa Fe, New Mexico.

Johnson, George. 1995. *Fire in the Mind: Science, Faith, and the Search for Order.* Vintage Books, New York.

Kelley, Klara, and Harris Francis. 1996. Navajo Stories About *Naazla*: Ethnohistory for the Red Rocks Regional Landfill. In *Archaeological and Ethnohistorical Data Recovery Investigations at OCA:CT:48 Within Northwest New Mexico Regional Solid Waste Authority Red Rocks Regional Landfill near Thoreau, New Mexico*, by Kurt F. Anschuetz, Klara B. Kelley, and Harris Francis, pp. 53–80. Southwest Archaeological Consultants Research Series 381b. Southwest Archaeological Consultants, Santa Fe, New Mexico.

Krall, Angie, and Lucinda Andreani. 2007. Western Pueblo Traditional Cultural Properties in El Segundo Mine Project Area. In *Ethnohistory*, edited by Cherie L. Scheick, pp. 1–61. Archaeological and Ethnohistorical Landscapes of El Segundo Mine: Continued Investigations into Land Patterning, McKinley County, New Mexico, Vol. 2. SW 459D. Southwest Archaeological Consultants, Santa Fe, New Mexico.

Küchler, Susanne. 1993. Landscape as Memory: The Mapping of Process and Its Representation in a Melanesian Society. In *Landscape Politics and Perspectives*, edited by Barbara Bender, pp. 85–106. Berg, Oxford.

Linford, Laurance D. 2000. *Navajo Places: History, Legend, Landscape.* University of Utah Press, Salt Lake City.

Marshall, Michael P. 1990. Punyana Pueblo—LA 79169: A 14th Century Pueblo of Ancestral Western Keresan Affinity. Survey Notes. Historic Research Associates, Missoula, Montana.

Morphy, Howard. 1993. Colonialism, History, and the Construction of Place: The Politics of Landscape in Northern Australia. In *Landscape Politics and Perspectives*, edited by Barbara Bender, pp. 205–243. Berg, Oxford.

Naranjo, Tessie. 1995. Thoughts on Migration by Santa Clara Pueblo. *Journal of Anthropological Archaeology* 14:247–250.

Naranjo, Tito, and Rina Swentzell. 1989. Healing Spaces in the Pueblo World. *American Indian Culture and Research Journal* 13(3–4):257–265.

Nelson, Ben A., and Steven A. LeBlanc. 1986. *Short-Term Sedentism in the American Southwest: The Mimbres Valley Salado.* Maxwell Museum of Anthropology and the University of New Mexico Press, Albuquerque.

Ortiz, Alfonso. 1969. *The Tewa World: Space, Time, Being, and Becoming in a Pueblo Society.* University of Chicago Press, Chicago.

Ortiz, Simon J. 2002. Epic. In *Out There Somewhere*, p. 65. University of Arizona, Tucson.

Ortman, Scott G. 2009. On the Dual Nature of Metaphor and Its Implication for an Archaeology of Worldview. Paper presented in the Amerind Foundation Seminar "Religious Ideologies in the Pueblo Southwest, A.D. 1250–1450," April 1–5, Dragoon, Arizona.

Parsons, Elsie Clews. 1996. *Pueblo Indian Religion*. 2 vols. University of Nebraska Press, Lincoln. (Originally published 1939, University of Chicago Press, Chicago.)

Peckham, Stewart. 1990. *From This Earth: The Ancient Art of Pueblo Pottery*. Museum of New Mexico Press, Santa Fe.

Roberts, Frank H. H., Jr. 1932. *The Village of the Great Kivas on the Zuñi Reservation, New Mexico*. Bureau of American Ethnology Bulletin 111. U.S. Government Printing Office, Washington, D.C.

Ruppé, Reynold J., Jr. 1990. *The Acoma Culture Province: An Archaeological Concept*. The Evolution of North American Indians: A 31-Volume Series of Outstanding Dissertations, edited by David Hurst Thomas. Garland, New York.

Silko, Leslie Marmon. 1995. Interior and Exterior Landscapes: The Pueblo Migration Stories. In *Landscape in America*, edited by George F. Thompson, pp. 155–169. University of Texas Press, Austin.

Silko, Leslie Marmon. 1996. Language and Literature from a Pueblo Indian Perspective. In *Yellow Woman and a Beauty of the Spirit: Essays on Native American Life Today*, pp. 48–59. Simon and Schuster, New York.

Snead, James E., and Robert W. Preucel. 1999. The Ideology of Settlement: Ancestral Keres Landscapes in the Northern Rio Grande. In *Archaeologies of Landscape: Contemporary Perspectives*, edited by Wendy Ashmore and Bernard Knapp, pp. 269–197. Blackwell, Malden, Massachusetts.

Tyler, Hamilton. 1964. *Pueblo Gods and Myths*. University of Oklahoma Press, Norman.

Williamson, Ray A. 1984. *Living the Sky: The Cosmos of the American Indian*. University of Oklahoma Press, Norman.

Young, M. Jane. 1987. Toward an Understanding of "Place" for Southwestern Indians. *New Mexico Folklore Record* 16:1–13.

2

Movement Encased in Tradition and Stone
Hemish Migration, Land Use, and Identity

Paul Tosa, Matthew J. Liebmann, T. J. Ferguson, and John R. Welch

North from Highway 4 outside the Pueblo of Jemez tribal headquarters, a mountain peak towers over the flat roofs of Wâala Tûuwa (figure 2.1). Modern maps label it Redondo Peak. Geologically, this mountain is a resurgent lava dome that rises out of a collapsed volcanic crater known as the Valles Caldera, a 22 km wide bowl of grass-carpeted meadows interlaced with meandering streams. When Jemez people gaze northward, however, they see more than a lava dome. Etched into the south side of the peak, defined by mottled patches of trees and stone, they see the silhouette of an eagle. Its beak opens toward the west, and a bolt of lightning issues from its screeching mouth whenever snow blankets the mountain. The Jemez refer to this sacred mountain as Sée Tôoky'aanu Tûukwâ (Place of the Eagle) or Wâavêmâ Ky'ôkwâ (Want for Nothing Peak) or simply Wâavêmâ.[1]

The eagle plays a key role in the Jemez migration saga, an epic tale spanning centuries of movement. As recounted in Jemez oral traditions, the spirits prophesied that a sacred eagle would reveal to the Jemez people their new homelands after their Emergence from the Underworld. After generations of travel across deserts, through canyons, and over mountain ranges, the Jemez finally arrived at the base of a large mountain. When they looked up at the peak, they saw the silhouette of the eagle standing guard above them—the sign that the spirits had foretold.

The prominent depiction of the Wâavêmâ eagle on the official tribal seal attests to its central significance to the Jemez, and nearly a century of ethnographic research provides details about the sacredness of Wâavêmâ (Anschuetz 2007; Ellis 1956, 1964; Parsons 1925; Sando 1982; Tosa and Steinbrecher 2017; Weslowski 1981). Given the astonishing natural beauty of the Valles Caldera and its environs, it is no wonder that the people of Jemez hold Wâavêmâ in particular esteem. A preeminent shrine adorns

Movement Encased in Tradition and Stone

Figure 2.1 Wâavêmâ (Redondo Peak) as seen from Jemez Pueblo, with an inset of the Pueblo of Jemez tribal seal. Photograph by Richard Krause.

the top of the sacred peak. Tribal members use the area surrounding the mountain for hunting, collecting plants and herbs, gathering minerals, and pasturing livestock, and for ceremonial and spiritual activities that include pilgrimage retreats and initiations (plate 2).

Wâavêmâ, however, is more than a pretty place to the Jemez people. It is a living entity and the source of all life. Like a mother, Wâavêmâ gives life to Jemez newborns and sustains them on earth. The waters flowing off its flanks irrigate Jemez fields and nourish Jemez bodies. At the end of life, Jemez spirits return to Wâavêmâ after shedding their earthly skins. Wâavêmâ is equivalent in Judeo-Christian belief to the Holy Spirit, the Garden of Eden, and Heaven all rolled into one: the domain where life began, from which life continues to spring forth, and to which the deceased return.

In this chapter, we consider how migration, travel, and landscape are key elements of Hemish (Jemez) identity. We then show how these can be investigated through the archaeological record of obsidian use. We begin with a summary of Hemish history as Paul Tosa, a member of the Fire Clan and Turquoise Moiety, learned it from his grandfather, Francisco Tosa, a medicine man. The lands described in Hemish traditions are conceived of as a Hemish footprint that includes all of the areas where Hemish ancestors traveled, settled, and used the land. Their use of obsidian provides a case study of how movement is documented in the archaeological record and what that means.

MOVEMENT ENCASED IN TRADITION: ORIGIN AND MIGRATION OF THE HEMISH PEOPLE

EMERGENCE

According to traditional Hemish history, handed down through many generations, Hemish culture began in an underworld known as Wâana Tûuta (figure 2.2). This is the place where the Hemish People were given their customs, medicines, and ceremonies. There were no clans in Wâana Tûuta.

Hwóotųyavêela (Hemish War Chief) led the People through rain and lightning to a place where they found corn, squash, pumpkins, and fruit. Here the Hemish feasted, then they dressed the sun and made the four seasons. Next, they made the four sacred mountains for Kópastéyá (Creator). Hwóotųyavêela then led the people south to a land with big canyons that the People called Ky'âawāamu ("Rock Canyon," said to be McElmo Canyon). Here they held their ceremonies again, and the ceremonies were good. It was here the first clans were formed.

The People lived at Ky'âawāamu for a long time. Peoples from other nations resided nearby, including the Hopi. From Ky'âawāamu, the Hemish saw Ky'âa Gíwē P'êtabu (Shiny Rock Mountain Range), the large snow-covered mountains to the east (said to be the San Juan and La Plata Mountains in what is now southwestern Colorado). To the southeast, beyond P'æ̀ Húlése ("Man Mountain," or Sleeping Ute Mountain), other peoples lived on the mesas (said to be Mesa Verde), where they traded with the Hemish. Some even joined Hemish clans. To the south, still other peoples lived in sagebrush canyons. The Hemish knew this because Dǽhæsǫma (War Captain) had cleared or marked four sacred roads at the request of Hwóotųyavêela, each leading in a sacred direction.

After the Hemish lived for a time at Ky'âawāamu, the rains and rivers became small, the crops grew poorly, and many became hungry. Foreigners started to raid Hemish settlements to steal food, and neighboring settlements began to argue. The Hemish held ceremonies again, and for a while things were good. The P'æ̀ækish Clan (Pecos people) was the first to leave Ky'âawāamu to search for new lands with more water. Other non-Hemish peoples also left to find places to live. However, the true Hemish stayed, joining together in larger settlements for safety.

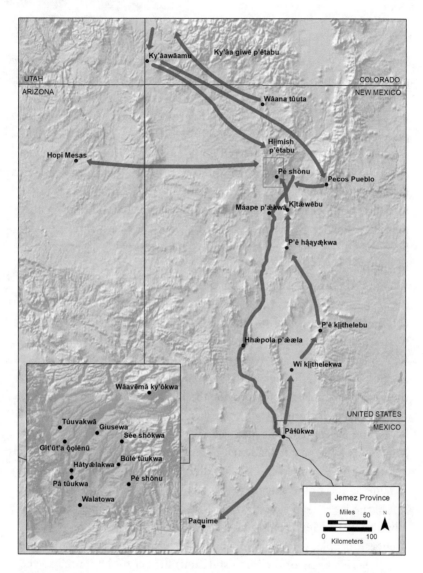

Figure 2.2 Jemez migration traditions in relation to the Jemez archaeological province.

MIGRATION

Eventually, less and less water came to Ky'âawāamu. The Hemish people became hungry and restless, so the Cacique informed the spirits of their desire to find a new home with bigger waters. The spirits told the Hemish that the Sacred Eagle (Sée) would show them where to place the sacred *tukwa* (shrine). Soon thereafter, the Hemish began to journey southeast along the Sacred Eagle and Red-Tailed Hawk feather roads that Dǽhæsǫma and Hwóotųųyavêela had marked. They walked toward distant mountains in the direction of the rising sun. They knew this direction because others had gone this way before. During this journey, a smaller group moved ahead to mark the path and to follow Sée. They moved in front of the main Hemish group, who were large in number.

Along the way, the people stopped and rested. They placed markers depicting birds and animals on stone cliffs to show their route, enabling other Hemish to follow. Clans and societies followed various roads to various places. Guiding markers were placed in the canyon path Ky'âawāamu ("Rock Canyon," said to be McElmo Canyon or possibly Largo Canyon). Offerings were made at each marker location so that the birds and animals would provide the Hemish all that they required.

Eventually, the canyon path took them to large mountains that could be seen on a clear day. This place is now called Hį́įmísh P'êtabu (Jemez Mountains). The people made temporary camps and placed more guide markers. They explored the surrounding area so they would know the terrain and meet others living nearby.

On the far eastern side, they saw familiar Têwêsh people (said to be Tiwa from the Mesa Verde area). To the south, they found Sǽyêsh and T'ų́ųtǽsh people, who were much smaller in number than the Hemish. They also knew of the Súunísh (Zuni) further to the south. To the north, they found scattered settlements of others who were not friendly. These others might have been the Gūmą̂achi (Comanche) or the Yílæ̂sh (Taos); they were Buffalo and Porcupine Quill People.

Once the rest of the Hemish arrived, they outnumbered the unfriendly ones, who were killed or defeated. These may possibly have been the ancestors of modern Comanche or Taos (known to archaeologists as the Gallina Culture).

The Hemish then entered the mountain from the west, near present-day Cuba and Gallina. They crossed the area of Shę́ęnap'ōbu (the Nacimiento Mountains, including the San Pedro Peaks) and Pę́ęshįįmû (Deer Mountain) to reach the top of what is now known as Barley Canyon. Here they held ceremonies and placed a marker for the others to follow. The Sacred Eagle showed them U̱ Kwâhoomînu (the land around Redondo Peak). The Sacred Eagle then took them up to Wâavêmâ Ky'ôkwâ (the top of Redondo Peak), and the sacred Tuukwa was reborn with eagle and hawk feathers painted with *toe-unsh* (red ochre). As they descended, they gathered sacred medicines and made offerings at the sacred springs.

The Hemish settled in areas to the south and southwest of Wâavêmâ Ky'ôkwâ, where no people lived. They built many small houses they called *Kay-tu-hah* and planted the first crops, many near the top of P'ę̂ Tyóosholunu Wâamu ("Water Descend Place Canyon," or Cañon de San Diego). They then built three large pueblos to guard Wâavêmâ and to protect the river and the people: Túuvakwā (Traditional Life-Renewal Place) to the west of Cañon de San Diego; Sée Shôkwa (Eagle Dwell Place) to the southeast of Wâavêmâ; and Hhó Kį̂įthelegi (Hole White Place), named for the white place on the side, near Battleship Rock.

From Hhó Kį̂įthelegi, Tyáaku̱zee (Arrow Mother) and Séeku̱zée (Eagle Mother) made the decision to continue following Hą̂ąyę̱ P'ę̂kwâ (South Water Place), the big river along the southern stretch of the Rio Grande. They promised that they would return and set off on a journey that took them many years to complete. Likewise, the Snake Society traveled west to the Húpésh (Hopi), and they, too, promised to return. They stayed with the Húpésh only for a short time.

Within a few years, the Hemish expanded by building more pueblos on the nearby mesas and in the upper reaches of the smaller canyons known as Wâalatū P'ę̂ægi ("Canyon Village Water," or the Vallecito drainage) and Gílawa ("Gate Place," or the Gilman drainage). This enlarged their hunting and gathering areas and gave them stronger control over the trails and the water. The population flourished, and the villages grew larger. The main Hemish village became the heavily guarded Gît'ūt'a Ǫǫlênū (Giant Footprint Place), which was also known as Kwę́ęgíyukwâ (Bark Beetle Place). It was there that the Hwóotu̱u̱yavêela, the Caciques, and many of the societies were based. The Dǽhæhwii Ky'óowísh (War Council comprised of prior War Captains) included members from the other villages.

Eventually, smaller trading villages were built along the Wâalatū P'ǽægi and near its junction with the P'ǽ Tyóosholunu Wâamu to facilitate trade with the neighboring Keresan people (Zia and Santa Ana). The Keresans built villages at Séeshįįnâ (Eagle Hill Place), near the present-day village of San Ysidro.

THE ARROW AND EAGLE MIGRATION TO THE SOUTH

The journey of Tyáakųzee (Arrow Mother) and Séekųzée (Eagle Mother) to the south, following Hąąyą̄ P'ǽkwâ (Rio Grande), took them to new lands occupied by people who were friendly with the Hemish and with whom the Hemish could trade.

After leaving the Hįįmísh P'êtabu (Jemez Mountains), the Eagle and the Arrow groups followed Hąąyą̄ P'ǽkwâ (Rio Grande) to Máape P'ǽkwâ ("Parrot Place" or "Macaw Place"—the Petroglyph National Monument in Albuquerque). They continued their journey to Hhǽpola P'ǽæla ("Far South Spring," the Truth or Consequences area) and to Wí Kįįthelekwa ("White Ridge Place," the White Sands area). It is said that they stayed in these locations to resupply and learn the area. They then continued their journey to the south to Pâlūkwa ("Place of Flowers," El Paso region). Here they stayed and traded for many years. Many Hemish lived with the Paquimé people at the junction of two rivers, where they met and traded with the Séyû T'ǽæsh (Bird People) for their parrot and macaw feathers. The Séyû T'ǽæsh were said to be the Aztec. The Hemish are good runners, so it is possible they maintained contact with the main body of Hemish people in Hįįmísh P'êtabu in the north.

After many, many years, the Arrow and the Eagle People knew they must return north back to Hemish Towa. However, many people made the decision to stay with the Paquimé and Séyû T'ǽæsh peoples because they had established families and homes.

The Arrow and the Eagle People who decided to leave Pâlūkwa journeyed north into the P'ê Kįįthelebu ("White Mountain Range," the Sierra Blanca on what is now the Mescalero Apache Reservation). From there, they traveled north into P'ê Hąąyą̄kwa ("Mountains to the Southeast," the Gran Quivira or Manzano Mountains region). They then journeyed north through the Kîtæwēbu (Sandia Mountains, including Cedar Crest and the North Peak) until they reached the place where the mountains touch the big river (Rio Grande, northeast of present-day Bernalillo). By this time it was late fall, so they rested at a village of friendly people whom they knew (San Felipe Pueblo). They were given food and supplies so they could continue their journey.

The Arrow and Eagle groups then proceeded toward the Borrego Mesa area and went to the place where the Sun lives at Pé Shônu (Sun Dwell Place). From there, they could see a village with big smoke and other villages with smaller amounts of smoke. Runners were sent to announce their arrival, and it was decided that Tyáakų̄zee (Arrow Mother) would go to Túuvakwā and Séekų̄zée (Eagle Mother) would go to the main Hemish village at Gît'ūt'a Ǫ̓ǫlênū (Giant Footprint Place), also known as Kwą́ægíyukwâ because that was where the Hwóotų̨yavêela and the Caciques lived.

THE SPANISH COLONIAL PERIOD, 1598–1703

In 1541 the Hemish discovered Europeans when members of the Francisco Vázquez de Coronado entrada first ventured into the Jemez province. Following this brief encounter, the Jemez pueblos hosted only sporadic foreign visitors over the next sixty years. When don Juan de Oñate colonized New Mexico in 1598, a Franciscan priest named Fray Alonso de Lugo became the first European to live among the Hemish. Fray Alonso established a small, temporary two-room mission at Giusewa (Jemez Historic Site in present-day Jemez Springs), but his tenure lasted less than three years. The rugged territory of the Jemez Plateau, combined with the reputed belligerence and recalcitrance of its inhabitants, colluded to keep the Spaniards at bay. In the 1620s, an enterprising young missionary named Fray Gerónimo Zárate Salmerón arrived in the Jemez province. Zárate Salmerón built the massive fortress-like mission church at Giusewa and founded a new settlement at the southern end of the valley. Called Wâala Tûuwa by the Jemez, the remains of this second mission village underlie the modern buildings of Jemez Pueblo.

The establishment of missions significantly impacted Jemez settlement patterns. The rugged landscape of Hį́įmísh P'êtabu (Jemez Mountains) proved to be an impediment to the evangelical progress of the Franciscans, causing them to adopt a policy of *congregación*. Under this policy, the friars attempted to induce the Hemish living in mesa-top pueblos to relocate into the valley bottom, where they could be proselytized. Attempts to concentrate the Hemish at missions initiated a complex ebb and flow of migrations among settlements in the floor of the canyon and on the tops of the mesas.

Migrations between valley-bottom and mesa-top settlements continued after the Spaniards were expelled from the Jemez province during the Pueblo Revolt era. Between 1681 and 1683, the Hemish left Wâala Tûuwa and constructed two new pueblos on the mesa tops—Pâ Tûukwa (Flower Shrine) and Búlé Tûukwa (Shell Shrine). In 1693 they left those villages and came together at Hâtyælakwa (Upright Wall Place). Following a battle with the Spaniards in 1694, the Hemish moved back to Pâ Tûukwa and Búlé Tûukwa. At Pâ Tûukwa, Franciscans constructed a new mission church in the northwest corner of the pueblo. Within eighteen months, Búlé Tûukwa was vacated, and the Hemish moved back to Wâala Tûuwa, where a second church was built. In 1696 the Jemez rebelled again and destroyed the missions. After a brief reoccupation of Hâtyælakwa and a final battle with Spanish forces, the Hemish left the valley, taking refuge with the Hopi, Zuni, Acoma, Taos, and Navajo. By August 1696, the Jemez province was depopulated. It remained essentially vacant for the next six years.

Beginning in 1703, however, the Hemish began to trickle back into the province, and two mission sites—Pâ Tûukwa and Wâala Tûuwa—were occupied until at least 1716. It was not until the second decade of the eighteenth century that the migration of the Hemish was completed and the Hemish people came together to occupy Wâala Tûuwa, where they remain today.

FROM PECOS PUEBLO TO JEMEZ PUEBLO, 1838

When Coronado visited Pecos Pueblo in the spring of 1541, the pueblo was one of the largest and most imposing Indian villages in New Mexico. In 1590 Gaspar Castaño de Sosa and his expedition attacked Pecos Pueblo, taking the place by storm. With the permanent colonization of New Mexico in 1598, friars began conversion of the Pecos people.

But their huge and splendid mission church, which took many years to build, was destroyed in the Pueblo Revolt of 1680. When the Spanish priests took up work at Pecos again, they built a new church on the ruins of the old one. New Mexico's governor, Juan Bautista de Anza, met the Comanche at Pecos in 1786. In a showy ceremony, de Anza negotiated a treaty of peace with the Comanche, which lasted into the next century.

After 1821, Americans moving westward over the Santa Fe Trail found Pecos Pueblo in a mournful condition. Years of warfare with Plains tribes and a series of epidemics had reduced the population to a mere handful. The old mission and many house blocks, long neglected, were falling into ruin. By 1838, the Pecos survivors walked away from their decaying village and moved west to Jemez Pueblo, where they were welcomed because they spoke the Towa language, like the Hemish people.

AN ANTHROPOLOGICAL PERSPECTIVE ON HEMISH MOVEMENT AND IDENTITY

As recounted in traditional history, the Hemish migration involved movement from the north to the Jemez Mountains. After arriving in the Jemez Mountains, several groups migrated to other areas before returning to rejoin their relatives living on the Jemez Plateau. Before the Spanish entrada, the Jemez Snake Society went to Hopi for a short period. The Arrow and Eagle groups traveled south along the Rio Grande to Paquimé. When Hemish people began a return migration, via a route that passed the Sierra Blanca and Manzano and Sandia Mountains, some of these people stayed at Paquimé. When they arrived back in the Jemez Mountains, Arrow Mother went to one village (Túuvakwā) and Eagle Mother went to another village (Gît'ūt'a Ôolênū, or Giant Footprint Place). These are two of the more than forty Hemish villages occupied on the Jemez Plateau between AD 1300 and 1700. These pueblos are situated in a vast landscape defined by several thousand one- to four-room field houses and hundreds of agricultural fields.

During the tumultuous Spanish colonial period, the Hemish people sought refuge at Hâtyælakwa (Upright Wall Place), Pâ Tûukwa (Flower Shrine), and Búlé Tûukwa (Shell Shrine). After 1700, the entire Hemish population, significantly reduced, moved from mesa villages to Wâala Tûuwa.

Hemish traditions encompass complex cultural developments that archaeologists need to take into account in developing models to explain the past. During their migration, the Hemish did not travel together en masse. Several migrating groups with differing constellations of clans and societies followed different routes. Hemish placed petroglyphs and pictographs on stone cliffs to show migration routes so that other Hemish could follow. These landmarks deserve more study. The historical trajectories described in traditions are intertwined in time and space, with groups splitting off from one another and later rejoining. After emergence, for instance, the P'ǽækish Clan (Pecos people) was the first to leave Ky'âawāamu (McElmo Canyon) to find new lands with more water. Centuries later, when Pecos Pueblo was vacated in 1838, the remaining P'ǽækish rejoined their linguistic and cultural relatives at Wâala Tûuwa. Hemish migrations expressed in archaeological records are sometimes linear and sometimes multifaceted and convoluted.

Hemish traditional history depicts a multiethnic social context, with peoples from other nations interacting in various ways. Social relations between these groups ranged from cooperation and trading to hostility and raiding. The Hemish journeyed to the Hopi Mesas prior to the arrival of the Spaniards and returned there and to other places as they sought refuge after the Pueblo Revolt. Hemish lived side-by-side with Kewa (Santo Domingo) people at Búlé Tûukwa and Athapaskan-speaking allies at Pâ Tûukwa in the late 1600s. More recently, Hemish leaders have journeyed to Zuni and vice versa to exchange ritual knowledge. Diverse settlement types are referenced in traditional history, including temporary camps, field houses, and large pueblos.

There is a striking difference in scale between the geographical areas referenced in traditional history and the post–AD 1200 archaeological signature of Jemez identity in the Jemez Mountains, an identity based primarily on architecture and Jemez Black-on-white ceramics (Elliot 1986). The Jemez archaeological province represents an intense occupation of the Jemez Mountains that lasted for four centuries, but this area encompasses only about 10 percent of the geography of Hemish emergence, migration, and settlement.

The archaeological record of the Hemish varies across time and space, including ancestors who lived in different areas in earlier times and groups who traveled southward along the Rio Grande before returning to the Jemez Mountains. Ultimately, a comprehensive archaeological study of the Hemish past needs to consider the full sweep of Hemish history that extends temporally and geographically beyond well-known Hemish villages, the Jemez Mountains, and the period between AD 1300 and 1700. The next section of our chapter advances this project by looking at the distribution of obsidian traceable to far-flung sources.

REVEALING ANCESTRAL JEMEZ MOBILITY THROUGH OBSIDIAN SOURCE PROVENIENCE

For several years, Matthew Liebmann has teamed with the Pueblo of Jemez Department of Natural Resources on the Wâavêmâ Archaeological Research Project (WARP). WARP focuses on documenting the obsidian assemblage at thirty-one large ancestral Hemish villages to learn about the dynamic nature of the Pueblo past. We do this using obsidian artifacts to document short-term movements across the Hį́įmísh P'êtabu (Jemez Mountains) landscape between AD 1300 and 1700.

We now know that mobility between Hemish villages and obsidian sources in the Valles Caldera was affected by Spanish colonialism in the seventeenth century. A network of ancient trails in the Hį́įmísh P'êtabu attests to centuries of movement between ancestral Hemish villages and the Valles Caldera. Exhaustively documented by Paul Tosa, Bill Whatley, and Chris Toya, and earlier by Detrich Fliedner (1975), this trail network links sixty ancestral Hemish villages and thousands of field houses with Wâavêmâ. One of the reasons Hemish people journeyed back and forth on these trails was to procure obsidian.

A literal mountain of obsidian, known to the Hemish as Ky'âagîwe Shį́į (Shiny Rock Mountain), rises out of a grassy meadow in the northeast corner of the Valles Caldera. On maps this mountain is labeled Cerro del Medio. It is the largest source of obsidian by volume in the southwestern United States (Shackley 2005:72). Unlike material from five other nearby sources, Cerro del Medio obsidian is not distributed in secondary contexts. That is, obsidian from Ky'âagîwe Shį́į (known technically as Valles Rhyolite) does not erode into the river drainages outside the caldera, and artifacts made of this obsidian had to have been procured at the source. Someone had to physically travel to Ky'âagîwe Shį́į to obtain this material. We can therefore use artifacts made of Cerro del Medio obsidian and found at ancestral Hemish pueblos as proxies for Hemish movements to and from Wâavêmâ in the past.

WARP collected 2,222 obsidian artifacts from midden contexts at thirty-one ancestral Hemish villages. We actively avoided collecting finished tools, such as projectile points, scrapers, and knives. Instead, we selected artifacts in the early stages of production (unmodified primary and secondary flakes, debitage, and shatter) to better represent patterns of acquisition and to minimize the impacts of trade on our sample. We then subjected these artifacts to X-ray fluorescence analysis to determine their source.

Our results show that ancestral Hemish people journeyed to Ky'âagîwe Shį́į́ more frequently than any other obsidian quarry. Hemish flint knappers made more artifacts from Cerro del Medio obsidian (n = 1,173) than from all other sources combined, representing more than half of the total number of analyzed artifacts. Cerro del Medio obsidian is the only source represented in the chipped-stone assemblage of each and every site sampled by WARP.

Patterns of obsidian acquisition varied through time at ancestral Hemish pueblos. Cerro del Medio obsidian acquisition increased dramatically between 1300 and 1700. At pueblos settled during the first half of this period, Cerro del Medio obsidian accounts for less than one-third of the total obsidian assemblage (29.2 percent, n = 291 of 997). But middens at sites occupied between 1500 and 1700 (as established by the presence of Rio Grande Glaze D, E, and F ceramics) have more than twice as much obsidian from Cerro del Medio (72 percent, n = 882 of 1,225). While some of this increase relates to the proximity of the early villages to the other obsidian sources, the intensification in use of Valles Rhyolite indexes a surge in Hemish travel to and use of the Valles Caldera in the sixteenth century (Liebmann 2017).

The 1598 colonization of New Mexico by Europeans transformed Hemish use of the Valles Caldera (figure 2.3). After the imposition of Spanish rule, the amount of Cerro del Medio obsidian at Hemish sites dropped to 28 percent at sites constructed between 1600 and 1680 (n = 46 of 164). In 1680 the Spaniards were expelled from New Mexico and use of the Cerro del Medio source returned to precolonial levels (rising to 54.2 percent, n = 52 of 96). When Spanish rule resumed in the

Movement Encased in Tradition and Stone

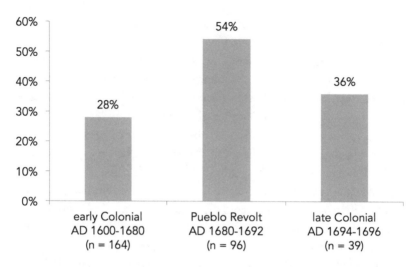

Figure 2.3 The percentage of Cerro del Medio obsidian (Valles Rhyolite) in the assemblages of ancestral Hemish pueblos, 1600–96.

mid-1690s, Cerro del Medio obsidian use plummeted once again, dropping to 36 percent (n = 14 of 39). The pattern is clear: under two separate periods of Spanish colonial rule (1598–1680 and post-1692), the Hemish reduced their use of Cerro del Medio obsidian. By comparison, during times when the Pueblos lived unfettered by settler colonialism (pre-1598 and 1680–92), quantities of Cerro del Medio obsidian at Hemish sites spike upward, indicating increased movement between Jemez villages and the Valles Caldera.

INTERPRETATION

Exactly why and how colonial rule constrained ancestral Hemish movement in and out of the Valles Caldera remains hazy. The introduction of metal does not seem to have affected this shift because obsidian from sources other than Cerro del Medio is found in similar proportions to precolonial contexts at seventeenth-century Hemish sites. The prevalence of rhyolite from three other nearby sources indicates that there was no significant decline in the overall use of obsidian during the first century of colonial occupation, when metal became more readily available.

Rather, the drop in Cerro del Medio obsidian probably resulted from increased labor demands on Hemish "subjects" of the crown, as well as increased raiding and violence during the colonial era (Liebmann 2017).

The escalation in raiding and violence that characterized seventeenth-century New Mexico likely transformed the Valles Caldera into a dangerous place. To access Ky'âagîwe Shı́ı̨, Hemish travelers would have crossed an open 5 km wide meadow. Historical records attest to the peril of this crossing, and clashes between Hemish and Navajo warriors in the Valles Caldera occurred throughout the 1800s (Brugge 2002; McNitt 1972:185, 256–257). Hemish oral traditions recount additional raids not mentioned in documentary records (Sando 1982:11–12). As Wâavêmâ became associated with bloodshed from clashes between Hemish and non-Pueblo groups during the Spanish colonial era, the quantity of Cerro del Medio obsidian at ancestral Hemish sites appears to have ebbed.

Use of Cerro del Medio obsidian surged following the Pueblo Revolt, when the Hemish helped evict Spanish colonizers from New Mexico. Apaches and Navajos allied with the Pueblos, taking up arms in the 1680 uprising. With the Spaniards gone, Pueblo trade with Navajo and Apache neighbors increased. Intergroup relations remained strong during the Spanish interregnum, and when the Spaniards returned to New Mexico in 1692 they found "Apaches" (likely Navajos) living side-by-side with the Hemish (Liebmann 2012:183–185). Rapprochement among the Indigenous peoples of New Mexico appears to have made the Valles Caldera safe once again, as borne out in the lithic assemblages of Pâ Tûukwa and Búlé Tûukwa, both occupied between 1680 and 1692. Yet when Spanish colonists returned to New Mexico in 1692, Hemish movement in and out of Wâavêmâ diminished again. The raiding that caused the decrease in Hemish use of Cerro del Medio obsidian prior to the 1680 revolt was renewed, and hostilities between the Pueblos and their Navajo and Apache neighbors increased during the years of Spanish reconquest (1692–96).

Even with decreased exploitation of Cerro del Medio obsidian in the 1600s, Hemish people continued to use the Valles Caldera to maintain Hemish culture and society. The prevalence of Cerro del Medio obsidian at ancestral Hemish sites shows that the Jemez frequently moved within the Valles Caldera between 1300 and 1700, and historical documents attest to the continued Jemez use of this landscape from the eighteenth century through today (Anschuetz 2007; Weslowski 1981).

Despite restrictions imposed on the Hemish use of Wâavêmâ by the colonial regimes of Spain, Mexico, and the United States, links between the Hemish people and Wâavêmâ remain unbroken over eight centuries. Since their arrival in Hį́įmísh P'êtabu (Jemez Mountains), the Hemish have always moved across and within the Valles Caldera.

CONCLUSION

Hemish traditions and archaeology provide rich sources of information for developing an anthropological understanding of history and social identity. A prominent theme in Hemish traditions is movement across the land, movement that led to Wâavêmâ and the occupation of Wâala Tûuwa. Ongoing Hemish cultural practices are tied to that same land, and hundreds of places with Towa names define the Hemish footprint as a cultural landscape and ancestral territory.

Language and religion are essential and inseparable elements of Hemish identity, and these are bound to the land with Towa place-names and stories that frame Hemish historical and cultural discourse. The named places that define the dimensions of Hemish ancestral geography are associated with the migrations that culminated in the occupation of Wâala Tûuwa. The same places link ancient migrations with contemporary religious pilgrimages, hunting, collecting, and other land uses that take Hemish people back to areas and sites where Hemish ancestors lived, often following trails that provide a physical connection between villages, shrines, and resource areas. Named places, including ancestral villages, are a prominent component of the Hemish traditions associated with the land, and these names are an important part of Hemish identity. Place-names are perpetuated in Hemish culture when people move, figuratively or literally, through the land and talk about the landforms and places they encounter.

The Hemish archaeological sites and trails that mark the landscape are physical expressions of past and present land use, and these figure prominently in the formation and transmission of Hemish identity. Movement over the land brought migrating Hemish people to the Jemez Mountains and Wâala Tûuwa, and sustained movement through and use of ancestral land continue to play a role in the retention and transmission of Hemish identity.

The archaeological record attests to the fact that the special relationship of the Hemish people with Wâavêmâ (Redondo Peak) developed in ancient times as people moved between Jemez pueblos and the Valles Caldera. The material culture of the Jemez province documents centuries of Jemez movement between the large ancestral villages that dot the mesa tops southwest of Wâavêmâ and the lush meadows and towering peaks of the Valles Caldera.

ACKNOWLEDGMENTS

We thank the Pueblo of Jemez for supporting our research, Dr. Logan Sutton for transcription of Hemish place-names, and Barry Price Steinbrecher for drafting the maps in this chapter. And special thanks to Richard Krause for permission to use his photograph of Eagle Dwelling Place.

NOTE

1. The term *Wâavêmâ* refers both to Redondo Peak specifically and the Valles Caldera region generally.

REFERENCES

Anschuetz, Kurt. 2007. Introducing a Landscape Approach for Evaluating Communities' Traditional Senses of Time and Place. In *More than a Scenic Mountain Landscape: Valles Caldera National Preserve Land Use History*, edited by K. Anscheutz and T. Merlan, pp. 249–262. USFS Rocky Mountain Research Station, General Technical Report RMRS-GTR-196, Ft. Collins, Colorado.

Brugge, David. 2002. Jemez Pueblo and the Navajos: Relations Prior to 1800. In *Forward into the Past*, edited by R. Wiseman, T. O'Laughlin, and C. Snow, pp. 5–16. Archaeological Society of New Mexico, Albuquerque.

Elliot, Michael. 1986. *Overview and Synthesis of the Archaeology of the Jemez Province, New Mexico*. Archaeology Notes 51. Museum of New Mexico Office of Archaeological Studies, Santa Fe.

Ellis, Florence Hawley. 1956. Anthropological Evidence Supporting the Claims of the Pueblos of Zia, Santa Ana, and Jemez. Manuscript on file at Laboratory of Anthropology, Museum of New Mexico, Santa Fe.

Ellis, Florence Hawley. 1964. *A Reconstruction of the Basic Jemez Pattern of Social Organization, with Comparisons to Other Tanoan Social Structures*. University of New Mexico Press, Albuquerque.

Fliedner, Dietrich. 1975. Pre-Spanish Pueblos in New Mexico. *Annals of the Association of American Geographers* 65(3):363–377.

Liebmann, Matthew. 2012. *Revolt: An Archaeological History of Pueblo Resistance and Revitalization in 17th Century New Mexico.* University of Arizona Press, Tucson.

Liebmann, Matthew. 2017. From Landscapes of Meaning to Landscapes of Signification in the American Southwest. *American Antiquity* 82(4):642–661.

McNitt, Frank. 1972. *Navajo Wars: Military Campaigns, Slave Raids, and Reprisals.* University of New Mexico Press, Albuquerque.

Parsons, Elsie Clews. 1925. *The Pueblo of Jemez.* Phillips Academy, Andover, Massachusetts.

Sando, Joe. 1982. *Nee Hemish: A History of Jemez Pueblo.* University of New Mexico Press, Albuquerque.

Shackley, M. Steven. 2005. *Obsidian: Geology and Archaeology in the North American Southwest.* University of Arizona Press, Tucson.

Tosa, Paul, and Barry Price Steinbrecher. 2017. The Hemish Footprint. *Archaeology Southwest* 30(4):7.

Weslowski, Lois Vermilya. 1981. Native American Land Use Along Redondo Creek. In *High Altitude Adaptations Along Redondo Creek: The Baca Geothermal Project*, edited by C. Baker and J. Winter, pp. 105–127. Office of Contract Archeology, University of New Mexico, Albuquerque.

Anshe K'yan'a and Zuni Traditions of Movement

Maren P. Hopkins, Octavius Seowtewa, Graydon Lennis Berlin, Jacob Campbell, Chip Colwell, and T. J. Ferguson

Migration and movement are of paramount importance in Zuni history and contemporary life. Zuni ancestors emerged into the present world at Ribbon Falls in the Grand Canyon and subsequently set out on a centuries-long journey in search of their spiritual and physical destination, Idiwan'a, the Middle Place, known today as Zuni Pueblo (figure 3.1). As they traveled, Zuni ancestors split into groups and moved in different directions. They acquired vast knowledge about the earth and sky—the plants and animals; the minerals; the sun, moon, stars; and the climate. They interacted with other people across the land, they formed and perfected their medicine societies, and they gained clan identities. Zuni ancestors learned the songs, prayers, and ceremonies during these migrations that now comprise the core of their religion.

Archaeologists who study settlement patterns in the American Southwest understand that past peoples coalesced and split and that groups carried knowledge with them as they moved from place to place. At varying magnitudes, archaeologists have studied the movement of people across the greater Southwest. The material record shows that migration and interaction occurred at large scales and across long distances and that people created and maintained meaningful relationships through time (Mills et al. 2015). Similarly, smaller-scale mobility interpreted in terms of environmental adaptation and social organization is also recognized by archaeologists as an important part of the ancient past (Gregory and Wilcox 2007; Mills et al. 2015; Schachner et al. 2011).

From the Zuni perspective, the terms *migration*, *movement*, and *mobility* evoke a sense of history that encompasses both pragmatic and spiritual aspects of life. Zunis also relate these concepts to ongoing traditions, such as resource collection, prayer, and pilgrimage, that serve as means by which contemporary Zunis sustain their religious and ceremonial lives

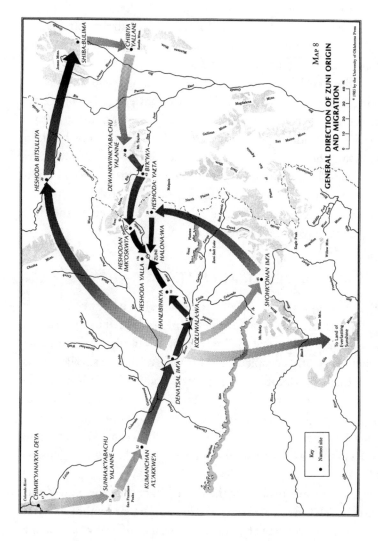

Figure 3.1 A schematic of the Zuni origin and subsequent migrations to the Middle Place. Map by Lucio and Stauber in *A Zuni Atlas* by T. J. Ferguson and E. Richard Hart. Copyright © 1985 by the University of Oklahoma Press, Norman. Reprinted by permission of the publisher.

today. Such traditions occurred in the past, just as they do now, and they are anchored in historical events and places. For example, many of the springs, stopping places, and mountains encountered by Zuni ancestors as they migrated to the Middle Place became sacred shrines, remembered in prayers, that the people returned to for ritual pilgrimages after they moved on (Ferguson and Hart 1985). In this sense, both the concept and the act of movement are part of remembering, retaining, and transmitting Zuni culture; they are part of being Zuni.

In 2014 the Pueblo of Zuni completed an ethnographic study at the Fort Wingate Depot Activity (FWDA) in northwestern New Mexico. This project has provided examples that tangibly demonstrate the history and longevity of traditions of movement and the connections between past places and contemporary cultural practices. Moreover, it shows how the Zuni people have maintained connections with their larger world in the face of restrictions to access and movement, as the FWDA has been closed to the public for decades and portions of it served as an active military testing range for explosive ordnance.

FORT WINGATE DEPOT ACTIVITY

The FWDA occupies about 24 mi^2 (15,277 acres) in northwestern New Mexico (figure 3.2). It is located about 7 mi north of the Zuni Indian Reservation and 8 mi east of Gallup. Anshe K'yan'a is the Zuni name for the land currently occupied by the FWDA. This area, called Bear Springs in English, is located within the tribe's aboriginal land as recognized by the United States in a 1987 ruling by the U.S. Court of Federal Claims (Yanello 1995). As early as 1846, U.S. Army personnel acknowledged that Bear Springs, the area that eventually became Fort Wingate and the FWDA, was situated "in the territory of the Zunis" (Jenkins 1995:78).

In the mid-nineteenth century, the U.S. military and other non-Zunis began to establish forts, settlements, and livestock ranges within and near Anshe K'yan'a. The entirety of Zuni ancestral lands officially became the territory of the United States in 1848, after the signing of the Treaty of Guadalupe Hidalgo with Mexico. Fort Wingate was established near present-day Gallup, New Mexico, in 1860, and over the last century it has been subject to various military undertakings that have gradually

Anshe K'yan'a and Zuni Traditions of Movement

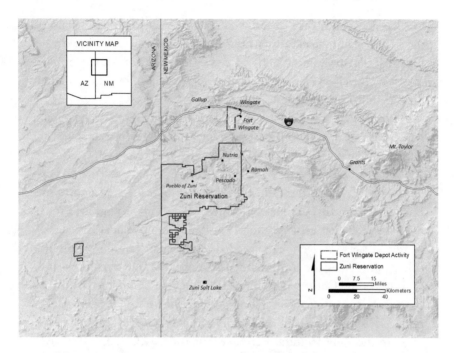

Figure 3.2 The location of the Fort Wingate Depot Activity in relation to the Zuni Reservation.

reduced the Pueblo of Zuni's traditional use of lands within the military reservation.

Zuni religious leaders consider Anshe K'yan'a to be integral to understanding Zuni history and traditions. As perceived by Zuni religious leaders, the name Anshe K'yan'a refers to a large landscape, as well as a specific water source. This area is recalled by its place-name in the prayers of Zuni medicine societies that recount the migrations of Zuni ancestors from the Grand Canyon to the Middle Place of Zuni Pueblo. Zuni cultural advisers suggest the place-name Anshe K'yan'a is associated with the medicine societies that use the bear, the Bear Clan, the younger brother War God associated with the Bear Clan, and the abundance of bears that once lived in the region. The water located within the cultural landscape of Anshe K'yan'a was first consecrated by members of Zuni medicine societies during their migrations to the Middle Place. This leads Zuni religious leaders today to seek out these water sources so they can reconnect with their ancestors and again make offerings to ensure the well-being of the natural environment (Perlman 1997:11). The Anshe K'yan'a landscape is important to Zuni people today because it continues to be used by religious societies, which collect plants, minerals, and water for traditional ritual purposes.

Fort Wingate was decommissioned as a military reservation in 1993, which began a process to transfer suitable land to the Bureau of Indian Affairs to benefit the Pueblo of Zuni and Navajo Nation. In 2011 the Army Corps of Engineers, Fort Worth District Office, issued a task order to identify properties of historical or traditional significance to the Pueblo of Zuni that are located on the FWDA and to evaluate these properties for their eligibility for inclusion on the National Register of Historic Places. To acquire the needed baseline data on Zuni traditional cultural properties, the army awarded a contract to HDR Environmental, Operations and Construction Inc. (HDR Environmental) to conduct an inventory of traditional cultural properties at the FWDA. HDR Environmental subcontracted the inventory of Zuni traditional cultural properties to the Zuni Cultural Resource Enterprise (ZCRE), and ZCRE then solicited Anthropological Research LLC to assist in this work. The inventory of Zuni traditional cultural properties that was compiled as a result of this work provides the army with the information it needs for consultation with the Pueblo of Zuni during ongoing and future planning of cleanup and closure actions at the FWDA.

A cultural resource survey of the FWDA conducted by the Office of Contract Archeology, University of New Mexico, between 1991 and 1994 identified 603 archaeological sites, representing 808 cultural and temporal components (Chapman et al. 1994:8). These sites have been categorized as including 22 Archaic components, 279 prehistoric Pueblo components, 294 historical Native American components, 3 Euro-American components, and 210 components of unknown cultural and temporal association. Historic Zuni ceramics were found at twenty-nine sites, with some assemblages dating to the 1930s (Daniel 1997:210). Some archaeologists have concluded that the Zuni have continuously occupied this area for over eleven hundred years (Perlman 1997:21). Although this survey provides insight about a sample of the cultural resources within the FWDA, it is not a complete inventory. The survey was undertaken with a 10 percent stratified random sample, and extensive areas were not surveyed at all (Chapman et al. 1994:2, 4).

Between 2003 and 2005, the ZCRE undertook ethnographic and ethnohistoric research to identify and assess Zuni traditional cultural properties and other cultural and natural resources on the FWDA (Dongoske and Nieto 2005). This research documents Zuni traditional use of the FWDA and explains why the Zuni believe that the well-being of Anshe K'yan'a is dependent on their traditional use of the area. Zuni aboriginal lands, as recognized by the United States, encompass numerous sacred sites, including Anshe K'yan'a, and these sacred sites are important in the cultural perpetuation of the Zuni people. The continued use of Zuni aboriginal lands is rooted in a long historical relationship that the Zuni have with their cultural landscape.

A 2014 ethnographic study expanded on the earlier research by ZCRE to provide additional documentation of the traditional cultural properties associated with Anshe K'yan'a and the FWDA and to discuss how these historic properties have significant historical, cultural, natural, and religious associations for Zuni people (Hopkins and Ferguson 2014). This work included a combination of archival research, ethnographic interviews with knowledgeable Zuni cultural advisers, and field visits to document specific sacred and traditional culturally important places within Fort Wingate. A significant component of the research included the identification of Zuni foot trails, wagon roads, and general routes of travel (plate 3). The identification of Zuni travel routes is important because trails are the product of movement and mobility, and when trails are viewed in connection with other sites and features on the landscape, one can begin to understand the meaningful relationships that exist between people and places through time.

THE ANSHE K'YAN'A CULTURAL LANDSCAPE

Cultural landscapes encompass both the land itself and how people perceive land given their particular cultural values and beliefs. As Carl Sauer (1963:343) observed, "The cultural landscape is fashioned from a natural landscape by a culture group. Culture is the agent, the natural area is the medium, and the cultural landscape is the result." Zuni cultural landscapes have complexity and power as a result of their creation through Zuni experience and encounters with the world. Zuni cultural landscapes are contextualized because the Zuni people understand them in light of specific events and historical conditions (Ferguson and Anyon

2001). Zuni cultural landscapes situate tribal members in historical time and space, providing a spatial conception of history. Importantly, each Zuni religious group has its own account of history that provides information for traditions and ceremonial events, thus connecting people to the land in different ways (Ferguson and Hart 1985:21). Concordance between narratives binds all Zunis to a general history and a broader landscape.

When Zuni people visit ancestral sites, the history of their migration is called to mind. In some instances, the very land itself was formed during past events involving spiritual beings. The land is thus part of historical memory, and it informs the conceptual framework of historical knowledge. As Jane Young (1988:2) observed, the Zuni "regard the land as a living being and themselves as part of this living being" because, according to traditional history, the Zuni people were born from the womb of Mother Earth. The Zuni consequently treat the land as a relative and feel a spiritual responsibility to care for the land as stewards.

Zunis traditionally view the land as a dynamic combination of natural and cultural elements and physical and spiritual entities. From the Zuni perspective, archaeological features are interconnected, springs are linked to shrines, lithic scatters are linked to animal resources, and ancient pueblos are linked to ancestral spirits (Dongoske and Nieto 2005). Zuni cultural landscapes are created and maintained by a traditional culture that instills in the community of Zuni tribal members values, beliefs, and historical memory about the importance of ancestral spirits, historical events, and the innate connection between people and the physical environment. Zuni cultural landscapes can consequently be sustained for long periods without physical use. Even after a long absence, Zunis maintain the social processes of collective memory, ceremony, and traditional history to renew cultural links with places that have been forgotten, irregularly used, or since occupied by other groups (Ferguson and Anyon 2001:104). Perceiving and talking about landscapes are ways that Zuni people "do" history and share the past with others, and this process helps create the unique Zuni identity.

The Zuni cultural landscape in its entirety encompasses all of the places where the Zuni people have lived, migrated through, or visited during economic or ritual activities. Called A:shiwi A:wan Dehwa:we in the Zuni language, this area encompasses Zuni aboriginal land as recognized by the U.S. Court of Federal Claims and extends far beyond that to include shrines and cultural sites in distant areas.

Cultural landscapes are created when people assign meaning to distinct places, and these individual components are spatialized at varying scales ranging from discrete sites and landforms to large tracts of land whose precise boundaries can be difficult to delineate. Places at various scales are thus the elements of composition for larger units of cultural landscapes. The Anshe K'yan'a cultural landscape has a coherent meaning for the Zuni people, and at the same time, it composes one building block used in conceptualizing a more comprehensive cultural landscape. The Anshe K'yan'a cultural landscape is an integral part of the larger cultural landscape of all Zuni aboriginal lands.

The cultural landscape that includes Fort Wingate and the FWDA is referred to as Anshe K'yan'a, translated approximately as "Bear Springs." Although Zunis use the name Anshe K'yan'a to refer to the Fort Wingate region, the place-name actually encompasses a larger area that extends beyond the boundaries of the military reservation. Some Zunis describe Anshe K'yan'a as including an area extending from Church Rock in the north, to Mount Taylor in the east, to Kebi'la:we ("Sheer Dry Sandstone Sitting Up," the Hogback, also known as Kedina:wa) and Ahmawuna (the west side of the Hogback near Bread Springs) in the west, to Ramah in the south (Dongoske and Nieto 2005:77). Most Zuni cultural advisers, however, are reluctant to delineate specific boundaries for Anshe K'yan'a other than pointing out that it is larger than the Bear Springs depicted on historic and contemporary maps of the FWDA.

The cultural meaning of the Anshe K'yan'a cultural landscape for the Zuni people is intimately associated with Zuni origins and the ancient migration to the Middle Village at Zuni Pueblo. Zuni traditions hold that after the world was formed, their ancient ancestors emerged at Chimik'yana'kya Dey'a (Ribbon Falls) in the Grand Canyon (see figure 3.1). These ancestors, known as the Ino:de:kwe, then began a lengthy migration across the American Southwest and beyond (Cushing 1896; Dongoske and Nieto 2005:18–19; Ferguson 2007; Ferguson and Hart 1985:21–23). On their sojourn the Ino:de:kwe separated into different groups at a location known today as Chavez Pass in Arizona. One segment went northward to Utah and Colorado and eventually arrived at Shiba:bulima on the Pajarito Plateau west of the Rio Grande, where the

Zuni medicine societies were perfected—including the Shi:wa:na:kwe, Newe:kwe, Halo:kwe, Chikk'yali:kwe, Uhuhu:kwe, Make:łana:kwe, Shu:ma:kwe, Łewe:kwe (now extinct), Sahniyakya:kwe (Hunter's Society), and associated religious groups. These societies traveled southward along the Rio Grande River to Chi:biya Yalanne (Sandia Mountains), where they gained more knowledge. The ancestors then trekked to Dewankwin K'yaba:chu Yalanne (Mount Taylor), where they settled for a time before moving west and passing through the land that would become Fort Wingate and the FWDA. The travels of the Zuni ancestors were never straightforward: groups sometimes scattered and moved in spirals and circles. Finally, the groups came together at Idiwan'a—the Middle Place of Zuni Pueblo—which would become their permanent home. The journey would not be forgotten, however. It has been recalled ever since in Zuni songs, prayers, ceremonies, and spoken traditions. Anshe K'yan'a is still referenced in the medicine songs sung today that recount the ancient Zuni migrations.

This remembered history is the lens through which Zunis interpret the distant past and give contemporary meaning to the places that make up their traditional land. Archaeological sites ranging from the Paleoindian and Archaic periods through the Pueblo occupation of the Southwest are understood to be the tangible vestiges—the footprints and markers—of the Zuni ancestors (Dongoske and Nieto 2005:52–54). In this way, pottery, stone tools, architecture, middens, shrines, burials, rock art, and villages come to have a dual purpose in Zuni society in that they provide a source of historical knowledge and a sign of their unique spiritual charter (Ferguson 1984, 2007, 2008).

Terms like *Paleoindian, Archaic,* and *Basketmaker* that archaeologists apply to some sites are often confusing to Zunis. From the Zuni perspective, all of the ancient sites that exist within their traditional homeland are conceptually grouped together and identified as *ino:de heshoda:we* (literally, "ancient homes"), and Zunis believe that the people who resided at these sites were Pueblo ancestors. Zuni historical traditions acknowledge a time when the people were learning and developing their current lifeways, which Zunis today correlate with the Paleoindian and Archaic archaeological traditions. The ancestors who lived a mobile or nomadic lifestyle are referred to as K'yabin A:ho'i, "Raw People," in the Zuni language (Roscoe 1992:128). The people who were "civilized or cultured" are known as Akna'A:ho, "Cooked Persons" (Roscoe 1992:128). Zuni ancestors became "cooked" when they learned their religion, economic, social, and kinship roles. These concepts of "raw" and "cooked" are complex, and they extend beyond people and eras (Roscoe 1992; Seowtewa, personal communication 2016; Tedlock 1979).

The Zuni consider ancient sites—Paleoindian through the Pueblo periods—within the FWDA to be monuments that commemorate the lives of their ancestors. They believe that these sites are important sources of information and are still occupied by the spirits of Zuni ancestors. Zuni tribal members explained that even light artifact scatters are important because they show that Zuni ancestors passed through the area. In addition to the ancient sites on the FWDA, other shrines, petroglyphs, springs, and plant and mineral sources are of value to the Zuni people.

ANSHE K'YAN'A TRAILS AND ZUNI TRADITIONS OF MOVEMENT

> The fences stopped us from coming here [to] Fort Wingate. The shrines and sites are not abandoned, though. Our ancestors are waiting for their souls to be nourished with our offerings. To do so gives us a sense of security, because they bless us and purify us— and bring peace and harmony to our families, our A:shiwi people, the world. Our grandfathers always talked about these areas, so we always have them in our minds as we go out. And when we find a shrine it feels good because then we recognize what we were told about in oral form [Ronnie Cachini in Hopkins and Ferguson 2014:19].

A primary goal of the ethnographic research conducted on the FWDA was to identify and ground verify the travel routes that linked Zuni villages on the reservation with the Anshe K'yan'a landscape (figure 3.3). Learning about Zuni values related to travel is essential in interpreting the trails and features across the land. Even as access to important places was cut off, Zunis stayed connected through prayer and by making offerings to their ancestors, who still reside in these distant locations. As access is being restored, Zunis are returning and establishing a physical presence once again.

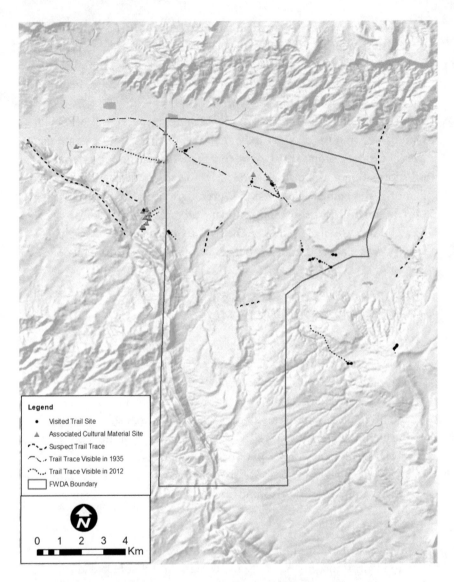

Figure 3.3 Trails and roads identified during ethnographic fieldwork on the Fort Wingate Depot Activity.

Multi-date aerial photographs, historical maps, U.S. Geological Survey topographic orthophotos, and interview information from Zuni tribal members were used to document the tangible traces of eighteen distinct prehistoric and historic roads and trails associated with Anshe K'yan'a (Hopkins and Ferguson 2014). In addition to the eighteen roads and trails inspected on the ground, two suspected pedestrian trails were identified in the 1935 aerial photography, and these appear to be associated with a large multistory Pueblo III period pueblo. Other trails were identified in the aerial photography and topo maps, including one pedestrian trail in the 1935 photography that corresponds to a trail on a General Land Office Special Plat map labeled as an "Indian Trail" (GLO n.d.) This map is undated, but it postdates the 1860 establishment of Fort Wingate. These trails could not be inspected in the field due to access restrictions and safety concerns (unexploded ordnance).

The trails and roads identified follow a general north–south, or northwest–southeast trajectory through the FWDA (figure 3.3). They were spatially associated with the Zuni Mountains, the Hogback, which is a prominent geological formation that defines the western boundary of the FWDA, archaeological sites, and springs (figure 3.4). According to Zuni cultural advisers, the spring they mainly refer to as Anshe K'yan'a is situated at the base of the Hogback within the FWDA. A foot trail leading from the Zuni village of Doya (Upper Nutria) to Fort Wingate comes directly to this place, and a portion of this trail was identified during fieldwork. Zuni cultural advisers have visited this spring in the past to leave offerings and collect water, and they knew of their relatives from generations past doing the same.

Another foot trail identified on the FWDA was associated with a large Pueblo site with a plaza, nine small kivas, and a great kiva. This site has been described by archaeologists as the "Zuni/Cibolan" site (Marshall et al. 1979; Schutt 1997:174–182). The Zuni cultural advisers unambiguously identified this site as a Zuni ancestral pueblo, with numerous features that they identify as uniquely Puebloan (Dongoske and Nieto 2005:37). In addition to the pottery and other artifacts seen on the surface, Zuni advisers said the two kinds of ceremonial chambers at the site resonate with contemporary cultural practices. The small "kivas" identified by archaeologists at the site are understood by Zunis to be *dikyan k'yakwenne*, chambers used for the curing rituals of medicine

Figure 3.4 Octavius Seowtewa points to a travel corridor leading to a natural spring on the Fort Wingate Depot Activity, April 11, 2012. Photograph by T. J. Ferguson.

groups. The large "kivas" archaeologists identified are *ki:wihtsinne* and are used for events like night dances and Kokko ceremonies. Zuni cultural advisers interpreted figures in petroglyphs near the site as depictions of Zuni ceremonies conducted in the winter, specifically, representations of ceremonial figures associated with the Zuni Sword-Swallowing Society.

Cultural advisers located a shrine at the southeastern edge of the same site (Dongoske and Nieto 2005:37). Zuni shrines have varied morphology. This particular shrine, constructed using rocks, has three sides. The cultural advisers knew that this shrine was constructed during Zuni migrations to the Middle Place and explained that these features today serve as spiritual umbilical cords that link ancestral sites to present-day people at Zuni Pueblo. Shrines are sacred places, with an everlasting spiritual value (Dongoske and Nieto 2005:76; Mills and Ferguson 1998; Perlman 1997:53). When a shrine is rediscovered, Zunis believe their ancestors are at that place waiting for them. The spiritual power of shrines never expires, and the sanctity of these shrines has been maintained through generations by Zuni prayers and, when possible, through offerings left during pilgrimages or visits to ancestral areas. The cultural advisers observed turquoise and shell offerings within this shrine, indicating use by Zuni religious practitioners in the past. They left another offering here during their fieldwork visit.

Zuni cultural advisers noted that Zuni religious leaders have made regular offerings for and at Anshe K'yan'a through the years. Ronnie Cachini explained, "Although Zunis had not visited this shrine for hundreds of years it has been talked about in our prayers. Zunis used to visit shrines like this but had to stop when White Man came." Zuni traditionalists believe the safety and well-being of the Zuni people is provided for by their ancestors. If shrines are destroyed or not properly respected, innocent people will be harmed. "Shrines give us a stronghold on the land. Not to 'control' the land, but a stronghold to ask for rain and an abundance of wildlife so that nature can flourish," Mr. Cachini continued.

These long-standing traditions of pilgrimage to and revisitation of important places are one way the Zuni people stay connected to the land. Places established during the ancient past, including ancestral sites, shrines, and other features on the land, provide a venue for Zuni religious leaders to fulfill and maintain their spiritual and religious obligations of nourishing the ancestors that fortify the Zuni people today.

Several wagon roads were identified during the ethnographic work at the FWDA. In discussions about the roads and foot trails that passed through the Zuni Mountains, cultural advisers recalled hearing stories from their grandfathers about traveling to this area for hunting and gathering plants and minerals. Some of the cultural advisers had personal recollections from when they were very young of traveling to Fort Wingate. One participant said his grandfather used to talk about how Zunis would go to Anshe K'yan'a to gather plants for the medicine societies, and he also described conflicts the Zunis later had with Navajos when gathering timbers in the area. Another cultural adviser reported that he collected bear root around the edges of the FWDA, and another recalled collecting aspen and piñon and other evergreens just south of the study area.

Much Zuni travel to Anshe K'yan'a and Fort Wingate in the nineteenth and twentieth centuries involved farming, hunting, trapping, sheepherding, trading at the Fort Wingate Trading Post and attending the boarding school at Fort Wingate (Hart 1980). When the U.S. Army settled Fort Wingate in the nineteenth century, the Zuni people provided food and supplies to the military outpost under the direction of Zuni leader Pedro Pino (Hart 2003). The trails and roads the Zunis traveled from their villages on the Zuni Reservation were already familiar to them because they used them when they traveled to the area to collect resources for religious purposes. One cultural adviser said he used to walk to the trading post, taking the trail from Nutria north along the Hogback, which led to the original Bear Springs.

Many other trails, roads, and travel corridors exist on the FWDA and merit further investigation to determine what associations they may have with Zuni history and traditions. These are important features of the Zuni cultural landscape because they connect present-day Zuni people with places of their past, and they represent long-standing traditions of movement across the land at varying scales.

SUMMARY AND CONCLUSION

Movement and mobility are an essential part of what sustains and fortifies Zuni traditional culture, which instills values, beliefs, and historical memory in community members about the importance of ancestral spirits, historical events, and the innate connection between people and the physical environment. The Anshe K'yan'a landscape is infused with diverse resources that are used to both remember the past and maintain living traditions.

Over the last century, the Zuni people, like other Native peoples, have become increasingly alienated from their use of many traditional places because of the impacts of colonialism on Native American heritage, including exclusion from private land, federal policies requiring permits to collect natural resources, fences that impede access, and development of roads. These processes, and others, make the continuation of traditional land use and cultural practices ever more difficult (Coder et al. 2005; Dongoske and Damp 2007; Record 2008).

Zuni use of the Anshe K'yan'a landscape is no exception. For more than a generation, a large part of Anshe K'yan'a has been cut off from Zuni use. However, even after a long absence Zunis maintain the social processes of collective memory, ceremony, and traditional history to renew their connections with places that have been forgotten, irregularly used, or since occupied by other groups (Ferguson and Anyon 2001:104). Ethnographic work with the members of the Pueblo of Zuni has enabled Zuni cultural advisers to discuss Zuni history and traditions related to this area and to reconnect with places that are significant in the retention and transmission of Zuni culture. It has also enabled Zunis to engage in meaningful discourse with land managers and archaeologists about concepts and terminology used by each group when describing history and heritage. The value of Anshe K'yan'a for the Zuni people extends back to the period in which their ancestors migrated across the land in search of the Middle Place. The identification of petroglyphs, shrines, ceremonial structures, ancestral habitations, and trails provides a means for Zuni religious practitioners to maintain their ongoing traditions that are rooted in these past places. Understanding the history associated with Zuni mobility across time and space is essential for grasping the "has been," the "being," and the "becoming" of the Zuni people.

REFERENCES

Chapman, Richard C., Carolyn L. Daniel, and Jeanne A. Schutt. 1994. *Cultural Resources Inventory of Fort Wingate Depot Activity, New Mexico: Executive Summary*. OCA/UNM Report No. 185–477A. Office of Contract Archeology, University of New Mexico, Albuquerque.

Coder, Christopher, Vincent Randall, Elizabeth Smith-Rocha, and Rozella Hines. 2005. Chi Ch'il (Acorns): Dissolution of Traditional Dilzhe'e Gathering Practice(s) Due to Federal Control of the Landscape. Paper presented at Connecting Mountain Islands and Desert Seas: Biodiversity and Management of the Madrean Archipelago II, Tucson, Arizona.

Cushing, Frank Hamilton. 1896. Outlines of Zuni Creation Myths. In *13th Annual Report of the Bureau of Ethnology for the Years 1891–1892*, pp. 321–447. Government Printing Office, Washington, D.C.

Daniel, Carolyn L. 1997. Historical Archaeology and the History of Fort Wingate. In *Cycles of Closure: A Cultural Resources Inventory of Fort Wingate Depot Activity, New Mexico*, edited by Jeanne A. Schutt and Richard C. Chapman, pp. 191–235. OCA/UNM Report No. 185–551. Office of Contract Archeology, University of New Mexico, Albuquerque.

Dongoske, Kurt E., and Jonathan E. Damp. 2007. Recognizing Zuni Place and Landscape Within the Fort Wingate Military Depot Activity. *SAA Archaeological Record* 7(2):31–34.

Dongoske, Kurt E., and Davis Nieto Jr. 2005. *Anshe Ky'an'a*: Zuni Traditional Places Located Within the Fort Wingate Military Depot Activity, McKinley County, New Mexico. Zuni Cultural Resource Enterprise, Zuni, New Mexico.

Ferguson, T. J. 1984. Archaeological Values in a Tribal Cultural Resource Management Program at the Pueblo of Zuni. In *Ethics and Values in Archaeology*, edited by Ernestene L. Green, pp. 224–235. Free Press, New York.

Ferguson, T. J. 2007. Zuni Traditional History and Cultural Geography. In *Zuni Origins: Toward a New Synthesis of Southwestern Archaeology*, edited by David A. Gregory and David R. Wilcox, pp. 377–403. University of Arizona Press, Tucson.

Ferguson, T. J. 2008. Zuni Traditional History. *Archaeology Southwest* 22(2):4–5.

Ferguson, T. J., and Roger Anyon. 2001. Hopi and Zuni Cultural Landscapes: Implications of Social Identity and Cultural Affiliation Research for Cultural Resources Management. In *Native Peoples of the Southwest: Negotiating Land, Water, and Ethnicities*, edited by Laurie Weinstein, pp. 99–122. Bergin and Garvey, Westport, Connecticut.

Ferguson, T. J., and Richard E. Hart. 1985. *A Zuni Atlas*. University of Oklahoma Press, Norman.

GLO (General Land Office). n.d. *Milit: Reservation, of Fort Wingate, N.M.* (Survey title: *Fort Wingate*). Digital GLO Collection, DM ID: 95750. Electronic document, www.glorecords.blm.gov.

Gregory, David A., and David R. Wilcox (editors). 2007. *Zuni Origins: Toward a New Synthesis of Southwestern Archaeology*. University of Arizona Press, Tucson.

Hart, E. Richard. 1980. *Zuni and the Courts: A Struggle for Sovereign Land Rights*. University Press of Kansas, Lawrence.

Hart, E. Richard. 2003. *Pedro Pino: Governor of Zuni Pueblo 1830–1878*. Utah State University Press, Logan.

Hopkins, Maren P., and T. J. Ferguson (editors). 2014. *Anshe Ky'an'a: Zuni Traditional Cultural Properties on the Fort Wingate Depot Activity*. ZCRE Report No. 1167. Zuni Cultural Resource Enterprise, Zuni Pueblo, New Mexico.

Jenkins, Myra Ellen. 1995. Zuni History During the Early U.S. Period. In *Zuni and the Courts*, edited by Richard E. Hart, pp. 46–59. University Press of Kansas, Lawrence.

Marshall, Michael P., John R. Stein, Richard W. Loose, and Judith E. Novotny (editors). 1979. *Anasazi Communities of the San Juan Basin*. Public Service Company of New Mexico, Albuquerque, and New Mexico Historic Preservation Bureau, Santa Fe.

Mills, Barbara J., and T. J. Ferguson. 1998. Preservation and Research of Sacred Sites by the Zuni Indian Tribe of New Mexico. *Human Organization* 57(1):30–42.

Mills, Barbara J., Matthew A. Peeples, W. Randall Haas Jr., Lewis Borck, Jeffery J. Clark, and John M. Roberts Jr. 2015. Multiscalar Perspectives on Social Networks in the Late Prehispanic Southwest. *American Antiquity* 80(1):3–24.

Perlman, Susan E. 1997. *Fort Wingate Depot Activity Ethnographic Study*. OCA/UNM Report No. 185–477B. Office of Contract Archeology, University of New Mexico, Albuquerque.

Record, Ian W. 2008. *Big Sycamore Stands There: The Western Apaches, Aravaipa, and the Struggle for Place*. University of Oklahoma Press, Norman.

Roscoe, Will. 1992. *The Zuni Man-Woman*. University of New Mexico Press, Albuquerque.

Sauer, Carl O. 1963. *Land and Life: A Selection from the Writings of Carl Ortwin Sauer*. University of California Press, Berkeley.

Schachner, Gregson, Deborah L. Huntley, and Andrew I. Duff. 2011. Changes in Regional Organization and Mobility in the Zuni Region of the American Southwest During the Pueblo III and IV Periods: Insights from INAA Studies. *Journal of Archaeological Science* 38(9):2261–2273.

Schutt, Jeanne A. 1997. Prehistoric Settlement on Fort Wingate. In *Cycles of Closure: A Cultural Resources Inventory of Fort Wingate Depot Activity, New Mexico*, edited by Jeanne A. Schutt and Richard C. Chapman, pp. 149–189. OCA/UNM Report No. 185–551. Office of Contract Archeology, University of New Mexico, Albuquerque.

Tedlock, Dennis. 1979. Zuni Religion and World View. In *Southwest*, edited by Alfonso Ortiz, pp. 499–508. Handbook of North American Indians, Vol. 9. Smithsonian Institution Press, Washington, D.C.

Yanello, Judith Ann. 1995. Appendix A: Findings of the United States Claims Commission Docket 161–79L, Aboriginal Area. In *Zuni and the Courts: A Struggle for Sovereign Land Rights*, edited by E. R. Hart, pp. 241–282. University Press of Kansas, Lawrence.

Young, M. Jane. 1988. *Signs from the Ancestors*. University of New Mexico Press, Albuquerque.

Tewa Origins and Middle Places

Samuel Duwe and Patrick J. Cruz

The Tewa Pueblo people know their own history. It is remembered in song and story and lived by dancing in the plaza and traveling through the mountains and valleys of northern New Mexico. We as archaeologists are fortunate that the broad outlines of these traditions have been shared outside the Tewa villages. First recorded by anthropologists a century ago, and then in more recent years by the Tewa themselves through scholarly work and collaborative relationships, these traditions do much more than record the long arc of Tewa history. They also act as a charter for the complex and nuanced social and ceremonial organization of Tewa life. And, most importantly, these ancient oral traditions encapsulate and demonstrate the Tewa philosophy of "seeking life," or the continual movement and ongoing negotiation of the people with the world as they attempt to achieve harmony between the complementary dichotomies of existence: summer and winter, female and male, life and death (Naranjo and Swentzell 1989).

For the Tewa, movement is an essential metaphor. It is particularly embedded in complex and disparate histories of the Tewa ancestors' journeys from the north and their eventual meeting and negotiation of Tewa society in the Rio Grande valley (Naranjo 2008). For archaeologists, however, the paths and consequences of this movement are up for debate. Renewed interest in population movement, and particularly migration, in southwestern archaeology has reopened old arguments regarding the identity of Tewa ancestors (Mills 2011). These include the in situ development of the Tewa world as the natural extension of many hundreds of years of Pueblo occupation and history in the Rio Grande valley and, conversely, the idea that Tewa identity was the result of large-scale population movement from the Mesa Verde region in southern Colorado in the late thirteenth century. Inherent in these explanations are questions about the roots of the Tewa language, the seeds of Tewa cosmology and dual-division social organization, and the relationship between archaeological data and Tewa oral tradition.

In searching for Tewa origins, archaeologists have found evidence that is messy, contradictory, and incomplete. We take a different approach in this chapter and attempt to reframe the debate in light of the Tewas' own view of history. Our inspiration comes from Rina Swentzell's (1991:177) discussion contrasting how archaeologists and Pueblo people view truth. She explains that archaeologists tend to accept the existence of an absolute truth (a real world observable by science) that can be uncovered through the collection of enough facts (and artifacts). The Pueblos, on the other hand, view truth as dynamic, multifaceted, and relative. There is never one truth but many, just as there are multiple people, levels of being, and middle places. From this latter perspective the messiness of the archaeological record fits comfortably within the fluid and relative bounds of Tewa history and philosophy. The modern Tewa world is hardly monolithic and is comprised of six autonomous Tewa-speaking villages along the Rio Grande and its tributaries. Whereas each village shares the common experience of distantly related yet disparate people coming together and negotiating Tewa society, each has done so in a unique, historically contingent, way (Anschuetz and Wilshusen 2011). And it is for precisely this reason that we think it so difficult to write a Tewa history, let alone have clear consensus on Tewa origins. There is no one Tewa history. These histories, manifested in the material record, differ considerably throughout the Tewa homeland and reflect the ways that various peoples lived in new worlds.

The entire Southwest experienced a dramatic social and demographic transformation in the thirteenth and fourteenth centuries. Thousands of individuals migrated from the Four Corners region in the north to the far-flung regions of the Pueblo world, including the already occupied northern Rio Grande valley. And people had been moving between regions for hundreds of years prior. In this context we examine how interaction, negotiation, and competition between migrant and local groups led to diversity and unity across the Tewa world. We discuss two distinct areas of the Tewa homeland: the middle northern Rio Grande valley, near Pojoaque Pueblo in the south and east, and the Rio Chama valley in the northwest. By incorporating diverse Tewa origin traditions with new archaeological research, we demonstrate that each area has a unique history of diverse groups joining to create new villages. By comparing and synthesizing these areas, we acknowledge both cultural continuity with ancient Rio Grande traditions, as well as large-scale changes catalyzed by emigration from the north. We shift from asking who was Tewa to asking how these different people created new worlds. Rather than viewing Tewa history as a local or migrant development, we can begin to see Tewa history as the Tewa do: as constantly moving, attempting to achieve harmony, and always in a state of becoming.

ORIGINS

While each of the six modern Tewa-speaking villages, located along the Rio Grande and its tributaries between the cities of Santa Fe and Taos (figure 4.1), has a unique history, the most important elements are shared by all (Harrington 1916; Ortiz 1969; Parsons 1994 [1926]). The origin traditions begin with how the Tewa emerged into the world in the distant north (plate 4). The place is Sandy Place Lake, thought to be located in southern Colorado. Soon after emergence, the Tewa were split into two people, the Summer and Winter People, and were sent to opposite places on the landscape and tasked with finding the "middle place," or the locations of their eventual historic villages. The Summer People traveled along the western side of the Rio Grande eating fruits, and the Winter People journeyed along the eastern side eating deer and elk. On their travels southward the people stopped twelve times, and these stops are represented as ancient villages. Eventually the two peoples came together in the Rio Grande valley and built their homes with a unique social arrangement; each village was united *and* divided as both the Summer and Winter People maintained their identities but worked together for the benefit of the entire village. In subsequent years the Tewa established their historic and modern homes but have continued to maintain this unique arrangement to the present day.

In its barest form, Tewa history details two core realities. The first is that Tewa ancestors, while likely distantly related, have disparate histories and took separate paths prior to coming together in the middle place of the Rio Grande. The second is that these groups, upon meeting, negotiated a unique social and ceremonial organization distinct from their

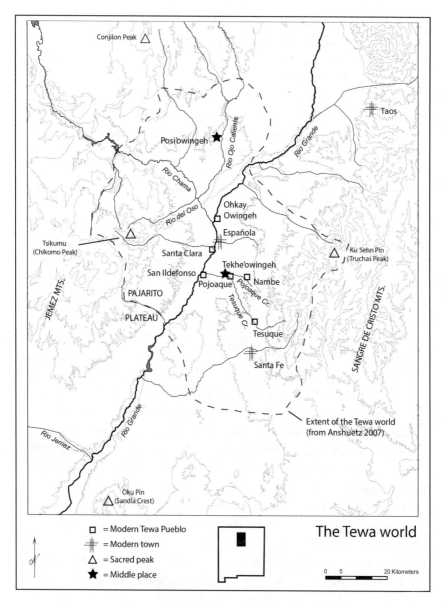

Figure 4.1 The Tewa world with the location of the various middle places.

Pueblo neighbors. It seems reasonable, then, to assume that the dramatic reshuffling of Pueblo demographics and the creation of new Pueblo villages and identities in the thirteenth and fourteenth centuries—including those of the Tewa—were not coincidental.

Archaeologists over the past century have been keenly aware of the impact of this demographic transformation, particularly in the development of the historic and modern Tewa world(s). Recently, a new generation of scholars has revisited these debates that can roughly be grouped into three categories: in situ development of Tewa society in the Rio Grande valley, large-scale population movement from the northern San Juan Basin and particularly the central Mesa Verde region, and hybrid models that incorporate elements from both. While each model acknowledges the demographic and social transformations that occurred in the Pueblo Southwest in the thirteenth century (if not before), they vary in emphasizing where and when the essential elements of Tewa language and culture were created and introduced.

Proponents of the in situ development model argue that Tewa society and language emerged from a proto-population of both ancestral Tewa- and Tiwa- (represented by the modern villages of Taos, Picuris, Isleta, and Sandia) speaking people who have lived in the Rio Grande valley since at least AD 900 (Boyer et al. 2010; Mera 1935; Steen 1977; Wendorf and Reed 1955). Recent research has demonstrated that sometime around AD 900 the Tewa language diverged from Tiwa (Schillaci et al. 2017) and the Tewa people began a long and seemingly unbroken chain of cultural continuity through the present day. This is reflected by the long-lived and conservative Tewa pottery tradition (Schillaci and Lakatos 2017), a continuity of architectural forms in the northern Rio Grande valley that are substantially different from those in the Mesa Verde region (Lakatos 2007) and in Late Developmental period (AD 900–1200) sites in the southern portion of the Tewa homeland. Possible Tewa names suggest their great antiquity (Schillaci et al. 2017). In addition, a review of regional population estimates (Boyer et al. 2010; Schillaci and Lakatos 2016) suggests that while the thirteenth-century migrants may have added to the population and cultural richness of Rio Grande Tewa people, they did not overwhelm or replace the existing people (contra Ortman 2012, 2014).

The contrasting model is that of large-scale population movement from the upper San Juan Basin to the northern Rio Grande region in the mid- to late thirteenth century (Jeançon 1923; Ortman 2012; Reed 1949). This out-migration was caused by extreme climatic and social upheaval in north, which led to the complete depopulation of the region (Ortman 2010, 2012) and a refugee crisis: tens of thousands of people joining distant relatives across the Pueblo world (Ortman 2014). These people spoke the Tewa language, a claim that Scott Ortman supports with Tewa place-names remembered in the Mesa Verde region (Ortman 2012) and shared Tewa metaphors in the archaeology of the Mesa Verde region and the northern Rio Grande valley (Ortman 2011). Additional supporting evidence includes craniometric similarities between the regions (Ortman 2012) and the potential introduction of particular domestic turkeys in the Rio Grande (Kemp et al. 2017). The strongest arguments for this migration, however, have historically and recently (Ortman 2012, 2014) been based on evidence for the movement of population. Ortman (2012) suggests that populations of Tewa-speaking migrants began to settle in the northern Rio Grande, particularly on the Pajarito Plateau in the western half of the Tewa homeland, first as a trickle and then as a flood by the end of the thirteenth century. The migrant population may have totaled ten thousand people and effectively overwhelmed the genes and language of local populations, thereby catalyzing the process of Tewa ethnogenesis (Ortman 2012).

This local/migrant dichotomy necessarily glosses over the more nuanced positions of archaeologists studying Tewa origins. For example, Michael Schillaci and Steven Lakatos (2016) reintroduce a hybrid model that acknowledges long-term and small-scale migration from the San Juan Basin and adjacent regions throughout the Developmental period, culminating in migration from the Mesa Verde region in the thirteenth century (Cordell 1979; Habicht-Mauche 1993; Kidder 1924). These people would have contributed to the northern Rio Grande valley's population growth but would have been incorporated into the existing ancestral Tewa world. And Ortman's (2012) position, while advocating for the large-scale replacement of local tongues with the Tewa language, acknowledges that many processes (from all models) may have happened together through earlier small-scale migration and through negotiations and adoptions of elements of native Rio Grande culture.

Inherent, but not necessarily central, to these arguments are implications for how these people (from whatever model) transformed their society and created the Tewa world. The great towns built at the beginning of the Classic period (AD 1350–1598) were very different from the small hamlets and villages of both migrant and local communities a century earlier. These fourteenth-century towns were substantially larger (some with over one thousand residents) and closely resemble historic and modern Tewa pueblos. Researchers advancing the in situ hypothesis point toward the unbroken continuity in material culture (Lakatos 2007; Schillaci and Lakatos 2017), and substantial pre–AD 1270 population (Boyer et al. 2010), to explain that Classic period Tewa society was the result of centuries of cultural development in the Rio Grande. The Rio Grande Tewa would have accommodated refugees and incorporated them into their villages and lives. Proponents of migration explain this continuity, and the lack of definitive Mesa Verde–style material culture, through another social process. Ortman (2012) views the Mesa Verde migration as analogous to a later event of Tewa cultural revitalization—the Pueblo Revolt—and argues that the migrants purposely abandoned their failed lifeways to return to an idealized past still lived by their distant cousins to the south and east. By adopting the Rio Grande Pueblos' lifeways they returned to the old ways to start anew, although they likely carried with them their previous ways of seeing and speaking about the world.

It strikes us, however, that these models have tended to focus on different areas (and times) of the ancestral Tewa homeland. The proponents of local Tewa origins draw heavily from the cultural and population continuity in the southern and eastern portions of the region, whereas the migrant models rely heavily on the dynamic histories of the north and west. If the Tewa world is neither historically nor ethnographically monolithic (including today), then neither, we assume, are Tewa histories and their associated archaeological records. To make sense of this we suggest looking to Tewas' own history for guidance. While all of the Tewa villages' histories remember the coming together of the Summer and Winter People, each village remembers the places, and the factors, of this coalescence differently. *There are multiple middle places.* For example, in one tradition the village of Tekhe'owingeh, located near Pojoaque Pueblo, was viewed by advisers from Nambe, San Ildefonso, and Ohkay Owingeh as the middle village where, after the peoples' migrations from the north, "some on the west side liked the east side and walked over, some on the east side liked the west side and walked over" (Parsons 1994[1926]:15). In another history from Ohkay Owingeh the middle place is remembered as the village of Posi'owingeh in the Rio Chama valley (Ortiz 1969). Each Tewa village also has a unique history of coalescence and becoming; for example, San Ildefonso's relationship to ancestral villages on the Pajarito Plateau (Aguilar and Preucel, this volume). This disparity suggests that the ways, and the locations, in which the Summer and Winter People came together varied across the Tewa world. Likely, so too did the various populations who interacted and negotiated their identities in the thirteenth and fourteenth centuries. The recounting of multiple middle places also implies that the Tewa are remembering not just a single event of coalescence, but rather an entire history of seeking life—and finding harmony—between disparate peoples in a constantly changing social landscape of northern New Mexico.

TEKHE'OWINGEH

We argue that the seeds of Tewa society originated from many places and came together in unique and historically contingent ways across the Rio Grande valley. Even so, when looking at Tewa history through the lens of the southern and eastern portions of the Tewa world, we are struck by both the antiquity of Pueblo occupation and the continuity of Tewa-like material culture from AD 900 to the present day. Based on the material culture of the middle northern Rio Grande region, defined as the area north of Santa Fe and south of Santa Cruz, archaeologists have made a strong case for cultural continuity from the Late Developmental period onward. This continuity, of course, has been taken as evidence for the in situ development of Tewa society (Lakatos 2007; Schillaci and Lakatos 2017) and against Tewa culture being heavily influenced by migrant populations. But when we turn to the Tewas' own history, a more complex picture emerges. All of the Tewa villages, including those in the middle northern Rio Grande (Pojoaque, Nambe, and Tesuque), share similar origin traditions of the Summer and Winter People traveling separate routes along the western and eastern sides of the Rio Grande, respectively (Harrington 1916; Parsons 1994[1926]). And one of the places that the Tewa specifically cite as the village where the Winter and Summer People first came together after traveling independently from the north—Tekhe'owingeh—is located adjacent to Pojoaque Pueblo (Harrington

1916:336–337). Tekhe'owingeh, based on its geographic centrality and historic significance, is both literally and figuratively the middle place.

Identifying the Summer and Winter People archaeologically, including where and how they came together, is challenging, but emerging archaeological research supports our reading of Tewa oral tradition. While the cultural history of this area runs deep, as far back as Clovis times (Warren 1974), occupation was generally sporadic and small in scale until AD 900. At the start of the Late Developmental period, the middle northern Rio Grande, along with much of the surrounding region, experienced an uptick in population. Ortman (2014) estimates that the area housed approximately nine hundred people in the years between AD 900 and 1050 but that this population more than doubled by the end of the eleventh century. We follow others (Ford et al. 1972; Reed 1949) in thinking that this increase may be related to an early migration from the north or west, perhaps including Tiwa speakers from the San Juan Valley. The majority of the residences were small pueblo hamlets (under twenty rooms in size) with the notable exception of the Pojoaque Grant Site with twenty house units, one hundred rooms, and a great kiva (McNutt 1969).

We believe that the people who immigrated into the middle northern Rio Grande in the Late Developmental period are remembered, at least in an abstract way, as the Winter People by the Tewa. This is supported by Florence Hawley Ellis's (1974a:1) recording of the Nambe tradition: "The Tewa people came into the Rio Grande in two major groups, one arriving from the northwest (San Juan drainage) by way of the Chama Valley and the other coming up the San Juan River but eventually leaving it to cut across the Conejos and reach the Rio Grande in southern Colorado. They then followed the Rio Grande south to the western high foothills of the Sangre de Cristos, where they settled in a number of pueblos built on high ridges, far above water." Those who journeyed down to the eastern side of the Rio Grande and lived high on the flanks of the mountains are remembered as the Winter People (Ortiz 1969; Parsons 1994[1926]). And the archaeology of the region—small sites located in high-elevation locales on the eastern side of the Rio Grande with San Juan origins—also fits this narrative neatly.

The Winter People, then, were possibly among the firstcomers. They likely shared cultural affinity with other contemporary Tiwa-speaking people in Rio Grande valley, such as people ancestral to Taos and Picuris (Fowles 2004), and may have produced the same Kwahe'e Black-on-white pottery (Schillachi and Lakatos 2016). However, in the thirteenth century the middle northern Rio Grande was affected by the demographic and social trends that impacted the entire region as migrants from the north and west arrived. While population size remained steady in the first half of the century, the number of residents tripled to roughly six thousand people by 1315 (Ortman 2014). Populations were never very large in the middle northern Rio Grande, and the thirteenth-century increase in size has been explained away as the product of internal growth (Boyer et al. 2010; Schillachi and Lakatos 2017). However, during this period a number of larger villages were built across the landscape, often on terraces overlooking drainages, and demonstrate considerable variability in architecture with both L-shaped and C-shaped plaza pueblos (Dickson 1975). This heterogeneity in material culture suggests the possibility of disparate peoples inhabiting the highlands in the southeastern portion of the Tewa world. Could it signal the coming of migrant populations or Summer People? And if so, how and where did these peoples meet?

While the research is still preliminary, one of us (Cruz) believes he has possibly located Tekhe'owingeh, the middle place where the Summer and Winter People joined. John Harrington (1916:337), after consulting with Tewa collaborators, mapped the site as being at or very near Pojoaque Pueblo. The archaeological history of Pojoaque is complex and includes multiple sites with many components dating from the Developmental to Historic periods. The vicinity has been razed and rebuilt many times, and much of the area has been bulldozed to create space for pasturelands and orchards (Ellis 1974b:18). However, upon a low hill that overlooks the Rio Pojoaque and has clear views to the mountains on both sides of the Rio Grande sits a small site, originally recorded by Ellis (1974b) and named the "Winter Village" by locals (LA 12271). While the eastern and northern portions of the site have likely been disturbed by development, as well as geologic processes, initial survey has identified multiple small adobe structures and possibly two kivas (figures 4.2 and 4.3). Ellis (1974b) identifies a hillside immediately north of the site on which the ground has either dropped or split, resulting in a series of parallel gullies running perpendicular to the hillslope. This process appears to have impacted the northern portion of the site, which has dropped away. Pottery observed

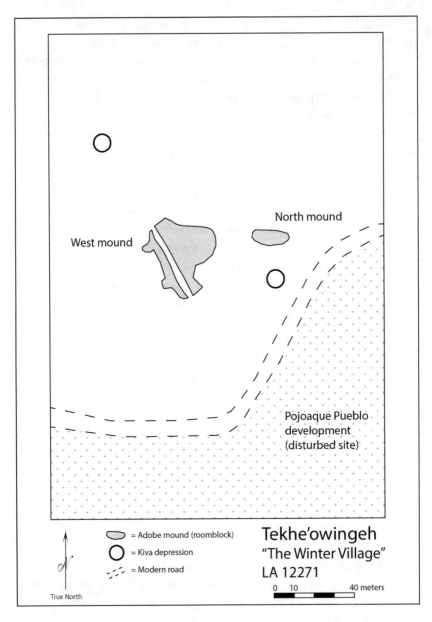

Figure 4.2 A plan map of LA 12271, the "Winter Village" and the possible location of Tekhe'owingeh.

Figure 4.3 A view of the Pojoaque Valley, with the sacred Tewa mountain Tsikumu in the distance, from Tekhe'owingeh. Photograph by Patrick J. Cruz.

on the ground surface is predominately Santa Fe Black-on-white with small amounts of Kwahe'e Black-on-white and Abiquiu Black-on-gray, suggesting that the site dates to the earliest parts of the Coalition period and into the Classic period. The name Winter Village suggests that this site was inhabited by people associated with the Winter moiety. This begs the question of the existence of a "Summer Village." There are numerous village sites located west of the Winter Village, some with Coalition-associated ceramics, but the area has been highly disturbed, and multiple overlapping occupations date right up to the present. While we cannot be certain that the Winter Village is Tekhe'owingeh, the site's placement at Pojoaque (the location of the village studied by Harrington) and early date support the possibility that the Winter Village, and the many similar Coalition period sites throughout the middle northern Rio Grande, were places where the Summer and Winter People came together.

Unlike the history of Posi'owingeh, a large Classic period village built in the social tumult of the unification of the peoples (see following), Tekhe'owingeh is small and unassuming. It is also considerably older, dating to the beginning of the Coalition period. We imagine a scenario in which the earliest migrants from the north and west, traveling in small numbers, possibly as "scouts" (Ortman 2012), encountered the Winter People on the skirts of the Sangre de Cristo Mountains. They would have settled at existing villages and been incorporated into the Winter People's world throughout the thirteenth century. While the number of migrants increased through the end of the century (concurrent with the final depopulation of the Mesa Verde region), the presence of similar material culture traditions from the Developmental to the Classic periods implies a continuing presence of the Winter People's traditions. This fits the "hybrid" model by acknowledging both in situ development of Tewa culture and the relatively small-scale, but still substantial, in-migration of Summer People.

This trajectory continued through the Classic period, as evidenced by people's gradual transition to larger sites in the fourteenth century; many communities moved from their terraced locations down along rivers and streams (Dickson 1975). The area's population had peaked by the mid-fourteenth century and steadily declined through the 1600s (Ortman 2014). The movement of people out of the middle northern Rio Grande coincided with a rise in the numbers of sites and rooms in other areas of the Tewa world, such as the Chama Valley, suggesting that the people, after resting for a while at Tekhe'owingeh, were again on the move. While some remained in the area and founded Pojoaque, Nambe, and Tesuque, others traveled to the north and west.

POSI'OWINGEH

On the northwestern frontier of the Tewa world a very different history played out. Whereas the middle northern Rio Grande was occupied for hundreds of years before the large-scale social and demographic changes of the thirteenth century, the Rio Chama valley, with its verdant, well-watered tributaries, was settled relatively late in the mid-thirteenth century. However, within a hundred years the valley had become a population center of the Tewa world and was the place, according to Ohkay Owingeh's tradition, where the Summer and Winter People came together to forge a new society.

The Chama Valley includes the mighty Rio Chama, a major tributary of the Rio Grande. Within the valley are multiple tributaries of the Chama itself, and along these green ribbons running through the high desert are the homes of ancestral Tewa people, which span the Late Coalition (AD 1250–1350) and Classic periods. While multiple Tewa villages claim the Chama as part of their ancestral homeland, Ohkay Owingeh has a particularly well-documented history in the valley. Some of the earliest sites, such as Tsipin'owingeh (established in AD 1312; Duwe 2011), are remembered in song and dance (Richard Ford, personal communication 2009). And all of the Classic period villages, built in the mid-fourteenth century, have Tewa names and well-remembered histories (Harrington 1916). These include Sapa'owingeh, located on El Rito Creek, whose people joined their relatives at Ohkay Owingeh in the sixteenth century (Ellis 1968:29, 1970:4); Te'ewi'owingeh and Pesede'owingeh along the Rio del Oso, which are visited by priests from Ohkay on pilgrimage (Anschuetz 2014); and finally, Posi'owingeh along the Rio Ojo Caliente, which sits above a symbolic place of emergence and is the place where the peoples congregated (Ortiz 1969) and later traveled to Ohkay Owingeh (Schroeder 1979:250; Wozniak 1992:50). According to Ohkay Owingeh, after emergence the Summer and Winter People traveled along either side of the Rio Grande and came together at Posi'owingeh. It was at this village that the Summer and Winter People lived in one place for many years. Eventually, an epidemic struck the village and catalyzed a move down to the historic Tewa villages, where the Tewa continued the system of one village, multiple peoples.

Recent archaeological research suggests that the Chama was settled by various groups of people, in waves, in the century preceding the building of Posi'owingeh. The first settlers opportunistically spread across both the highland and lowland areas and built small villages. The earliest secure date—an architectural timber that was cut in AD 1231—was recovered at Tsama'owingeh, then a small site along the north bank of the Rio Chama. It is difficult for archaeologists to assign identities to these first settlers. In many ways the architecture of Tsama'owingeh appears similar to contemporary sites south of the Chama (Kidder 1958; Stubbs and Stallings 1953). However, we also have indications that the original settlers of Tsama'owingeh were coming from much further afield. Ortman (2012) suggests that the earliest inhabitants were migrants from the northern San Juan region based on his stylistic reanalysis of Santa Fe Black-on-white pottery from the site. Supporting this claim is the fact that the earliest-dated kiva is D shaped and can therefore be viewed as part of a Chacoan or Mesa Verde tradition (Windes and McKenna 2006). It is quite possible that Tsama'owingeh and other small sites located in the highland areas south of the Chama (Bremer 1995) were built by migrants and represent people either traveling directly down the Chama or traveling north from the Pajarito Plateau after their initial migration. Samuel Duwe (2011) has previously suggested that these migrants, based on their travels on the western side of the Rio Grande, were remembered as the Summer People in Tewa memory.

Settlement continued sporadically throughout, and particularly in the later parts of the thirteenth century. Multiple sites were built along the Rio del Oso, the creek that both metaphorically and literally links Ohkay Owingeh to Tsikumu, the sacred Tewa peak of the west (Anschuetz 1998; Duwe 2011). These sites were small, and population density continued to be low. However, the Chama again experienced an upsurge in settlement activity, this time a fourfold increase in the number of architectural rooms, in the early part of the fourteenth century. The Wiyo phase (AD 1300–1350) in the Chama is best known from the introduction of a new site type in the valley: the C-shaped plaza pueblo. First described in detail by Frank Hibben (1937) in his excavation and analysis of Riana Ruin, similar sites were discovered along the Rio Chama in the vicinity of Abiquiu (Luebben 1953; Peckham 1959). A recent reexcavation and reanalysis of Palisade Ruin have painted a picture of a small settlement that was self-sufficient, growing its own food and making its own pottery (Duwe 2017). However, 17 percent of the painted pottery was Pindi Black-on-white, a distinctive type from the Santa Fe area, which suggests that this group of sites was socially and economically connected with areas to the south and east and may represent settlers with origins in the Rio Grande valley.

In the eighty years since Hibben's analysis, archaeologists working in the Tewa world have learned (1) that population influx during the Wiyo phase was much greater than originally anticipated (Anschuetz 1998; Beal 1987; Duwe 2011; Marshall and Walt 2007); and (2) architecture, ceramic, and ritual landscape patterns suggest that populations were not as culturally homogenous as initially believed (Duwe 2011). There is a great deal of variability between contemporary sites in size (thirty to five hundred rooms), layout (quadrangular plaza, linear and multi-roomblock pueblos), and number and types of kivas. Of particular interest is the striking comparison of Tsiping'owingeh, a linear, sprawling site that may have five hundred rooms and thirteen kivas (Trott and Taylor 1994), and Palisade Ruin, a C-shaped village with fifty rooms and one kiva. Both villages were built in AD 1312 and are located only 8 km apart. While we are still assessing their relationship, a preliminary lithic analysis has demonstrated very different frequencies of raw material use that suggest differential relationships with the physical and cultural landscape (Duwe 2017). What we do know, however, is that the Chama was occupied by many different people in the first half of the fourteenth century. These people likely include migrant settlers (Summer People) who were later joined by Wiyo phase populations from the Rio Grande valley, at least some of whom may have originated in the middle northern Rio Grande. The latter would have made contact with earlier migrants at places like Tekhe'owingeh but may have been remembered as the Winter People based on their mountain origins on the east side of the Rio Grande.

How these different groups interacted and negotiated an eventual Tewa identity is still an open question, but it was likely a process of both cooperation and conflict. For all of their differences, the early thirteenth-century Pueblo people living in the Chama were producing and consuming the same types of pottery—Wiyo Black-on-white—a transitionary ceramic type and direct antecedent to Classic period Tewa biscuitware. While pots are not people, biscuitware and the greater Tewa series of black-on-white pottery have traditionally been viewed as markers of Tewa social identity (Mera 1934). However, our analysis of Wiyo Black-on-white pottery from Palisade Ruin (Duwe 2017) mirrors previous studies that observed a high degree of stylistic (Luebben 1953) and technological (Wilson 2007) variability at both the inter- and intrasite scales. We propose that the roots of this variability were different people learning and creating new pottery traditions as they also crafted new ideas of society and the cosmos, and we have evidence that this was not an easy transition. Many of these Wiyo phase sites are located in inaccessible and defendable architecture and sites (Mera 1934), and some villages, such as Kapo'uinge (Luebben 1953) and Riana Ruin (Hibben 1937), were sacked and burned by mid-century. Strife between the peoples is not a theme in the Tewa origin tradition, and many questions remain regarding the nature of these negotiations. What we do know, however, is by the mid-fourteenth century the Tewa world had fundamentally changed.

By AD 1350—the beginning of the Classic period—a major transformation had occurred in the size, density, and organization of residential settlements. People moved from highland mesa tops to coalesce near fertile valley bottoms and built very large villages that housed possibly hundreds, if not thousands, of individuals. This movement coincides with Ohkay's tradition of the Summer and Winter People joining together at the village of Posi'owingeh in the Chama. Posi'owingeh, as both tree-ring and ceramic dating demonstrates, was built in the mid-fourteenth century (Duwe 2011). The village's size and sprawling site plan, with over two thousand rooms, suggest that this was indeed a place of population coalescence (figures 4.4 and 4.5). And based on the presence of two large kivas, it is likely that Posi'owingeh represents both the Summer and Winter People cohabitating at the same village. The village also has additional importance as it sits on an alluvial bench directly above the Ojo Caliente hot springs, a sacred portal to the place of emergence (Ortiz 1969). To visit Posi'owingeh, as the Tewa continue to do today, is to remember the entirety of the origin tradition from emergence to reunification.

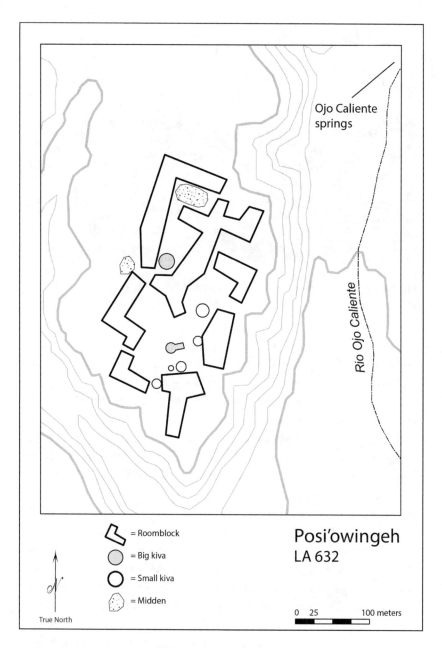

Figure 4.4 A plan map of Posi'owingeh.

Figure 4.5 A view of the Rio Ojo Caliente valley with Tsikumu in the distance, from Posi'owingeh. Photograph by Samuel Duwe.

Of course, Posi'owingeh was not the only place where this great coalescence of people occurred. In the mid-fourteenth century eleven additional large villages were built across the Chama with estimated populations ranging from five hundred to two thousand people (Duwe et al. 2016). These were places where earlier villagers had come together and were joined by additional settlers from the Pajarito Plateau (Duwe 2019). And these were also places where the historic and modern Tewa system of social and cosmological organization, based on the alternating leadership of the Summer and Winter People, is visible for the first time in the material record. This system is most easily identified by the presence of two large kivas at the majority of these villages, a pattern that matches historical and ethnographic descriptions of each people owning their own large kiva (Ellis 1950; Parsons 1929). Additionally, each Classic period village is surrounded by a similar sacred geography of shrines (Anschuetz 1998; Duwe 2011, 2016) that demarcates the historic and modern Tewa cosmography (Ortiz 1969).

This is not to say that the system was static (Duwe and Anschuetz 2013). Throughout the Classic period Chama residents continued to coalesce as villages broke apart and joined others or as people left the valley entirely. People may have also used Tewa moieties (the Summer and

Winter People) to detach from village life, either to join others or to create new homes, based on historic Tewa accounts (Ellis 1950). Following Ohkay's tradition, people continued to move and eventually joined their brethren at the villages along the Rio Grande, including Ohkay Owingeh. By the late sixteenth century, Spanish censuses recorded only a handful of sites in the valley and the majority of the Tewa people living in the newly missionized villages. The causes of this move are likely multivalent and include Spanish colonization (and perhaps disease [Ortiz 1969; Ramenofsky 1988]), incursions by Navajos and Apaches (Carrillo 1992), and a continuation of the gradual population coalescence that began in the fourteenth century. However, the Chama was never "abandoned" and has remained an essential part of Ohkay Owingeh's world as a place of refuge, pilgrimage, and social memory. And the system of Tewa social organization and way of life that were created at Posi'owingeh have persisted and been reproduced countless times in the years since, even in the face of changing environmental and social pressures from the contemporary world.

SEEKING LIFE

The Tewa believe that they live in a world in which they have always been present, yet they are forever in a state of becoming. The cosmos is in a state of "constant re-creation and transformation" (Swentzell 1993:141) as the people seek harmony and balance between essential dualities, including Summer and Winter (Naranjo and Swentzell 1989). To find this balance, a process the Tewa refer to as "seeking life," is to avoid stasis and embrace movement and the transformation of life that results from the tension of opposites (Laski 1959; Swentzell 1993:45). The stories told of the distant past—of great migrations and the joining of the peoples—not only link the modern people to their ancestors but also demonstrate the essentials of Tewa philosophy both historically and in present community life (Naranjo 2008). This fluidity of movement is both temporal (the seasonal transfer of authority between the Summer and Winter People) and spatial (the movement of people, animals, spirits, and blessings across the Tewa world). And this movement is ongoing as the Tewa seek to achieve balance in a rapidly changing and interconnected world (Naranjo and Swentzell 1989).

The search for Tewa origins is understandable, particularly as archaeologists engage with "grand narratives" and the effects of large-scale population movement. The questions posed in the northern Rio Grande have great potential for helping us understand social and demographic transformations, the evolution and nuance of languages and meaning, and cultural affiliations with contemporary Pueblo people. But we wonder if debates about *who* the Tewa were (migrants or locals) are sidestepping another perhaps more crucial question: *how* did Tewa society come to be?

It is increasingly hard to deny the cosmopolitan and chaotic nature of the thirteenth-century Rio Grande valley. The world must have seemed strikingly out of balance. The people's prayers for rain were met with extreme drought, and the subsequent migrations created new neighbors. For us it comes as no surprise that the bedrock principle of being Tewa that emerged from this tumult—seeking life—is based on finding complementarity and harmony. This is not to say that these Pueblo principles did not extend much further into the past, but they were likely cemented in the ontology and cosmology of Tewa life as these groups began to cultivate their world.

Our comparison of two areas of the Tewa world—the middle northern Rio Grande and the Chama Valley—demonstrates three main points. First, both areas were directly impacted by the social and demographic transformations of the thirteenth and fourteenth centuries as migrants from the Four Corners region and elsewhere moved into a previously occupied landscape. While these histories varied between the eastern and western sides of the Rio Grande, attributing Tewa origins to either migrants or local people becomes too simplistic if we take the Tewa history seriously. However (and whenever) we define Tewa identity, the Tewa likely share cultural affiliation with Pueblo ancestors across the American Southwest. Second, once we accept that these negotiations were occurring across the ancestral Tewa world and are crucial to understanding the resulting Tewa identities, we can begin to focus on the unique historical contingencies of each area and each village. And third, we believe that elements of the many arguments for Tewa origins are likely correct depending on their historical and geographic context. Tewa identity and society can be traced to *both* in situ development *and* migration from the north as traditions were mixed and mapped onto the landscape in a process of continuing *ensoulment* (Anschuetz and Wilshusen 2011). It is how these groups developed their eventual world that is important to us and has become an ongoing focus of research as we explore our respective areas of the Tewa homeland.

The middle northern Rio Grande area and the Chama have strikingly different histories of the Summer and Winter People coming together. The middle northern Rio Grande has been inhabited for millennia, and the Winter People were only minimally impacted by emigrants (Summer People) joining their communities in the thirteenth century. Tekhe'owingeh, remembered in Tewa history as the place where the peoples joined, dates to the early 1200s and may have been a place where these early settlers from the north and west first made their homes. Their populations must have been small, and based on the continuity of Tewa material culture from the Developmental period onward, these migrant communities may have readily adopted the cultural norms of their hosts. In this case the Winter People appear to have heavily influenced the resulting identities. The history of the Chama, however, is quite different. Rather than a history of one people joining another at their ancestral home, it is a story of the two peoples settling separately and coming together in a "new world" of sorts. Although first settled in the mid-thirteenth century by migrants (Summer People), the Chama became a culturally heterogeneous landscape with the later waves of colonists, likely from the Rio Grande valley (Winter People). By around AD 1350 these disparate peoples had coalesced and built massive villages including Posi'owingeh, remembered in Ohkay Owingeh's history as the place where the Summer and Winter People rejoined. We can imagine that the negotiations between these peoples must have been complex, and regardless of what language they spoke and their relative population sizes, elements of many cultural traditions were mixed. However, even the Chama appears to have material cultural continuity with older Rio Grande traditions, and we agree with Ortman (2012) that the migrants were readily adopting local customs.

Based on these two examples, we argue that Tewa history included multiple episodes of diverse peoples coming together, first in the early parts of the Coalition period and then later in the Classic period. The recounting of multiple middle places, first at Tekhe'owingeh and then at Posi'owingeh, likely represents the diversity in histories across a heterogeneous Tewa world. But it also suggests that the Tewa oral traditions are preserving a pattern of "serial coalescence" in which the Summer and Winter People, however defined, joined and rejoined multiple times. While the Tewa origin traditions are useful as historical narratives that shape archaeological questions, perhaps their true strength is in encapsulating a *process* rather than an *event*. This process is, of course, known as seeking life: the continuous transformation of society through movement and finding harmony among opposites. Our examples show how this life was sought through the encounters of diverse people, some old and some new, in the thirteenth and fourteenth centuries. Similar encounters, and the continual remaking of the Tewa world, occurred many times afterward, including during Spanish conquest, the Pueblo Revolt and its aftermath, and American colonization. And the same process continues through the modern day and will continue into the future as Tewa people seek to find balance in an ever-changing world.

We have chosen to highlight the heterogeneity of the Tewa world in the past and present to advance current debates regarding Tewa origins. But it is important to not lose sight of the interconnectedness of the Tewa people and their histories. Swentzell (1991:177) argued that archaeologists often focus on the differences between the Pueblo people in both space and time. Conversely, a Tewa perspective begins with the idea that everything and everybody has a context or a whole in which they belong. The primary question is not "Why are people different?" but rather "How does one, or one's group, activity, or place, fit into the larger whole?" While the Tewa peoples took different paths to finding the middle place and establishing their villages, their journeys took place in an interconnected, and uniquely Tewa, world. It is probably not coincidence that both middle places, Tekhe'owingeh (see figure 4.3) and Posi'owingeh (see figure 4.5), share clear views of Tsikumu, the sacred peak of the west. We imagine Tewa histories that are diverse, multifaceted, and relative. But these histories are also vitally interconnected through a shared landscape and philosophy, and they encapsulate the ever-continuing process of becoming Tewa.

ACKNOWLEDGMENTS

Sam would like to thank Ohkay Owingeh for their willingness to engage in discussions of the Pueblo's long-term and ongoing history in the

Chama. Patrick would like to thank Scott Ortman for his advice and encouragement, Bruce Bernstein (the tribal historic preservation officer for Pojoaque Pueblo) for his support, and the Pueblo of Pojoaque for guidance and assistance of this continuing research regarding their land and history.

REFERENCES

Anschuetz, Kurt F. 1998. Not Waiting for the Rain: Integrated Systems of Water Management by Pre-Columbian Pueblo Farmers in North-Central New Mexico. PhD dissertation, Department of Anthropology. University of Michigan, Ann Arbor.

Anschuetz, Kurt F. 2014. Toward an Archaeology of Pueblo Ritual Landscapes: A Forthcoming NMAC Continuing Education Program. *NewsMAC: Newsletter of the New Mexico Archaeological Council* 2014(1):9–15.

Anschuetz, Kurt F., and Richard H. Wilshusen. 2011. Ensouled Places: Ethnogenesis and the Making of the Dinétah and Tewa Basin Landscapes. In *Movement, Connectivity, and Landscape Change in the Ancient Southwest: The 20th Anniversary Southwest Symposium*, edited by Margaret C. Nelson and Colleen Strawhacker, pp. 321–344. University Press of Colorado, Boulder.

Beal, John D. 1987. *Foundation of the Rio Grande Classic: The Lower Chama River, A.D. 1300–1500*. Report Submitted to the Office of Cultural Affairs, Historic Preservation Division, by Southwest Archaeological Consultants, Inc., Albuquerque, New Mexico.

Boyer, Jeffrey L., James L. Moore, Steven Lakatos, Nancy J. Akins, C. Dean Wilson, and Eric Blinman. 2010. Remodeling Immigration: A Northern Rio Grande Perspective on Depopulation, Migration, and Donation-Side Models. In *Leaving Mesa Verde: Peril and Change in the Thirteenth-Century Southwest*, edited by Timothy A. Kohler, Mark D. Varien, and Aaron M. Wright, pp. 285–322. University of Arizona Press, Tucson.

Bremer, J. Michael. 1995. AR-03-10-06-1230. Site form on file, Archaeological Records Management System, Historic Preservation Division and Museum of New Mexico, Santa Fe.

Carrillo, Charles M. 1992. Oral History/History of the Abiquiu Reservoir Area. In *History and Ethnohistory Along the Rio Chama*, edited by Frank. J. Wozniak, Meade F. Kemrer, and Charles M. Carrillo, pp. 109–176. Prepared by J. D. Shelberg and R. R. Kneebone for Albuquerque District, U.S. Army Corps of Engineers, Albuquerque, New Mexico.

Cordell, Linda S. 1979. Prehistory: Eastern Anasazi. In *Southwest*, edited by Alfonso Ortiz, pp. 131–151. Handbook of North American Indians, Vol. 9. Smithsonian Institution Press, Washington, D.C.

Dickson, D. Bruce. 1975. Settlement Pattern Stability and Change in the Middle Northern Rio Grande Region, New Mexico: A Test of Some Hypotheses. *American Antiquity* 40(2):159–171.

Duwe, Samuel. 2011. The Prehispanic Tewa World: Space, Time, and Becoming in the Pueblo Southwest. PhD dissertation, School of Anthropology, University of Arizona, Tucson.

Duwe, Samuel. 2016. Cupules and the Creation of the Tewa Pueblo World. *Journal of Lithic Studies* 3(3):147–168.

Duwe, Samuel. 2017. Re-excavation of Palisade Ruin (LA 3505). Manuscript on file, Albuquerque District, U.S. Army Corps of Engineers, Albuquerque, New Mexico.

Duwe, Samuel. 2019. The Economics of Becoming: Population Coalescence and the Production and Distribution of Ancestral Tewa Pottery. In *Re-framing Northern Rio Grande Pueblo Economies*, edited by Scott G. Ortman. University of Arizona Press, Tucson.

Duwe, Samuel, and Kurt F. Anschuetz. 2013. Ecological Uncertainty and Organizational Flexibility on the Prehispanic Tewa Landscape: Notes from the Northern Frontier. In *Mountain and Valley: Understanding Past Land Use in the Northern Rio Grande Valley, New Mexico*, edited by Bradley J. Vierra, pp. 95–112. University of Utah Press, Salt Lake City.

Duwe, Samuel, B. Sunday Eiselt, J. Andrew Darling, Mark D. Willis, and Chester Walker. 2016. The Pueblo Decomposition Model: A Method for Quantifying Architectural Rubble to Estimate Population Size. *Journal of Archaeological Science* 65:20–31.

Ellis, Florence H. 1950. Big Kivas, Little Kivas, and Moiety Houses in Historical Reconstruction. *Southwestern Journal of Anthropology* 6:286–302.

Ellis, Florence H. 1968. San Juan Pueblo's Water Use. Bound copy of 27-page draft with bibliography. Catalogue No. 2010.41.1968f, Maxwell Museum, University of New Mexico, Albuquerque.

Ellis, Florence H. 1970. San Gabriel del Yunque, Window on the Pre-Spanish Indian World. Revision of 1960 paper. Catalogue No. 2010.41.1970e, Maxwell Museum, University of New Mexico, Albuquerque.

Ellis, Florence H. 1974a. Nambe: Their Past Agricultural Use of Territory. Prepared for the USDI, Bureau of Indian Affairs. Manuscript on file, New Mexico Office of the State Engineer, Santa Fe.

Ellis, Florence H. 1974b. Pojoaque: A Casualty of the Pueblo Rebellion. Prepared for the USDI, Bureau of Indian Affairs. Manuscript on file, University of New Mexico, Albuquerque.

Ford, Richard I., Albert H. Schroeder, and Stewart L. Peckham. 1972. Three Perspectives on Puebloan Prehistory. In *New Perspectives on the Pueblos*, edited by Alfonso Ortiz, pp. 19–39. University of New Mexico Press, Albuquerque.

Fowles, Severin M. 2004. The Making of Made People: The Prehistoric Evolution of Hierocracy Among the Northern Tiwa of New Mexico. PhD dissertation, Department of Anthropology, University of Michigan, Ann Arbor.

Habicht-Mauche, Judith A. 1993. *The Pottery from Arroyo Hondo Pueblo, New Mexico: Tribalization and Trade in the Northern Rio Grande*. Arroyo Hondo Archaeological Series 8. School of American Research Press, Santa Fe, New Mexico.

Harrington, John P. 1916. *Ethnogeography of the Tewa*. 29th Annual Report of the Bureau of American Ethnology. Government Printing Office, Washington, D.C.

Hibben, Frank C. 1937. *Excavation of the Riana Ruin and Chama Valley Survey*. Anthropological Series Bulletin 300. University of New Mexico Press, Albuquerque.

Jeançon, J. A. 1923. *Excavations in the Chama Valley, New Mexico*. Bureau of American Ethnology Bulletin 81. Government Printing Office, Washington, D.C.

Kemp, Brian M., Kathleen Judd, Cara Monroe, Jelmer W. Eerkens, Lindsay Hilldorger, Connor Cordray, Rebecca Schad, Erin Reams, Scott G. Ortman, and Timothy A. Kohler. 2017. Prehistoric Mitochondrial DNA of Domesticate Animals Supports a 13th Century Exodus from the Northern US Southwest. *PLOS ONE* 12(7):e0178882.

Kidder, Alfred V. 1924. *An Introduction to the Study of Southwestern Archaeology with a Preliminary Account of the Excavations at Pecos*. Yale University Press, New Haven, Connecticut.

Kidder, Alfred V. 1958. *Pecos, New Mexico: Archaeological Notes*. Papers of the Robert S. Peabody Foundation for Archaeology 5. Phillips Academy, Andover, Massachusetts.

Lakatos, Steven. 2007. Cultural Continuity and the Development of Integrative Architecture in the Northern Rio Grande Valley of New Mexico, A.D. 600–1200. *Kiva* 73(1):31–66.

Laski, Vera. 1959. *Seeking Life*. American Folklore Society, Philadelphia.

Luebben, Ralph A. 1953. Leaf Water Site. In *Salvage Archaeology in the Chama Valley, New Mexico*, edited by Fred Wendorf, pp. 9–33. Monographs of the School of American Research. School of American Research Press, Santa Fe, New Mexico.

Marshall, Michael P., and Henry Walt. 2007. *The Eastern Homeland of San Juan Pueblo: Tewa Land and Water Use in the Santa Cruz and Truchas Watersheds; An Archaeological and Ethnogeographic Study*. Cibola Research Consultants Report No. 432. Corrales, New Mexico.

McNutt, Charles H. 1969. *Early Puebloan Occupation at Tesuque By-Pass and in the Upper Rio Grande Valley*. Anthropological Papers No. 40. Museum of Anthropology, University of Michigan, Ann Arbor.

Mera, Harry P. 1934. *A Survey of the Biscuit Ware Area in Northern New Mexico*. Technical Series Bulletin No. 6. Laboratory of Anthropology, Santa Fe, New Mexico.

Mera, Harry P. 1935. *Ceramic Clues to the Prehistory of North Central New Mexico*. Technical Series Bulletin No. 8. Laboratory of Anthropology, Santa Fe, New Mexico.

Mills, Barbara J. 2011. Themes and Models for Understanding Migration in the Southwest. In *Movement, Connectivity, and Landscape Change in the Ancient Southwest*, edited by Margaret C. Nelson and Colleen Strawhacker, pp. 345–362. University Press of Colorado, Boulder.

Naranjo, Tessie. 2008. Life as Movement: A Tewa View of Community and Identity. In *The Social Construction of Communities: Agency, Structure, and Identity in the Prehispanic Southwest*, edited by Mark D. Varien and James M. Potter, pp. 251–262. AltaMira Press, New York.

Naranjo, Tito, and Rina Swentzell. 1989. Healing Places in the Tewa Pueblo World. *American Indian Culture and Research Journal* 13(304):257–265.

Ortiz, Alfonso. 1969. *The Tewa World: Space, Time, Being, and Becoming in a Pueblo Society*. University of Chicago Press, Chicago.

Ortman, Scott G. 2010. Evidence of a Mesa Verde Homeland for the Tewa Pueblos. In *Leaving Mesa Verde: Peril and Change in the Thirteenth-Century Southwest*, edited by Timothy A. Kohler, Mark D. Varien, and Aaron M. Wright, pp. 222–261. University of Arizona Press, Tucson.

Ortman, Scott G. 2011. Bowls to Gardens: A History of Tewa Community Metaphors. In *Religious Transformation in the Late Pre-Hispanic Pueblo World*, edited by Donna M. Glowacki and Scott Van Keuren, pp. 84–108. University of Arizona Press, Tucson.

Ortman, Scott G. 2012. *Winds from the North: Tewa Origins and Historical Anthropology*. University of Utah Press, Salt Lake City.

Ortman, Scott G. 2014. Uniform Probability Density Analysis and Population History in the Northern Rio Grande. *Journal of Archaeological Method and Theory* 23(1):95–126.

Parsons, Elsie Clews. 1929. *The Social Organization of the Tewa of New Mexico*. American Anthropological Association, Menasha, Wisconsin.

Parsons, Elsie Clews. 1994 [1926]. *Tewa Tales*. University of Arizona Press, Tucson.

Peckham, Stewart L. 1959. LA 3505: Archaeological Salvage Excavations near the Abiquiu Dam, Rio Arriba County, New Mexico. Manuscript on file, U.S. Army Corps of Engineers, Albuquerque, New Mexico.

Ramenofsky, Ann F. 1988. *Vectors of Death: The Archaeology of European Contact*. University of New Mexico Press, Albuquerque.

Reed, Erik K. 1949. Sources of Rio Grande Culture and Population. *El Palacio* 56:163–184.

Schillaci, Michael A., and Steven A. Lakatos. 2016. Refiguring the Population History of the Tewa Basin. *Kiva* 82(4):364–386.

Schillaci, Michael A., and Steven A. Lakatos. 2017. The Emergence of Kwahe'e Black-on-white Pottery in the Tewa Basin, New Mexico. *Journal of Field Archaeology* 42(2):152–160.

Schillaci, Michael A., Steven A. Lakatos, and Logan D. Sutton. 2017. Tewa Place Names for Early Habitation Sites in the Northern Rio Grande Valley, New Mexico. *Journal of Field Archaeology* 42(2):142–151.

Schroeder, Albert H. 1979. Pueblos Abandoned in Historic Times. In *Southwest*, edited by Alfonso Ortiz, pp. 236–254. Handbook of North American Indians, Vol. 9. Smithsonian Institution Press, Washington, D.C.

Steen, Charles R. 1977. *Pajarito Plateau Archaeological Survey and Excavations*. Los Alamos Scientific Laboratory Report 77–4. Los Alamos National Laboratory, Los Alamos, New Mexico.

Stubbs, Stanley A., and William A. Stallings. 1953. *The Excavation of Pindi Pueblo, New Mexico*. Monographs of the School of American Research and the Laboratory of Anthropology 18. School of American Research Press, Santa Fe, New Mexico.

Swentzell, Rina. 1991. Levels of Truth: Southwest Archaeologists and Anasazi/Pueblo People. In *Puebloan Past and Present: Papers in Honor of Stewart Peckham*, edited by Meliha S. Duran and David T. Kirkpatrick, pp. 177–181. Archaeological Society of New Mexico, Albuquerque.

Swentzell, Rina. 1993. Mountain Form, Village Form: Unity in the Pueblo World. In *Ancient Land, Ancestral Places: Paul Logsdon in the Pueblo Southwest*, edited by Stephen H. Lekson, pp. 139–147. Museum of New Mexico Press, Santa Fe.

Trott, J. James, and Michael Taylor. 1994. Tsiping Ruin: Stabilization Assessment and Preservation Plan. Report No. 1994-10-010. Manuscript on file, National Park Service, Southwest Regional Office, Santa Fe, New Mexico.

Warren, A. Helene. 1974. The Ancient Mineral Industries of Cerro Pedernal, Rio Arriba County, New Mexico. In *Guidebook, Ghost Ranch Central-Northern New Mexico*, edited by C. T. Siemers, pp. 87–93. 25th Field Conference, New Mexico Geological Society, New Mexico Bureau of Mines and Mineral Resources, Socorro.

Wendorf, Fred, and Erik K. Reed. 1955. An Alternative Reconstruction of Northern Rio Grande Prehistory. *El Palacio* 62(5–6):131–173.

Wilson, Gordon P. 2007. *Guide to Ceramic Identification: Northern Rio Grande Valley and Galisteo Basin to A.D. 1700*. 2nd ed. Laboratory of Anthropology Technical Series Bulletin No. 12. Laboratory of Anthropology, Santa Fe, New Mexico.

Windes, Thomas C., and Peter J. McKenna. 2006. The Kivas of Tsama (LA 908). In *Southwestern Interludes: Papers in Honor of Charlotte J. and Theodore R. Frisbie*, Vol. 32, edited by Regge N. Wiseman, Thomas C. O'Laughlin, and Cordelia T. Snow, pp. 233–253. Archaeological Society of New Mexico, Albuquerque.

Wozniak, Frank J. 1992. Ethnohistory of the Abiquiu Reservoir Area. In *History and Ethnohistory Along the Rio Chama*, by Frank J. Wozniak, Meade F. Kemrer, and Charles M. Carrillo, pp. 1–65. Prepared by J. D. Shelberg and R. R. Kneebone, Albuquerque District, U.S. Army Corps of Engineers, Albuquerque, New Mexico.

5

To and From Hopi

Negotiating Identity Through Migration, Coalescence, and Closure at the Homol'ovi Settlement Cluster

Samantha G. Fladd, Claire S. Barker, E. Charles Adams, Dwight C. Honyouti, and Saul L. Hedquist

The Hopi emerged into this world—the Fourth World—following travels through earlier worlds characterized by disorder and corruption. Upon emergence, Hopi ancestors encountered Màasaw, a guardian deity. Màasaw allowed the Hopi to live on his land if they agreed to be humble farmers who served as stewards of the earth. He instructed the Hopi to travel the world in search of their rightful place, leaving footprints as evidence of their journey. As Hopi ancestors moved and lived throughout the land—gaining important knowledge of places and resources—they left material traces as "physical evidence that they had vested the land with their spiritual stewardship and fulfilled their pact with *Màasaw*" (Kuwanwisiwma and Ferguson 2009:93; see also Ferguson et al. 2000). Known in the Hopi language as *itaakuku* (literally, "our footprints"), these traces include the many ancestral villages, petroglyphs, and other archaeological sites that mark the migrations of Hopi ancestors prior to their arriving at their ultimate destination on the Hopi Mesas (Hedquist et al. 2014; Kuwanwisiwma and Ferguson 2009; Whiteley 2011). Collectively, all areas of ancestral travel are considered Hopitutskwa (Hopi land), an extensive landscape defined by innumerable cultural and natural features.

While the overarching theme of emergence is the same, the Hopi did not move across the landscape en masse. Rather, ancestral groups moved in varying configurations through the region prior to the "gathering of the clans" at the Hopi Mesas (Bernardini 2005; Courlander 1971; Fewkes 1904; Nequatewa 1936). Each clan possesses unique stories regarding their nonlinear migration route and maintains distinct ties to ancestral villages and landscape features. Archaeologists have come to recognize that migrant groups were often small, consisting of a household or group of households (e.g., Bernardini 2005; Ferguson and Colwell-Chanthaphonh 2006). This scale of movement supported the persistence of subgroup identities, while large community identities remained more flexible and variable in form (Bernardini and Fowles 2011). Members of these groups accumulated individual and group identities through shared memories and experiences, as well as relationships with objects and landscapes (e.g., Basso 1996; Mills and Walker 2008). For the Hopi, migrations remain an important aspect of history and clan identity and a foundation on which current social relationships and participation in ceremonies are based.

About 80 km south of the Hopi Mesas, just outside of Winslow, Arizona, the Homol'ovi Settlement Cluster (AD 1260–1400) consists of seven villages ranging from fifty to over one thousand rooms (figure 5.1). *Homol'ovi* is a Hopi term meaning to "be mounded up" or the "place of small hills," referencing the local topography (Adams 2002:3; Hopi Dictionary Project 1998:92; Lyons 2003:39). The oral traditions of numerous Hopi clans identify the region as an important stop along their respective migration routes (Ferguson and Lomaomvaya 1999; Fewkes 1904; see also Hedquist 2016:214).

We explore the differential formations and expressions of Hopi identities within the Homol'ovi Settlement Cluster through a focus on three forms of movement: immigration, village reorganization, and depopulation/emigration. Immigrants from diverse backgrounds founded the large villages and had to negotiate their places within these communities. However, movement did not stop after immigration as the smaller villages were quickly depopulated and their former residents joined larger pueblos in the area. Constant population movements were also evident within the large pueblos as new rooms were built and existing rooms were reconstructed or closed, in part tied to the coming of the *katsina* religion (Adams 1991). Closure practices—"a suite of practices with material manifestations that ends the occupation of a structure or settlement with the added intent of either remembering or forgetting associated people, groups, or events" (Adams 2016a:43)—served as material markers of the memories and meanings tied to these rooms. Finally, emigration to the Hopi Mesas occurred gradually and affected the remaining village residents. Ritualized closure practices signified the depopulation of these villages, memorializing their place in Hopi history (e.g., Adams 2002, 2016b).

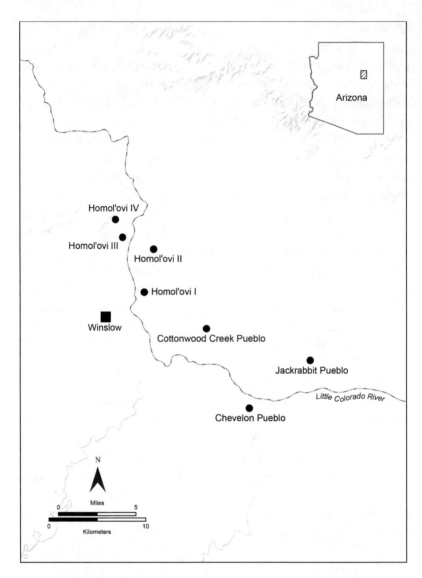

Figure 5.1 A map of the Homol'ovi Settlement Cluster villages. Based on Adams 2016a:Figure 1.2.

HOPI MOVEMENT IN ARCHAEOLOGICAL PRACTICES

Stewart Koyiyumptewa and Chip Colwell-Chanthaphonh (2011:445) describe how "the Hopi experience geography as cultural landscapes that constitute the memory of the people." The complexity of the interweaving movements of clans toward the Hopi Mesas is difficult to directly map onto the archaeological record. While petroglyphs in the Homol'ovi region include clan symbols that support oral traditions of migration (Bernardini 2005), the precise locations of these groups within each village continue to evade archaeologists' grasp. Despite our inability to locate clans or named social groups in the archaeological record, we can incorporate Hopi views into our research. At Homol'ovi, Hopi understandings of movement, space, and memory figure prominently in the creation of a nuanced picture of the past (e.g., Adams 2002, 2016a, 2016b; Bernardini 2005; Hedquist 2016, 2017; Lyons 2003).

The inclusion of Indigenous information in archaeological analyses is a complex and multifaceted issue that continues to be reworked and redefined (e.g., Colwell 2016; Ferguson 1996; Liebmann 2017). In part, this can be accomplished through altering our vocabulary and subsequent treatment of the material record during analyses. Specifically, we exclude two terms from our lexicon in an attempt to better represent Hopi views of the past: *abandonment* and *trash*. Archaeologists frequently view the "trash" fill of "abandoned" rooms as practical—the use of meaningless spaces to discard useless materials. Legally, claims to ancestral sites and materials can be negatively affected by the use of this terminology (e.g., Colwell-Chanthaphonh and Ferguson 2006; Kuwanwisiwma and Ferguson 2009), but why are they problematic for archaeological research and interpretation?

Both terms imply disregard, disinterest, and discontinuity, which vastly misrepresent the views of descendent communities. The Hopi people believe that archaeological sites remain inhabited by their ancestors, and they actively use these places to construct identities today (Kuwanwisiwma and Ferguson 2009:105). The deposition of materials similarly carries ritual significance, including the proper acknowledgment of memories, and actively contributes to the creation of meaningful spaces (e.g., Fladd et al. 2018; Hays-Gilpin and Ware 2015:328; Silko 1996:26). Hopi migration histories speak to the deliberate and directed movements that led to the Hopi Mesas and demarcated the broader landscape. Room and site closures and the placement of materials within those settings contributed to the creation of the Hopi cultural landscape, serving as "footprints" of ancestral movement. Thus, considerations of the deliberate placement of materials and closure of rooms and villages reveal insights into the development of Hopi identities through time and across space.

BECOMING HOPI AT THE HOMOL'OVI VILLAGES

Human occupation in the Homol'ovi area has great time depth (Lange 1998). The permanent water flow and wide floodplain of the Little Colorado River created a prime region for agriculture and served as a source of abundant riparian resources (Adams 1996, 2002). Fieldwork conducted at nearby Rock Art Ranch has recovered multiple Clovis points near Chevelon Canyon (Fladd et al. 2017), and an earlier project found evidence for farming by 800 BC (Huckell and Huckell 2004; plate 5). Occupation of the region was sporadic from AD 600 to 1225; ceramic assemblages and radiocarbon dating indicate an occupational hiatus of about forty years, just prior to the founding of the pueblos discussed herein (Adams 1996, 2002; Lange 1998; Young 1996). We examine the village life histories—from founding to closure—of the Homol'ovi Settlement Cluster in order to better understand the negotiations of identities that occurred within the villages throughout their occupation (figure 5.1), providing insights on the social groups that emigrated around AD 1400 and continue to occupy the Hopi Mesas today.

AGGREGATION AT HOMOL'OVI

The founding of the seven villages that comprise the Homol'ovi Settlement Cluster (table 5.1) was unique in that migrants settled into a largely uninhabited landscape, which allowed these new groups to decide precisely how they would structure their lives within this space. For the most part, the material culture of the villages suggests that immigrants had a northern origin, tied to communities on or near the Hopi Mesas (Adams 2002; Barker 2017; Lyons 2003). The two areas have many similarities in terms of the size and layout of villages, the style of kiva construction, and the presence of katsina religion.

Table 5.1 Homol'ovi Settlement Cluster Villages

Village	Number of Structures	Structures Excavated	Occupation Period
Chevelon Pueblo	500	39	1290–1400
Cottonwood Creek	120	0	1285–1360
Homol'ovi I	1100	70	1290–1400
Homol'ovi II	1200	34	1360–1400
Homol'ovi III	45	20	1285–1305; 1325–75
Homol'ovi IV	200	10	1260–90
Jackrabbit Pueblo	120	5	1285–1305; 1350–75

Source: Based on Adams 2016a:Table 1.

Ceramics have proven particularly useful in understanding the origins of the people who resided at Homol'ovi. The locally produced decorated ware, Winslow Orange Ware, is stylistically similar to pottery produced by contemporaneous groups on the Hopi Mesas. Northern vessel forms, including colanders and babe-in-cradle ladles, were also produced with materials local to the Homol'ovi region (Lyons 2003). The local production of decorated pottery greatly diminished through time as the importation of Jeddito Yellow Ware, made on the Hopi Mesas, increased drastically; this imported ware comprised the majority of the decorated assemblage at Homol'ovi after AD 1350 (Adams 2002; LaMotta 2006).

Unlike analyses of the decorated ceramics, those of the locally produced utilitarian ware—Homolovi Utility Ware—suggest greater diversity (Barker 2017). A recent examination of the way that corrugated vessels were made identified two distinct styles of production (figure 5.2): local parallel (representing 73 percent of the sampled assemblage) and local oblique (representing 27 percent of the sampled assemblage). These production styles are delineated by statistically significant differences in technological attributes such as indentation shape and dimensions (Barker 2017). The appearance of diverse manufacturing practices indicates the presence of at least two social groups who possessed unique histories and traditions. An interregional comparison of technological style shows the abundant local parallel style to be associated with communities from the Hopi area, corresponding with the decorated ceramics, while the local oblique style is more similar to pottery produced in the Puerco

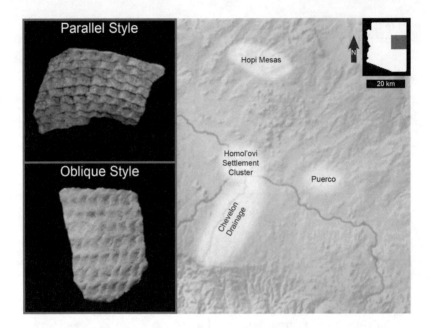

Figure 5.2 Examples of corrugated pottery styles and corresponding areas around Homol'ovi where they were produced in greatest abundance (see Barker 2017).

area to the east or the Chevelon Drainage to the south (Barker 2017). The local oblique style also resembles the imported Mogollon Brown Ware at Homol'ovi, which was likely produced in many areas to the east, south, and southeast. Additionally, imported utilitarian wares from Puerco and Hopi appear in the ceramic assemblages, likely brought with immigrants who moved to Homol'ovi or representative of intermarriage and the existence of close social ties among regions of the Western Pueblo world (e.g., Barker 2017; Duff 2002; Schachner 2012; Triadan 1997). Thus, the utilitarian ceramics indicate that immigrants arrived from the north, as well as the east, south, or southeast.

Migrants from both of these areas resided in all seven Homol'ovi villages throughout their occupation. Both decorated and utilitarian ceramics indicate that the majority of the occupants came from the Hopi Mesas area, although their prior migration paths were likely varied and these populations may have moved throughout the Southwest prior to reaching the mesas. The less common local oblique tradition became more abundant at later Homol'ovi pueblos, indicating the intensification of immigration from the east, south, or southeast through time. These findings support the presence of multiple groups with unique migration histories who continued to accumulate their diverse identities at the Homol'ovi villages (see also Adams 2002, 2016a; Barker 2017; Lyons 2003).

INTRA-VILLAGE MOVEMENT

Studies of movement in the Southwest tend to focus on migrations between distant villages and regions, but small-scale and internal movement within villages and settlement clusters also played an important role in identity development and negotiation. Two of the smallest and earliest pueblos of the Homol'ovi Settlement Cluster, Homol'ovi IV and Homol'ovi III, were founded in the mid- to late thirteenth century (figure 5.3). Occupation lasted for only a few decades before residents joined one of the nearby larger villages, likely Homol'ovi I (Adams 1989, 1996, 2002, 2016a), but initial settlement within these pueblos remained an

Figure 5.3 A contemporary view of Homol'ovi IV, looking east. Photograph by Samantha G. Fladd.

important component of the former residents' identities. Homol'ovi III, the smaller of the two villages, included a great kiva, indicating some efforts at coalescence (Adams 2002; Birch 2012). Depopulation was likely tied to flooding issues, as the village was located in the floodplain, but reuse occurred in the mid-fourteenth century with its conversion to a field house and, later, a farming hamlet (Adams 2001, 2002; Lange 1998; Young 1996). Reoccupation of the area may indicate efforts by the former occupants or descendants of the former occupants to reassert their rights to the area based on their links to the initial occupation of the pueblo. Whether or not these individuals reused the pueblo, occupation of the smaller Homol'ovi villages prior to settlement within the larger communities distinguished the migration path of certain groups, adding an extra spatial layer to their accumulated identities.

Significant remodeling and reorganization are also evident architecturally, particularly within two of the largest and longest-occupied villages: Homol'ovi I and Chevelon Pueblo (figure 5.4; Adams 2002, 2016a; LaMotta 2006). Initial construction at these villages consisted of discrete roomblocks, suggesting greater social divisions among occupants and the maintenance of distinctive spaces (Adams 2002, 2016a). The freestanding roomblocks were eventually connected to form contiguous pueblos of five hundred to one thousand rooms as coalescent communities were formed. The processes of construction, reconstruction, and use of these rooms served as important markers of the development of identities associated with spaces within the villages.

At a small scale, groups moved frequently within the pueblos. These shifting relationships with space required commemoration of the social memories housed by each room. Rooms, as the spatial settings for events and the containers of memories, often become members of the family or group, experiencing their own life histories marked by specific rituals (e.g., Fogelin and Schiffer 2015; LaMotta and Schiffer 1999). Commemoration was often achieved through multiple layers of room fill, including ceremonially important objects and sediments, such as ash (Adams and Fladd 2017). These practices can serve as material mediums through which to develop identity as it relates to understandings of the proper treatment of space and discard of materials, as well as access to or knowledge of the social memories encapsulated by each room (e.g., Adams 2016b; Mills and Walker 2008; Walker 2002).

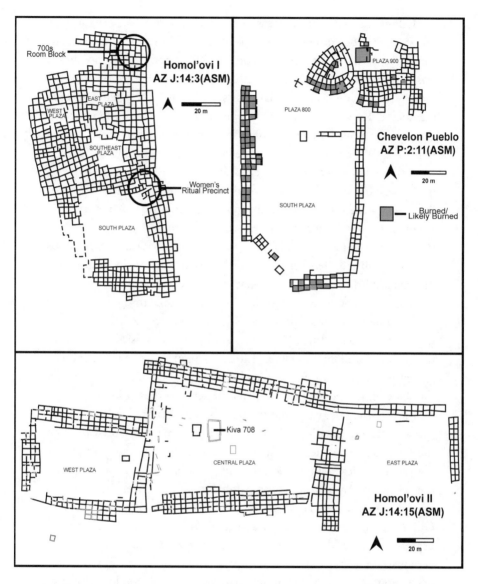

Figure 5.4 Plan maps of Homol'ovi I, Homol'ovi II, and Chevelon Pueblo. Areas discussed in the text are labeled. Base maps provided by ASM-HRP.

Built in the 1290s, the northeast roomblock of Homol'ovi I (figure 5.4), known as the 700s roomblock, represents one of the earliest independent constructions at the site (Adams 2002; LaMotta 2006). This roomblock was later connected to nearby roomblocks, but depositional patterns indicate that its role as a foundational space within the pueblo was remembered. Room 733 was filled by alternating deposits of ash and sand through a ceiling hatchway, which formed a cone of material on the floor. The deliberate patterning of sediments of contrasting colors suggests that their placement was carefully controlled and knowledge of the underlying materials (social memory) factored into the subsequent introduction of fill (Adams and Fladd 2017:1107–1109; Miljour 2016). Room 701, a habitation room, was converted to a clan room partway through its occupation (Adams 2002:118–119; LaMotta 2006:112). To mark this shift and reorient the space for use in a new way, a thick layer of ash and bird bones, largely turkey, was added before the construction of the second floor surface. Conversion of this space through the use of ritually important materials served either to memorialize past uses or to sanctify the area for future purposes. In either case, depositional practices that would be hidden from later visitors signified the movement of social groups within Homol'ovi I as membership could be reinforced through the shared knowledge of the materials underlying these rooms.

The extension of group identity to pueblo spaces is further emphasized in room closure practices. For example, Room 704 was closed through the continual deposition of ash and cultural materials, including projectile points, ladles, manos, and miniature vessels. At some point during the accumulation of materials, a painted mountain sheep cranium and several manos were placed in a cluster through a still open doorway. Closure practices in this room and many others formed a long-term process involving discrete, although often related, depositional events demonstrating the continuation of personal ties to space. The repeated deposition of similar types of materials suggests a shared knowledge of the lower contents within the room and the identification of this space with certain objects, practices, and groups within the village. Depositional patterns also serve to reaffirm relational ties to and between spaces. Room 729, connected to Room 704 by a doorway, included a mountain sheep cranium placed with ground stones that were deposited later in time. The relation of these deposits affirms the spatial tie between the two rooms, the social link between these spaces, and the shared memory possessed by the associated group(s). Thus, identities were marked by and negotiated through materials and sediments in particular combinations placed within rooms that acted as the setting for group activities.

At a larger scale, these villages underwent episodes of drastic construction and reconstruction that altered the size and shape of the pueblos themselves around AD 1360—contemporaneous with the founding of Homol'ovi II. Homol'ovi II was built more quickly than the other villages and had rooms oriented around two large enclosed plazas and a third partially enclosed plaza. The reconstruction of Homol'ovi I and Chevelon Pueblo focused on the addition of large enclosed plazas to the south, an architectural space tied to the katsina religion that promoted village coalescence through public dances and ceremonies (Adams 1991, 1994). Concurrently, in the roomblocks surrounding the South Plaza of Homol'ovi I, distinctive, spatially clustered rooms speak to the development of ritual precincts (Adams 2002:131). For example, the northeast corner of the plaza (figure 5.4) contained abundant evidence of ritual use by women, including the presence of corn-grinding rooms, a *piiki* room (used to cook corn-based wafer bread) containing a whole piiki stone, and a room filled with disarticulated rabbit bones and large cooking vessels associated with feasting, as well as large quantities of whole groundstone, *pukis* (shallow plates used to support ceramic vessels during construction), and ceramic vessels. Thus, a female group, complementary to the male groups often associated with rituals and ceremonies in kivas in the Southwest, established the importance of their identity through spatial proximity to the plaza and kivas. Clear patterns of gendered closure of these spaces marked their former use and continued association with women (see also Crown 2000; Heitman 2016).

At the same time, small, more exclusive plazas were added over razed rooms in the northern half of the site. The fill within these rooms contained significant numbers of whole and rare artifacts, including ladle handles, mano fragments, and turquoise (Adams 2002; Adams and LaMotta 2006; Hedquist 2017; LaMotta 2006). While the spaces could have been leveled with any type of fill, large quantities of culturally significant objects and ash were selected and deliberately placed within the area. The material content used to fill the former storage rooms suggests that the ritual preparation for the construction of the plaza was as important as, and likely more important than, the physical preparation of the space. While invisible during later uses of the plazas, the processes undertaken to sanctify these spaces would have been remembered by the occupants. In laying the necessary groundwork for the plaza and partaking in the associated ritual practices, the residents of Homol'ovi were establishing social expectations and acceptable interactions with spaces, objects, and each other. Demonstrating these material protocols and social networks was an important part of the accumulation of daily practices that informed identity. In other words, identity was, quite literally, built into the pueblo itself with movement explicitly and materially marked in part to signify the continued associations between certain groups and spaces.

PATTERNS OF CLOSURE

Rooms within the Homol'ovi Settlement Cluster generally received some degree of formal closure, suggesting that the cessation of use required clear material markers to honor the importance of and signify a new relationship with that space (Fladd et al. 2018). Closure practices could be used to determine how the groups, activities, and meanings associated with a given room would be remembered. While room closures occurred continuously throughout occupation, the treatment of twenty-six excavated kivas was particularly notable as 69 percent (18/26) were ritually closed (Adams 2016b).[1] Ash and burning are often associated with acts of purification or cleansing and can be used to close or rededicate a space (Walker et al. 2000); 58 percent (15/26) of excavated kivas evidenced burning or the addition of ash (Adams and Fladd 2017:1107). Even more common than the burning of kivas is the burial of the floor and/or features, which occurred 61 percent (16/26) of the time (Adams 2016b). Burning and burial often co-occurred. For example, Kiva 708 at Homol'ovi II (figure 5.4) underwent several episodes of closure, including the filling and sealing of the ventilator, the placement of a bowl with a katsina face on the bench, the burning of the roof, burial through the deposition of cultural materials, and the removal of the primary roof beams (Walker 1995:92). Thus, the closure of kivas involved the accumulation of ritual practices in addition to materials.

Continuity through time and space is evident when we consider documented examples from the Hopi Mesas, specifically Antelope Mesa

Table 5.2 Kiva Closure Patterns from Villages in the Homol'ovi Settlement Cluster and on Antelope Mesa

Region	Date (AD)	Excavated Kivas	Ritually Closed	Burned/ Ash	Buried[a]	Unknown[b]
Antelope Mesa	1000–1275	12	2 (17%)	1 (8%)	1 (8%)	10 (83%)
Antelope Mesa	1275–1450	26	13 (50%)	3 (12%)	11 (42%)	13 (50%)
Antelope Mesa	Post-1540	9	7 (78%)	2 (22%)	7 (78%)	2 (22%)
Homol'ovi	1260–1400	26	18 (69%)	15 (58%)	16 (61%)	5 (19%)

Source: Based on Adams 2016b; Adams and Fladd 2017; Smith 1972.
[a] Notes on kiva fill from Antelope Mesa were sparse. Suspected kiva burial is based on descriptions of the density, speed, or diversity of materials found in the fill.
[b] This category covers a wide range of possible limitations to the data. For Homol'ovi, kivas in this category were vandalized. For Antelope Mesa, kivas were either destroyed or partially tested, or the publication contained insufficient information to make a determination.

(east of First Mesa). Although percentages are less revealing due to the lack of detailed records describing room fill, Antelope Mesa kivas dating to after the thirteenth century were frequently burned or closed through the introduction of ash or other materials (table 5.2). For example, a kiva at Awatovi, Room 2, contained a cone of material deposited through the roof hatchway, similar to the ash- and sand-layered cones encountered at Homol'ovi (Adams and Fladd 2017; Smith 1972:17). William Walker (1995:109) notes that the elaborate closure treatment of kivas at Homol'ovi II mirrored their importance as ceremonial spaces; this treatment sometimes highlighted the potential danger of the remnants of practices that occurred in those spaces to uninitiated members of society. Kivas took on the identities of the groups who used them and the practices that they encased. When those groups moved on, efforts needed to be taken to mark the importance of these places within the village and region and to protect future visitors from the powers they contained (Walker 1995). Closures of kivas generally increased in prevalence through time on Antelope Mesa, likely supported in part by immigrants from Homol'ovi, who carried these traditions with them to Hopi.

The final closures of the villages of the Homol'ovi Settlement Cluster varied but demonstrated the importance of the careful treatment of space and demarcation of identity and meaning within pueblo structures. At Homol'ovi I, several instances of the deliberate breakage of ceramic vessels have been identified (Adams 2016b; Plumlee 2000). While possibly tied to the practical limitations of emigration, this act also served to create and reinforce the "footprints" left behind during migration to the Hopi Mesas (Hedquist et al. 2014; Kuwanwisiwma and Ferguson 2009). Most distinctively, it is estimated that one hundred of five hundred structures at Chevelon Pueblo (figure 5.4) were intentionally burned (Adams 2016a). This practice appears to be part of a broader effort to close the entire village prior to emigration and is likely linked to the same efforts at purification or rededication as was suggested for kiva closures. While the specific forms and types of closure varied within and among Homol'ovi pueblos, closure practices demonstrate the importance of these spaces as preservers of memory and markers of social ties to ancestral homes.

Archaeological and ethnographic research suggests that many alterations to village life were intended to preserve key components of internal social identities (Ferguson and Colwell-Chanthaphonh 2006; Kaldahl et al. 2004). Through the careful structuring of social practices and relationships, village residents can actively shape who they become. At Homol'ovi, the observed material patterns speak to the importance of the use and organization of space in order to regulate social memory and promote certain forms of identity, both at the communal and small group levels. Closure practices allowed residents to express their sustained material links with these villages and rooms, while also signaling their continual movement through the landscape.

DISCUSSION

Efforts to integrate immigrants into the Homol'ovi settlements resulted in repeated restructurings of the uses of space throughout the villages. These changes often focused on the creation of a community identity, albeit temporarily, for residents of the pueblos. Community efforts are evident in the century-long occupation of these villages, their aggregated forms, and the construction of large plazas for group gatherings and ceremonies. However, ongoing movements into and throughout the villages supported the maintenance of distinct group identities (see also Bernardini and Fowles 2011). As noted by Wesley Bernardini (2008:497), "Firstcomers to a village (and their descendants) had an interest in emphasizing 'clan' distinctiveness to maintain their hold on the best land and their status as gatekeepers . . . even latecomers would have an incentive to embrace clan distinctiveness to safeguard their land rights and ceremonial status from subsequent arrivals." The importance of movement to Pueblo identity was not suspended during occupation of settled villages; rather, groups expressed themselves through movement among villages within various regions and through intra-village reorganization. As such, the occupation of Homol'ovi is marked by a concurrent emphasis on stability and movement.

Distinctive identities were spatially situated, and changes in group location or composition were marked by depositional practices, spanning several years to decades. Deposition also served to safeguard the knowledge and memories associated with each group and its space. The importance of the identities formed, negotiated, and contested within the walls of these villages necessitated that spaces and associated memories be treated appropriately. The focus on the proper closure of space is unsurprising when the importance of movement and migration between villages and regions is considered. The closure of rooms serves as the initial material marker of that movement but is often classified by archaeological analyses as "trash" formed as the haphazard result of "abandonment." The findings from Homol'ovi demonstrate the deliberate and directed actions of closure that represent continued interactions with spaces and materials and result in distinctive patterns of practice (Fladd et al. 2018).

Similar to the accumulation of materials at archaeological sites, groups accumulate aspects of their identity as they make active decisions about elements to preserve and build upon. Migration stories that discuss the specific links of many Hopi clans to the Homol'ovi villages demonstrate this active accumulation through time and across space (Adams 2002; Bernardini 2005; Fewkes 1904:24; Lyons 2003). The care with which rooms and villages were closed and the preserved memories of these places in oral traditions support the importance of and contributions to Hopi identities that developed during migration to the mesas.

LASTING TIES

While intensive occupation of the Homol'ovi area ceased around AD 1400, the region remains an important part of the Hopi cultural landscape.

Ancestral places such as Homol'ovi endure because they are remembered and commemorated by people in the present (see Koyiyumptewa and Colwell-Chanthaphonh 2011). As Patrick Lyons (2003:39) writes, "The Hopi maintain strong connections to Homol'ovi, returning occasionally to gather water, plants, and animals for use in ritual activities and making pilgrimages to shrines in the area" (see also Beaglehole 1936:22–23; Fewkes 1898:525–526; Hough 1915:177). According to Titiev (1992:246), inhabitants of Orayvi maintain a katsina shrine at Homol'ovi. Alexander M. Stephen (1936:1155) recorded a ruined kiva named Homol'ovi at the base of First Mesa, "formally . . . belonging to the Patki clan and named after its early home." Jesse Walter Fewkes (1906:348), in discussing contemporary Hopi shrines, wrote that "even remote ruins like Homolobi [sic] . . . are still regarded as the property of the clans that once owned them, and their old shrines and springs still figure in the ceremonials of those clans." Bernardini (2005:77) notes that the Patkingyam (Water Clan) maintains access rights to eagle nests on their ancestral migration route from Homol'ovi to Wàlpi on First Mesa.

In 2010 the state of Arizona defunded the Homolovi State Park, forcing it to close. However, the Hopi Tribal Council voted to provide the funds necessary to reopen the park the following spring to protect these important ancestral villages. At around the same time, the name of the park was changed to remove the word *ruins* (previously Homolovi Ruins State Park). This change was made due to a petition by the Hopi Tribal Council calling for the park's name to better reflect the view that their ancestors continue to occupy these villages, reiterating the importance of language discussed earlier (Eatherly 2017).

Hopi involvement at the park continues today. For example, Susan Sekaquaptewa, a member of the Butterfly Clan from Sipaulavi, helped design the visitor center's exhibit, which highlights scholarly research within and around park boundaries, as well as continued Hopi connections to the place. The visitor center regularly hosts pottery demonstrations and employs one of the demonstrators, Gwen Setalla, a member of the Bear Clan from First Mesa, as a park ranger. An annual corn-roasting celebration—Suvoyuki Day—is held at the park in August. While Hopi individuals maintain different relationships with the Homol'ovi villages based on their clan migration histories, the pueblos form an important part of the Hopi landscape that warrants protection and respect. In these and many other ways, the histories and memories at Homol'ovi continue to constitute Hopi identities in the twenty-first century.

ACKNOWLEDGMENTS

This chapter would not have been possible without the Hopi Tribe's sustained commemoration of Homol'ovi and their decision to fund the current state park. Archaeological research has been supported by numerous organizations, including the Arizona State Museum, National Science Foundation (NSF), Earthwatch Institute, and Wenner-Gren Foundation, including recent NSF grants BCS-1405748 and BCS-1616970. We thank the many researchers, students, and volunteers (especially Jaye Smith, Byron Estes, Riley Duke, and Matt Hillin for their assistance with the ceramic analysis) involved in this project, and most notably Richard C. Lange, co-director of the Homol'ovi Research Program. We also thank Susan Sekaquaptewa and Gwen Setalla for allowing us to mention their relationships with the park. Finally, we are grateful to Samuel Duwe and Robert Preucel for organizing the session, the Amerind Foundation and Christine Szuter for hosting the subsequent seminar, and all of the authors in this volume for invaluable discussions that helped to improve our chapter.

NOTE

1. Proportions presented here vary slightly from those found in Adams 2016b and Adams and Fladd 2017 due to the inclusion of vandalized kivas, which allows for a more accurate comparison with those on Antelope Mesa in table 5.2.

REFERENCES

Adams, E. Charles. 1989. Homol'ovi III: A Pueblo Hamlet in the Middle Little Colorado River Valley. *Kiva* 54(3):217–230.

Adams, E. Charles. 1991. *The Origin and Development of the Pueblo Katsina Cult.* University of Arizona Press, Tucson.

Adams, E. Charles. 1994. The Katsina Cult: A Western Pueblo Perspective. In *Kachinas in the Pueblo World*, edited by Polly Schaafsma, pp. 35–46. University of New Mexico Press, Albuquerque.

Adams, E. Charles. 1996. Understanding Aggregation in the Homol'ovi Pueblos: Scalar Stress and Social Power. In *River of Change: Prehistory of the Middle Little Colorado River Valley, Arizona*, edited by E. Charles Adams, pp. 1–11. ASM Archaeological Series No. 185. University of Arizona, Tucson.

Adams, E. Charles (editor). 2001. *Homol'ovi III: A Pueblo Hamlet in the Middle Little Colorado River Valley*. Arizona State Museum Archaeological Series No. 193. University of Arizona, Tucson.

Adams, E. Charles. 2002. *Homol'ovi: An Ancient Hopi Settlement Cluster*. University of Arizona Press, Tucson.

Adams, E. Charles (editor). 2016a. *Chevelon: Pueblo at Blue Running Water*. Arizona State Museum Archaeological Series No. 211. University of Arizona, Tucson.

Adams, E. Charles. 2016b. Closure and Dedication Practices in the Homol'ovi Settlement Cluster, Northeastern Arizona. *American Antiquity* 81(1):42–57.

Adams, E. Charles, and Samantha Fladd. 2017. Composition and Interpretation of Stratified Deposits in Ancestral Hopi Villages at Homol'ovi. *Archaeological and Anthropological Sciences* 9(6):1101–1114.

Adams, E. Charles and Vince LaMotta. 2006. New Perspectives on an Ancient Religion: Katsina Ritual and the Archaeological Record. In *Religion in the Prehispanic Southwest*, edited by C. S. VanPool, T. L. VanPool, and D. A. Phillips Jr., pp. 73–94. AltaMira Press, Lanham, Maryland.

Barker, Claire S. 2017. Inconspicuous Identity: Using Everyday Objects to Explore Social Identity within the Homol'ovi Settlement Cluster, A.D. 1260–1400. PhD dissertation, School of Anthropology, University of Arizona, Tucson.

Basso, Keith H. 1996. *Wisdom Sits in Places: Landscape and Language Among the Western Apache*. University of New Mexico Press, Albuquerque.

Beaglehole, Ernest. 1936. *Hopi Hunting and Hunting Ritual*. Yale University Publications in Anthropology No. 4. Yale University Press, New Haven, Connecticut.

Bernardini, Wesley. 2005. *Hopi Oral Tradition and the Archaeology of Identity*. University of Arizona Press, Tucson.

Bernardini, Wesley. 2008. Identity as History: Hopi Clans and the Curation of Oral Tradition. *Journal of Anthropological Research* 64(4):483–509.

Bernardini, Wesley, and Severin Fowles. 2011. Becoming Hopi, Becoming Tiwa: Two Pueblo Histories of Movement. In *Movement, Connectivity, and Landscape Change in the Ancient Southwest: The 20th Anniversary Southwest Symposium*, edited by Margaret C. Nelson and Colleen Strawhacker, pp. 253–274. University Press of Colorado, Boulder.

Birch, Jennifer. 2012. Coalescent Communities: Settlement Aggregation and Social Integration in Iroquoian Ontario. *American Antiquity* 77(4):646–670.

Colwell, Chip. 2016. Collaborative Archaeologies and Descendant Communities. *Annual Review of Anthropology* 45:113–127.

Colwell-Chanthaphonh, Chip, and T. J. Ferguson. 2006. Memory Pieces and Footprints: Multivocality and the Meanings of Ancient Times and Ancestral Places Among the Zuni and Hopi. *American Anthropologist* 108(1): 148–162.

Courlander, Harold. 1971. *The Fourth World of the Hopis*. Crown, New York.

Crown, Patricia L. (editor). 2000. *Women and Men in the Prehispanic Southwest: Labor, Power, & Prestige*. School of American Research Press, Santa Fe, New Mexico.

Duff, Andrew I. 2002. *Western Pueblo Identities: Regional Interaction, Migration, and Transformation*. University of Arizona, Tucson.

Eatherly, Charles R. 2017. Homolovi State Park—Park History: Opened and Dedicated May 22, 1993. Arizona State Parks. Electronic document, https://azstateparks.com/homolovi/explore/park-history.

Ferguson, T. J. 1996. Native Americans and the Practice of Archaeology. *Annual Review of Anthropology* 25:63–79.

Ferguson, T. J., and Chip Colwell-Chanthaphonh. 2006. *History Is in the Land: Multivocal Tribal Traditions in Arizona's San Pedro Valley*. University of Arizona Press, Tucson.

Ferguson, T. J., Kurt E. Dongoske, Michael Yeatts, and Leigh J. Kuwanwisiwma. 2000. Hopi Oral History and Archaeology. In *Working Together: Native Americans and Archaeologists*, edited by Kurt E. Dongoske, Mark Aldenderfer, and Karen Doehner, pp. 45–60. Society for American Archaeology, Washington, D.C.

Ferguson, T. J., and Micah Lomaomvaya. 1999. *Hoopoq'yaqam niqw Wukoskyavi (Those Who Went to the Northeast and Tonto Basin): Hopi-Salado Cultural Affiliation Study*. Hopi Cultural Preservation Office, The Hopi Tribe, Kykotsmovi, Arizona.

Fewkes, Jesse Walter. 1898. Preliminary Account of an Expedition to the Pueblo Ruins near Winslow, Arizona. In *Annual Report of the Smithsonian Institution for 1896*, pp. 517–539. Smithsonian Institution, Washington, D.C.

Fewkes, Jesse Walter. 1904. Two Summers' Work in Pueblo Ruins. In *22nd Annual Report of the Bureau of American Ethnology for 1899–1900*, pp. 3–196. Smithsonian Institution, Washington, D.C.

Fewkes, Jesse Walter. 1906. The Sun's Influence on the Form of Hopi Pueblos. *American Anthropologist* 8(1):88–100.

Fladd, Samantha G., Saul L. Hedquist, and E. Charles Adams. 2018. Trash Reconsidered: A Relational Approach to Deposition in the Pueblo Southwest. Manuscript on file, Homol'ovi Research Lab, Arizona State Museum, University of Arizona, Tucson.

Fladd, Samantha, Richard C. Lange, and E. Charles Adams. 2017. Report of 2011–2016 Survey of Rock Art Ranch and Section 16, Navajo County, Arizona. Report on file, Arizona State Museum, Tucson.

Fogelin, Lars, and Michael Brian Schiffer. 2015. Rites of Passage and Other Rituals in the Life Histories of Objects. *Cambridge Archaeological Journal* 25(4):815–827.

Hays-Gilpin, Kelley, and John Ware. 2015. Chaco: The View from Downstream. In *Chaco Revisited: New Research on the Prehistory of Chaco Canyon, New Mexico*, edited by Carrie Heitman and Stephen Plog, pp. 322–345. University of Arizona Press, Tucson.

Hedquist, Saul L. 2016. Ritual Practice and Exchange in the Late Prehispanic Western Pueblo Region: Insights from the Distribution and Deposition of Turquoise at Homol'ovi I. *Kiva* 82(3):209–231.

Hedquist, Saul L. 2017. A Colorful Past: Turquoise and Social Identity in the Late Prehispanic Western Pueblo Region, A.D. 1275–1400. PhD dissertation, School of Anthropology, University of Arizona, Tucson.

Hedquist, Saul L., Stewart B. Koyiyumptewa, Peter M. Whiteley, Leigh J. Kuwanwisiwma, Kenneth C. Hill, and T. J. Ferguson. 2014. Recording Toponyms to Document the Endangered Hopi Language. *American Anthropologist* 116(2):324–331.

Heitman, Carrie C. 2016. "A Mother for All the People": Feminist Science and Chacoan Archaeology. *American Antiquity* 81(3):471–489.

Hopi Dictionary Project. 1998. *Hopi Dictionary/Hopìikwa Lavàytutuveni: A Hopi-English Dictionary of the Third Mesa Dialect*. University of Arizona Press, Tucson.

Hough, Walter. 1915. *The Hopi Indians: Mesa Folk of Hopiland*. Torch Press, Cedar Rapids, Iowa.

Huckell, Bruce, and Lisa Huckell. 2004. God's Pocket. Manuscript on file, Homol'ovi Research Program, Arizona State Museum, University of Arizona, Tucson.

Kaldahl, Eric J., Scott Van Keuren, and Barbara J. Mills. 2004. Migration, Factionalism, and the Trajectories of Pueblo IV Period Clusters in the Mogollon Rim Region. In *The Protohistoric Pueblo World, A.D. 1275–1600*, edited by E. Charles Adams and Andrew I. Duff, pp. 85–94. University of Arizona Press, Tucson.

Koyiyumptewa, Stewart B., and Chip Colwell-Chanthaphonh. 2011. The Past Is Now: Hopi Connections to Ancient Times and Places. In *Movement, Connectivity, and Landscape Change in the Ancient Southwest*, edited by Margaret C. Nelson and Colleen Strawhacker, pp. 443–455. University Press of Colorado, Boulder.

Kuwanwisiwma, Leigh J., and T. J. Ferguson. 2009. Hopitutskwa and Ang Kuktota: The Role of Archaeological Sites in Defining Hopi Cultural Landscapes. In *The Archaeology of Meaningful Places*, edited by Brenda J. Bowser and Maria Nieves Zedeño, pp. 90–106. University of Utah Press, Salt Lake City.

LaMotta, Vincent M. 2006. Zooarchaeology and Chronology of Homol'ovi I and Other Pueblo IV Period Sites in the Central Little Colorado River Valley,

Northern Arizona. PhD dissertation, Department of Anthropology, University of Arizona, Tucson.

LaMotta, Vincent M., and Michael B. Schiffer. 1999. Formation Processes of House Floor Assemblages. In *The Archaeology of Household Activities*, edited by Penelope Allison, pp. 19–29. Routledge, New York.

Lange, Richard C. 1998. *Prehistoric Land-Use and Settlement of the Middle Little Colorado River Valley: The Survey of Homolovi Ruins State Park, Winslow, Arizona*. Arizona State Museum Archaeological Series No. 189. University of Arizona, Tucson.

Liebmann, Matthew J. 2017. From Landscapes of Meaning to Landscapes of Signification in the American Southwest. *American Antiquity* 82(4):642–661.

Lyons, Patrick D. 2003. *Ancestral Hopi Migrations*. Anthropological Papers of the University of Arizona No. 68. University of Arizona Press, Tucson.

Miljour, Heather. 2016. Homol'ovi I Pueblo: An Examination of Plant Remains within Ash Closure, Renewal, and Dedication Deposits. MA thesis, School of Anthropology, University of Arizona, Tucson.

Mills, Barbara J., and William H. Walker (editors). 2008. *Memory Work: Archaeologies of Material Practices*. School for Advanced Research Press, Santa Fe, New Mexico.

Nequatewa, Edmund. 1936. *Truth of a Hopi*. Museum of Northern Arizona Bulletin No. 8. Museum of Northern Arizona, Flagstaff.

Parsons, Elsie Clews. 1936. Early Relations Between Hopi and Keres. *American Anthropologist* 38(4):554–560.

Plumlee, Scott. 2000. Experimental Approaches to the Study of Purposeful Vessel Breakage at Homol'ovi I. Paper on file, Homol'ovi Research Program, Arizona State Museum, University of Arizona, Tucson.

Schachner, Gregson. 2012. *Population Circulation and the Transformation of Ancient Zuni Communities*. University of Arizona Press, Tucson.

Silko, Leslie Marmon. 1996. *Yellow Woman and a Beauty of the Spirit: Essays on Native American Life Today*. Simon and Schuster, New York.

Smith, Watson. 1972. *Prehistoric Kivas of Antelope Mesa*. Awatovi Expedition Report No. 9. Peabody Museum, Harvard University, Cambridge, Massachusetts.

Stephen, Alexander M. 1936. *Hopi Journal of Alexander M. Stephen*. Edited by E. Clews Parsons. Columbia University Contributions to Anthropology 23. Columbia University Press, New York.

Titiev, Mischa. 1992. *Old Oraibi: A Study of the Hopi Indians of Third Mesa*. University of New Mexico Press, Albuquerque.

Triadan, Daniela. 1997. *Ceramic Commodities and Common Containers: Production and Distribution of White Mountain Red Ware in the Grasshopper Region, Arizona*. Anthropological Papers of the University of Arizona No. 61. University of Arizona Press, Tucson.

Walker, William H. 1995. Ritual Prehistory: A Pueblo Case Study. PhD dissertation, Department of Anthropology, University of Arizona, Tucson.

Walker, William H. 2002. Stratigraphy and Practical Reason. *American Anthropologist* 104(1):159–177.

Walker, William H., Vincent M. LaMotta, and E. Charles Adams. 2000. Katsinas and Kiva Abandonments at Homol'ovi: A Deposit-Oriented Perspective on Religion in Southwest Prehistory. In *The Archaeology of Regional Interaction*, edited by Michelle Hegmon, pp. 341–360. University Press of Colorado, Boulder.

Whiteley, Peter M. 2011. Hopi Place Value: Translating a Landscape. In *Born in the Blood: On Native American Translation*, edited by Brian Swann, pp. 84–108. University of Nebraska Press, Lincoln.

Young, Lisa. 1996. Mobility and Farmers: The Pithouse-to-Pueblo Transition in Northeastern Arizona. PhD dissertation, Department of Anthropology, University of Arizona, Tucson.

PART II
ALWAYS BECOMING

6

Seeking Strength and Protection
Tewa Mobility During the Pueblo Revolt Period

Joseph Aguilar and Robert W. Preucel

> Long ago in the north
> Lies the road of emergence!
> Yonder our ancestors live,
> Yonder we take our being.
> Yet now we come southwards.
> For cloud flowers blossom here
> Here the lightning flashes,
> Rain water here is falling!
> —Marta Weigle and Peter White, *The Lore of New Mexico*

So begins a Turtle Dance song sung on every winter solstice at Santa Clara Pueblo. Similar songs sung at many of the Tewa pueblos of northern New Mexico demonstrate the importance of north for the Tewa people. More than just a point on a compass, north is a dynamic pathway merging time, space, and history into a social claim about identity. As the song indicates, Tewa "being" is connected to the north since this is the place of emergence and where the ancestors lived before making their journey southward and eventually settling at the villages of today. The singing of these songs is a prayer and a way of constantly acknowledging and reestablishing the intimate ties between ancestors, deities, places, and people. We wish to use these insights to assist our interpretation of Tewa population movements during the Pueblo Revolt period (1680–96). We present our study as an example of the ways in which an Indigenous perspective can redirect research questions (Watkins 2000; Wilcox 2009).

The period following the Pueblo Revolt of 1680 was a time of considerable violence and social unrest (Knaut 1995; Liebmann 2012). Contrary to the popular narrative of Diego de Vargas's "peaceful reconquest" of 1692 commemorated each year during the Santa Fe Fiesta, Pueblo people actively resisted the Spaniards upon their return. In fact, in 1693 Vargas was forced to retake Santa Fe in a pitched battle (Kessell et al. 1995).

By this time, many Pueblo communities had evacuated their mission villages and moved up onto defensible mesas (Liebmann et al. 2005), which proved to be a major challenge during Vargas's reconquest campaign. Pueblo people also took refuge in other isolated upland areas in the plateau and mountain regions surrounding the Rio Grande valley (figure 6.1). Mobility became an important resistance strategy, and the landscape provided a place in which Pueblo communities could seek strength and protection.

In our chapter, we adopt an Indigenous perspective that integrates the practical and sacred dimensions of Tewa mobility during the Pueblo Revolt period by focusing on movements of San Ildefonso Pueblo people. Our approach is inspired in part by Greg Cajete's (2000) holistic approach to Native science in which different ways of knowing inform one another and create a more robust whole (see Aguilar and Preucel 2013). We pay particular attention to the movements to both mesa-top and upland areas that allowed the Tewa people to withstand Vargas's 1694 military campaigns. We also consider the sacred significance of these places, which are used in paying reverence to ancestors and as places for gathering strength. The decisions made by Pueblo leaders during this traumatic period are important to document; they are responsible for the survival of Pueblo people today.

PUEBLO RESPONSES TO SPANISH COLONIALISM

Pueblo people resisted Spanish authority from the very beginning of the Spanish colonization of New Mexico. When Governor Juan de Oñate arrived in Pueblo country in 1598, he found many of the Piro villages vacated and their storehouses empty (Simmons 1991:106). Their strategy of moving away to avoid the Spaniards was a reaction to Coronado's abuse of Pueblo people three generations earlier, an event that was undoubtedly still fresh in their memories. Oñate pushed on northward until he arrived in the northern Rio Grande valley, north of the modern town of Española. There he found the Tewa people were living in two villages on either side of the Rio Grande, one known as Ohkay Owingeh (Village of the Strong People) and the other as Yungé Owingeh (Mockingbird Village). Oñate designated Ohkay as San Juan de los Caballeros, his new

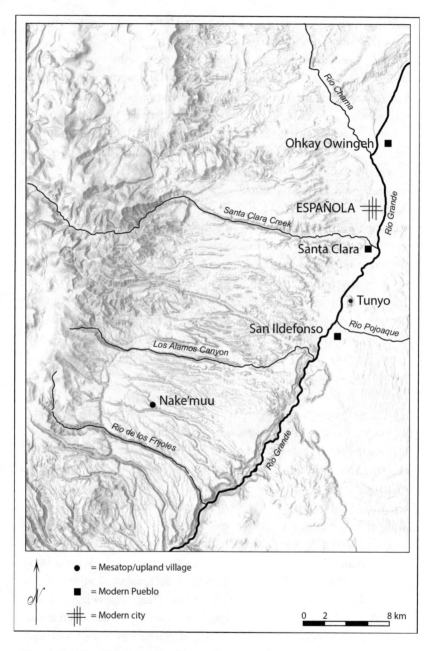

Figure 6.1 San Ildefonso Pueblo and associated mesa-top and upland villages discussed in the chapter.

capital, but then took over Yungé, renamed San Gabriel, as the site for his new colony (Simmons 1991).

Oñate's expedition included ten Franciscans—eight priests and two lay brothers—because his contract with the royal government stipulated that at least six Franciscans be part of the new colony (Norris 2000:8). This was also in accord with the Franciscan Order's desire to open up new mission fields. Thus, the church took over the financial responsibilities for the new colony. In 1609 Pedro de Peralta replaced Oñate as governor, moved the capital, and named it La Villa Real de la Santa Fe de San Francisco de Asís (Norris 2000:8). Franciscan priests were assigned to individual Pueblo villages and immediately required the Indians to convert to Catholicism, build missions, and provide tribute in the form of mantas and corn. These practices of subjugation infringed on Pueblo religious and economic sovereignty, and resentment quickly built up. There were major revolts at Jemez in 1623, at Zuni in 1632, and at Taos in 1639. Significantly, these revolts took place first in precisely those areas that were the most difficult for the Spaniards to control from Santa Fe.

Resistance to Spanish authority intensified at the end of the seventeenth century. On August 10, 1680, all of the Pueblo Indians of New Mexico (with the exception of the Piro) and their Navajo and Apache allies united in an armed revolt to drive the Spanish colonists from their homelands (Hackett and Shelby 1942). Pueblo warriors executed Franciscan priests and Hispanic settlers, burned missions and haciendas, and laid siege to the Spanish capital of Santa Fe. The turning point came when they diverted the Santa Fe River and cut off the water to the people and livestock (Sando 2005). Governor Antonio de Otermín and his colonists were forced to flee south to El Paso del Norte (present-day Ciudad Juárez, Mexico), where they temporarily reestablished their colony. The Pueblo warriors allowed them to leave peaceably and did not offer pursuit.

The Spaniards immediately made plans to retake their colony (Hackett and Shelby 1942). Otermín returned in 1681, eager to atone for his failure. He marched north to Isleta Pueblo and took the village without a battle. He then sent his lieutenant, Juan Domínguez de Mendoza, to subdue Cochiti Pueblo. There, however, Mendoza was turned back by a war party, and Otermín gauged the resistance so severe that he decided to return to El Paso. In 1687 Governor Pedro Reneros de Posada led a column up the Jemez River, which he then followed to Tamaya (Santa

Ana Pueblo). The people of Tamaya refused to surrender, and a battle followed. Posada retaliated by burning the village and returned to El Paso with four Pueblo leaders and ten other captives. In 1689 Governor Domingo Jironza Pétriz de Cruzate led an expedition in yet another attempt to reconquer New Mexico. The main event of the expedition was the destruction of Zia Pueblo. During the daylong battle, fifty of Cruzate's eighty men were wounded. An estimated six hundred Indians were killed, and seventy were taken back to El Paso as captives.

In 1692 Vargas succeeded in his "ritual repossession" of the colony. He arrived at Santa Fe on the evening of September 13 and established his *plaza de armas* within sight of the *villa* (Kessell and Hendricks 1992:385). The next day, he entered Santa Fe unarmed and publicly revalidated Spain's claim to the kingdom and provinces of New Mexico. He returned to his camp without having fired a shot. He then returned to El Paso to gather up people to participate in his recolonization program. Upon his return in 1693, however, Vargas found that the Pueblo Indians had fortified Santa Fe. He was forced to attack the villa and retake it in battle. Despite this victory, his authority remained precarious, and in the months following, Pueblo Indians continually raided his livestock. In 1694 he mounted a punitive campaign against the rebels, many of whom were living in the new mesa-top villages surrounding Santa Fe. He attacked Kotyiti on April 17, Astialakwa on July 24, and laid siege to Tunyo (Black Mesa) twice from March 4 to 19 and then again from September 4 to 6 (Hendricks 2002).

The Spanish reconquest is traditionally celebrated at Santa Fe Fiesta as peaceful and bloodless, and during Vargas's initial foray into the region in 1692, he in fact faced little resistance. But in 1693, the Pueblo people fortified Santa Fe, and he was forced to lay siege to the city. A year later he began a series of brutal military campaigns against the Pueblo mesa villages. What characterized the Pueblo response to the Spanish church and crown was not only its violence, but the people's adamant resistance to subjugation. While the Pueblos made some accommodations and even entered into strategic alliances with Vargas, their resistance was constant throughout the reconquest.

Over the last twenty years, considerable archaeological research has been conducted to investigate the social contexts of these mesa villages. Robert Preucel (2000, 2006; Preucel et al. 2002; Wilcox 2009) has mapped Kotyiti. Matthew Liebmann (2012; Liebmann and Preucel 2007) has mapped Patokwa on a low rise below Guadalupe Mesa, Astialakwa on the top of Guadalupe Mesa, Boletsakwa on San Juan Mesa, and Cerro Colorado village on Cerro Colorado Mesa. Joseph Aguilar (2013; Aguilar and Preucel 2013) is currently mapping Tunyo on San Ildefonso Mesa. In addition, T. J. Ferguson and Robert Preucel (2005) and Liebmann and colleagues (2005) have examined the mesa-village phenomenon within a broader postrevolt regional study.

MEANINGS OF THE MESAS

As Alfonso Ortiz has described, the Tewa world is delimited by a series of nested tetrads. The outermost of these are the sacred mountains. Closer to the villages are the sacred mesas located in each of the cardinal directions. Ortiz (1969:19) gives the names of these mesas for San Juan Pueblo as follows: to the north is Tema Yoh, located above the town of La Madera; to the west is Toma Yoh; to the south is Tun Yoh, also known as Black Mesa; and to the east is Tse Mayoh, near the Spanish town of Chimayo. He writes that each of these hills is sacred because each contains caves and tunnels where the supernatural beings known as *tsave yoh* live. This tetradic pattern, though not the specific mesa referents, is shared among the different Tewa villages.

At San Ildefonso Pueblo, Tunyo Pin, also called Black Mesa or Spotted Mountain, is the principal mesa of the north (figure 6.2). It figures prominently in San Ildefonso history. In San Ildefonso lore, Tunyo is home to the giant, who is known to visit the pueblo, where he threatens to capture misbehaving children and take them back to his cave in the mesa (Harrington 1916:295). The giant was defeated in an epic battle by the Twin War Gods, and his remains can still be seen on the mesa today in the form of shrines that are visited by the Tewa. The mesa is a remnant of a series of volcanic events that occurred over an extended period of geologic time. Traditional stories mention that the mountain once emitted smoke and fire. The mesa is also the location of one of the most famous of the Tewa Revolt period villages. This village is called Tunyo Kwaje Teqwakeji ("Old Houses on Top of Tunyo"; Harrington 1916:297). The importance of this place is perhaps best indicated by the fact that dances were traditionally performed on top of the mesa, and it

Seeking Strength and Protection

Figure 6.2 Tunyo (Black Mesa), the northern sacred mesa of San Ildefonso Pueblo. Photograph by Joseph Aguilar.

continues to be used for ceremonial purposes by the people of San Ildefonso (Harrington 1916:295).

Although Ortiz does not mention them, previously inhabited villages built by Tewa ancestors are also venerated as shrines. When Pueblo people visit these places, they make offerings to acknowledge and honor the ancestors who still dwell in them. The Pajarito Plateau is a sacred place for the San Ildefonso people because it is the location of ancestral Tewa villages that gave rise to the Rio Grande villages of today (Hewett 1906). These villages include Potsuwi (Village at the Gap Where the Water Sinks), Tsankawi (Prickly-Pear Cactus Gap Village), Tsiregeh (Bird Place Village), Navawi (Field Gap Village), and Nake'muu (Village on the Edge). Archaeological evidence reveals that these villages were occupied during the Coalition and Classic periods (Kohler 2004). Nake'muu is of special interest because it was rebuilt and temporarily reoccupied by the people of San Ildefonso during the Reconquest period (Vierra et al. 2003:142–143). Oral traditions about Nake'muu are still maintained within the community.

FIGHTING FOR SURVIVAL

Although occupied for only nine months during 1694, Tunyo was a major center of resistance during the Spanish reconquest of New Mexico. At the onset of Vargas's campaign, many of the Pueblos had already moved to upland areas, while others remained at their mission villages along the Rio Grande and Galisteo and Jemez Rivers. The choice to move a community to an upland or mesa-top location was important for each pueblo as each sought a strategy to deal with the reconquest in a way that made most sense to the community.

Tunyo was perhaps the largest of all the mesa villages established in the northern Rio Grande region. It hosted people from as many as nine different Tewa villages. At different times, it included people from Powhoge (San Ildefonso), Kha'po (Santa Clara), Nanbé (Nambe), P'osuwaege (Pojoaque), Tetsugeh (Tesuque), Kuyemuugeh (Cuyamungue), and Sakona (Jacona), as well as the two southern Tewa villages of San Cristobal and San Lazaro.

Vargas laid siege to the mesa for much of 1694, as part of his military campaign to reconquer the pueblos. On January 9 he learned that the Tewa had taken refuge on Tunyo. His interrogation of two prisoners named Diego and don Diego from Nambe Pueblo revealed that people from their home, along with those from San Ildefonso, Tesuque, Cuyamungue, Pojoaque, Jacona, and Santa Clara, had taken refuge on the mesa (Kessell et al. 1998:39–41). The move to the top of Tunyo, Vargas learned, was prompted by his victory at Santa Fe just weeks earlier, after which seventy Pueblo defenders were executed in its plaza. On January 10, Vargas traveled to Tunyo and spoke with Domingo, a Tesuque war captain, who by many accounts was a leader of the Tewa defenders. Domingo claimed that he and the others were not coming down since they were afraid of what happened to the Tanos in Santa Fe (Kessell et al. 1998:44). With the Tewa established in a strategically advantageous position and prepared to stay on the mesa indefinitely, Vargas decided to use military force. His first attack on Tunyo was in February of 1694. However, the combination of too few horses, a relentless defense of the mesa, and a heavy snow prevented Vargas from mounting a proper attack. After making camp at San Ildefonso Pueblo, just south of the mesa, Vargas gathered his troops for another assault on Tunyo on March 4, at which

Seeking Strength and Protection 157

time several skirmishes took place. By Vargas's account, fourteen Tewa defenders were killed and twenty-two Spanish soldiers were wounded. Despite all his efforts, Vargas and his allies were unable to take the mesa.

During the nine-month siege at Tunyo, Vargas carried out simultaneous military campaigns at the mesa-top villages of Astialakwa in the Jemez region and Kotyiti, just north of Cochiti. At Kotyiti, Vargas and his Pueblo allies overwhelmed the Keres defenders, many of whom broke and ran, escaping as best they could. The allied army captured the plaza and pueblo and seized 342 noncombatants and warriors as prisoners. The latter were absolved and shot. Eight others died in the battle. The Pueblo allies plundered the pueblo, and Vargas set it on fire (Hendricks 2002). Two months later, in July, Vargas led a campaign at Astialakwa against the Jemez and Kewa people who were living on the mesa. Vargas was able to gain access to the top via a back route, and he captured the village. Seventy Pueblo people died in battle, five were burned in their houses, seven leaped off the mesa to their deaths, and two were executed. There were 361 noncombatants taken prisoner.

After these battles, Vargas turned his attention back to Tunyo in another attempt to take the mesa. On September 4, Vargas and his allies departed Santa Fe for San Ildefonso. Accompanying him on this military campaign were approximately 150 allies from Santa Ana, San Felipe, Zia, Pecos, and Jemez Pueblos. As with the previous battle, the Tewa held off Vargas and his troops during several skirmishes in which the Tewa shot arrows, threw hooks, and hurled stones and slabs of rock onto the invaders while fortifying themselves behind stone ramparts. Approximately six Tewa defenders and two Spanish soldiers were killed, with many more wounded on each side. On September 8 of 1694, Tewa resistance came to an end. Domingo, the captain from Tesuque, negotiated with Vargas a cessation of hostilities on the condition that the Tewa were allowed to return to occupy their pueblos below. Most Tewa did just that, although others chose to take refuge with relatives in other villages, including villages as a far away as the Hopi Mesas.

MOBILITY ACROSS THE TEWA LANDSCAPE

The Spanish accounts indicate that the Tewa people were actively moving from their mission villages to many different mesa and plateau areas during the time of Vargas's military campaign. Vargas was aware that some people had retreated to the canyons west of San Ildefonso and that others sought refuge at a place called Embudo, north of Ohkay Owingeh, but because of the pressing threat of the mesa villages he did not begin a military campaign in either area until 1696 (Espinosa 1988). The Tewa people effectively mobilized across a landscape with which they were intimately familiar due to their traditional hunting and ritual practices. This deep knowledge of their landscape helped the Tewa as they sought protection from the onslaught of Vargas's campaigns.

Pueblo people also sought out these places as spiritual sanctuaries. As discussed previously, the Tewa cosmological landscape is marked by mountains, hills, springs, and ancestral villages that are home to Tewa ancestors and deities. The natural and built environments of the Tewa thus hold strong spiritual significance and are often evoked as places from which strength can be drawn with the correct preparations. When Pueblo people return to these places and perform certain ceremonies that involve acknowledging the different directions, they draw on the power of place. This aspect of Tewa mobility is not well appreciated by non-Pueblo scholars and must be considered alongside strategic and logistical motivations for mobilization.

The archaeological focus on the Pueblo Revolt mesa villages, while understandable given the available historical documentation, has tended to obscure the full range of Pueblo movement during this period. Many Pueblo people took refuge in upland areas and established temporary camps and rancherias. The lack of scholarship on these kinds of sites may in part be due to their low archaeological visibility: short-term occupations typically produce low density archaeological assemblages. One way forward is to turn to Pueblo oral history to gain a deeper understanding of Tewa mobility.

San Ildefonso oral histories, for example, provide evidence of a strategy of hiding women and children deep in the ancestral landscape. They relate the journey that women and children took first to Navawi and then up the canyons where they reoccupied Nake'muu (Vierra 2003:12). Nake'muu is a Late Coalition (AD 1275–1325) plaza pueblo (figure 6.3). Its name refers to the location of the village at the confluence of Water Canyon and Cañon de Valle, on the narrow point at the end of a mesa. The physiographic setting of Nake'muu is dramatic, with steep

Seeking Strength and Protection

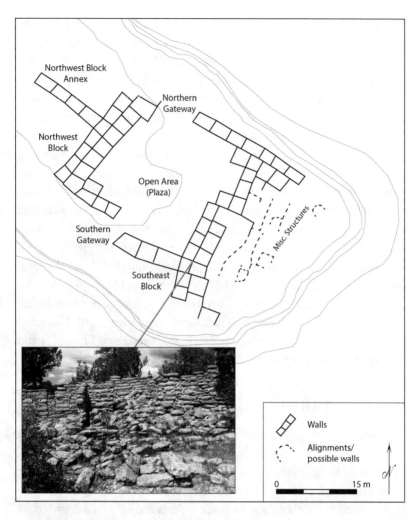

Figure 6.3 Nake'muu, the Coalition period village reoccupied by San Ildefonso women and children during the Pueblo Revolt period (map based on Vierra 2003:Figure 5). Photograph by Bradley Vierra.

cliffs directly adjacent to its roomblocks. This village was well off the radar of Vargas and his allies as he sought to subdue the mesa villages. Indeed, it proved to be so well hidden that it is not mentioned in any of the Spanish documents.

Edgar Lee Hewett (1906:25) visited Nake'muu and produced the first sketch maps of the village, calling it the "the best preserved ruin in this region." The site received this distinction because it is one of the few ancestral sites on the Pajarito Plateau to retain aboveground, standing masonry walls. Although no archaeological excavations have taken place at Nake'muu, its architecture has been extensively documented by Brad Vierra (2003) for the Los Alamos National Laboratory in a collaborative effort with San Ildefonso to monitor the effects of ambient environmental conditions and laboratory activities on the village.

Nake'muu contains at least fifty-five ground-floor rooms distributed in four roomblocks. A close inspection of the wall construction sequence indicates that two separate linear roomblocks were built initially. Sometime later a series of lateral northern and southern roomblocks was added, enclosing a central plaza. The outside doorways were subsequently sealed, and the focus of the pueblo became the central plaza area (Vierra 2003:3). The walls are constructed of shaped tuff blocks quarried from the local bedrock and held together by adobe mortar. One possible explanation for the excellent condition of the walls is that the roofs were repaired during the Revolt period reoccupation. Traditional knowledge about this sacred place has been passed down at San Ildefonso through oral histories and through annual visits to the village by tribal members.

MAPPING TUNYO

Virtually no systematic archaeological fieldwork has been conducted at Tunyo. This may be in part because of its characterization by Adolph Bandelier, who was skeptical of its archaeological value. He wrote, "The pueblo of San Ildefonso, or Po-juo-ge [sic], offers nothing of archaeological interest. Neither does the black mesa called Tu-yo [sic], two miles from the village, deserve attention except from an historic standpoint" (Bandelier 1892:82). What we know about the events that happened at Tunyo is drawn largely from Vargas's letters and reports. While they form a rich resource and are now widely available, thanks to John Kessell and the Vargas Project's translations, these documents can provide only a one-sided perspective on a multidimensional history.

In order to incorporate Tunyo into Pueblo Revolt history and archaeology, Joseph Aguilar is currently conducting research at the village with the support of the San Ildefonso leadership. In consideration of the pueblo's values and ethics, Aguilar has used noninvasive methodologies to minimize the impact on heritage resources. Using drone, or unmanned aerial vehicle (UAV), technology, Aguilar and his colleagues, Chet Walker and Mark Willis of Archaeo-Geophysical Associates (AGA), have produced high-resolution images and models of Tunyo that aid in a basic understanding of the archaeology of the mesa and the settlement on its summit (plate 6).

One of the goals of Indigenous archaeology is to broaden the interpretation and understanding of the archaeological record through the incorporation of Indigenous world views, histories, and science (Nicholas 2008:1660). Drone technology provides a suitable alternative for tribes who have a vested interest in archaeology but are concerned with the limitations of traditional site-based survey methods and wish to refrain from engaging in invasive archaeological practices. While providing a suitable alternative archaeological method to Indigenous people, drone technology also provides a more efficient and precise means of mapping sites and landscapes that should appeal to all archaeologists regardless of their methodological leanings.

Aguilar and AGA conducted an aerial photography survey at Tunyo to collect three-dimensional data from the site and the surrounding landscape. AGA used fixed-wing and multirotor UAVs, each equipped with a digital camera, GPS, and radio receiver—all controlled by a ground-based computer. The goal of using UAVs was to generate a very dense digital terrain model (DTM) and to provide stereo-images for highly detailed architectural mapping and mound volume measurements. The first stage of data collection used a digital process called photogrammetry that extracts three-dimensional data from a series of overlapping stereo-pair images, all spatially referenced to photo targets on the ground. Computer software then compared the overlapping areas from the photographs and re-created a high-resolution topography of the region.

The benefits of drone mapping at Tunyo were significant. Under optimal conditions, we were able to collect a large amount of high-resolution data in a fraction of the time it would have typically taken to collect these data using traditional archaeological survey methods. Moreover, drones collected data from above the ground surface, making the impacts on Tunyo virtually nonexistent.

Preliminary findings of the UAV mapping show that the architecture at Tunyo is distinct from other Revolt period mesa villages. There appear to be few visible formal architectural elements and no formal dual-plaza structure, as seen at the other mesa-top villages such as Kotyiti, Patokwa, and Boletsawka, which are interpreted as evidence of a moiety social organization. Instead, the analysis of three-dimensional models of the architecture reveals clusters of shallow pits with stone footings scattered across the mesa. This informal construction may be consistent with the fact that the move to Tunyo happened quickly and involved multiple social groups from different pueblos, in response to Vargas's military campaign against the Pueblos.

Tunyo's geologic history provides an important context for understanding the nature of the settlement. The mesa is capped with the remnants of an ancient riverbed, consisting of loose quartzite cobbles and river gravels. This formation is not particularly suitable for the construction of masonry walls. It is better suited for the excavation of shallow pits that, when topped with a temporary superstructure, could provide the temporary habitation space needed during the winter of 1694. It may be significant that the Tewa people used similar pit excavations or "dugouts" in the construction of their gravel mulch fields. This expedient architecture is in line with the San Ildefonso oral traditions that assert that Tunyo was only temporarily occupied in times of war.

San Ildefonso oral history suggests that the most vulnerable of the Tewa population sought refuge in upland areas like Nake'muu, whereas a fighting force occupied Tunyo. It was these warriors who attracted most of Vargas's attention, allowing other Tewa groups to seek sanctuary in the upland areas. Initial estimations of the total settlement size at Tunyo suggest that it is unlikely to have housed one thousand people, as Vargas reported. Aguilar's analysis of architectural data and associated defensive features reveals defensive strategies. Pueblo warriors fortified several areas where the mesa was the most vulnerable. They erected ramparts and blockades to prevent equestrian access and piled up caches of cobblestones at the trailheads to use as ammunition. These strategies were quite effective, and the Spanish accounts indicate that they were unable to scale the mesa and that several men were wounded by stone missiles.

CONCLUSIONS

Mobility is widely recognized as a key form of resistance to Spanish authority during the Pueblo Revolt period. However, the ways in which and reasons why Pueblo people mobilized need to be further investigated.

Mobilization to mesa tops and upland areas is typically interpreted as a strategic maneuver. While this certainly was the case, deeper meanings underlie this decision. Pueblo people chose to move in the direction from whence their ancestors came, which allowed them to draw spiritual strength from the power of place. This is well illustrated by the Tewa, who moved several times to sacred places on the landscape that were also strategically advantageous in their military defense against Vargas and his allies. San Ildefonso leaders sent some of their women and children to Nake'muu on the Pajarito Plateau at the same time that they established their fighting force on Tunyo. Incorporating this understanding of Tewa mobility into our work requires that we view mobility as a multifaceted undertaking that includes the spiritual and symbolic meanings of movement alongside its strategic considerations.

ACKNOWLEDGMENTS

We would like to express our gratitude to the San Ildefonso Pueblo Tribal Council for supporting this research on San Ildefonso history and heritage. We especially thank Chet Walker and Mark Willis for their assistance in conducting the drone mapping. We also thank Brad Vierra (tribal historic preservation officer for San Ildefonso Pueblo) for his advice and research on Nake'muu. Finally, we thank the University of Pennsylvania Museum and the School for Advanced Research for providing support for Aguilar's fieldwork.

REFERENCES

Aguilar, Joseph R. 2013. Researching the Pueblo Revolt of 1680. *Expedition* 55(3):34–35.

Aguilar, Joseph R., and Robert W. Preucel. 2013. Sacred Mesas: Pueblo Time, Space, and History in the Aftermath of the Pueblo Revolt of 1680. In *The Death of Prehistory*, edited by Peter Schmidt and Stephen A. Mrozowski, pp. 267–289. Oxford University Press, Oxford.

Bandelier, Adolph F. 1892. *Final Report of Investigation Among the Indians of the Southwestern United States, Carried on Mainly in the Years from 1880 to 1885: Part II*. Papers of the Archaeological Institute of America, American Series, Vol. IV. Cambridge University Press, Cambridge.

Cajete, Gregory. 2000. *Native Science: Natural Laws of Interdependence*. Clear Light Press, Santa Fe, New Mexico.

Espinosa, J. Manuel. 1988. *The Pueblo Indian Revolt of 1696 and the Franciscan Missions in New Mexico: Letters of the Missionaries and Related Documents*. University of Oklahoma Press, Norman.

Ferguson, T. J., and Robert W. Preucel. 2005. Signs of the Ancestors: An Archaeology of the Mesa Villages of the Pueblo Revolt. In *Structure and Meaning in Human Settlement*, edited by Joseph Rykwert and Tony Atkin, pp. 185–207. University Museum Press, Philadelphia.

Hackett, Charles W., and Charmion C. Shelby (editor and translator). 1942. *Revolt of the Pueblo Indians of New Mexico, and Otermín's Attempted Reconquest, 1680–1682*. 2 vols. Coronado Cuarto Centennial Publications. University of New Mexico Press, Albuquerque.

Harrington, John P. 1916. *Ethnogeography of the Tewa*. 29th Annual Report of the Bureau of American Ethnology. Government Printing Office, Washington, D.C.

Hendricks, Rick. 2002. Pueblo-Spanish Warfare in Seventeenth-Century New Mexico: The Battles of Black Mesa, Kotyiti, and Astialakwa. In *Archaeologies of the Pueblo Revolt: Identity, Meaning, and Renewal in the Pueblo World*, edited by Robert W. Preucel, pp. 180–197. University of New Mexico Press, Albuquerque.

Hewett, Edgar Lee. 1906. *Antiquities of the Jemez Plateau, New Mexico*. Bureau of American Ethnology Bulletin No. 32. Government Printing Office, Washington, D.C.

Kessell, John L., Rick Hendricks, and Meredith Dodge (editors). 1995. *To the Royal Crown Restored: The Journals of Don Diego de Vargas, New Mexico, 1692–1694*. University of New Mexico Press, Albuquerque.

Kessell, John L., Rick Hendricks, and Meredith Dodge (editors). 1998. *Blood on the Boulders: The Journals of Don Diego de Vargas, New Mexico 1694–1697, Book 1*. University of New Mexico Press, Albuquerque.

Knaut, Andrew L. 1995. *The Pueblo Revolt: Conquest and Resistance in Seventeenth-Century New Mexico*. University of Oklahoma Press, Norman.

Kohler, Timothy A. (editor). 2004. *The Archaeology of Bandelier National Monument: Village Formation on the Pajarito Plateau, New Mexico*. University of New Mexico Press, Albuquerque.

Liebmann, Matthew. 2012. *Revolt: An Archaeological History of Pueblo Resistance and Revitalization in the 17th Century, New Mexico*. University of Arizona Press, Tucson.

Liebmann, Matthew, and Robert W. Preucel. 2007. The Archaeology of the Pueblo Revolt and the Formation of the Modern Pueblo World. *Kiva* 73(2): 197–219.

Liebmann, Matthew, T. J. Ferguson, and Robert W. Preucel. 2005. Pueblo Settlement, Architecture, and Social Change in the Pueblo Revolt Era, A.D. 1680–1696. *Journal of Field Archaeology* 30:1–16.

Nicholas, George. 2008. Native Peoples and Archaeology. In *Encyclopedia of Archaeology*, vol. 3, edited by Deborah M. Pearsall, pp. 1660–1669. Academic Press, New York.

Norris, Jim. 2000. *After "The Year Eighty": The Demise of Franciscan Power in Spanish New Mexico*. University of New Mexico Press, Albuquerque.

Ortiz, Alfonso. 1969. *The Tewa World: Space, Time, Being and Becoming in a Pueblo Society*. University of Chicago Press, Chicago.

Preucel, Robert W. 2000. Living on the Mesa: Hanat Kotyiti, A Post-Revolt Cochiti Community in the Northern Rio Grande. *Expedition* 42:8–17.

Preucel, Robert W. 2006. *Archaeological Semiotics*. Blackwell, Oxford.

Preucel, Robert W., Loa P. Traxler, and Michael V. Wilcox. 2002. "Now the God of the Spaniards Is Dead": Ethnogenesis and Community Formation in the Aftermath of the Pueblo Revolt of 1680. In *Traditions, Transitions and Technologies: Themes in Southwestern Archaeology*, edited by Sarah H. Schlanger, pp. 71–93. University Press of Colorado, Boulder.

Sando, Joe S. 2005. The Pueblo Revolt. In *Po'Pay: Leader of the First American Revolution*, edited by J. S. Sando and H. Agoyo, pp. 5–53. Clear Light Press, Santa Fe, New Mexico.

Simmons, Marc. 1991. *The Last Conquistador: Juan de Oñate and the Settling of the Far Southwest*. University of Oklahoma Press, Norman.

Vierra, Bradley. 2003. *A Current Assessment of the Nake'muu Monitoring Program*. Cultural Resource Survey Report No. 188. Los Alamos National Laboratory, Los Alamos, New Mexico.

Vierra, Bradley, Larry Nordby, and Gerald Martinez. 2003. Nake'muu: Village at the Edge. In *Anasazi Archaeology at the Millennium: Proceedings of the Sixth Occasional Anasazi Symposium*, edited by Paul S. Reed, pp. 137–144. Center for Desert Archaeology, Tucson, Arizona.

Watkins, Joe. 2000. *Indigenous Archaeology: American Indian Values and Scientific Practice*. AltaMira Press, Walnut Creek, California.

Weigle, Marta, and Peter White. 2003. *The Lore of New Mexico*. University of New Mexico Press, Albuquerque.

Wilcox, Michael V. 2009. *The Pueblo Revolt and the Mythology of Conquest: An Indigenous Archaeology of Contact*. University of California Press, Berkeley.

7

Apache, Tiwa, and Back Again
Ethnic Shifting in the American Southwest

Severin Fowles and B. Sunday Eiselt

As with so many late nineteenth-century photographs of Indigenous people in the colonized world, we do not know the names of the individuals in figure 7.1. According to the National Anthropological Archives (NAA) of the Smithsonian Institution, where the photographs are now stored, each was taken in 1877 and each is affiliated with the Northern Tiwa–speaking community of Taos Pueblo in New Mexico. "Taos" has even been written along the bottom of each image. They appear to have been captured in rapid succession; at least, one is labeled "5th" and the other "6th," and the walls in the backgrounds of the images are identical, even down to the shadows. Moreover, the breastfeeding mother on the left bears an uncanny facial similarity to the girl on the right. One can reasonably assume, then, that all three individuals are related: mother, infant, and adolescent daughter.

Those who are familiar with the cultural traditions of the American Southwest, however, will immediately observe that something is awry. The hairstyles may be Puebloan: the adolescent girl, in particular, is done up in butterfly hair whorls, signifying that she has reached puberty and is a maiden of marriageable age. But the hide garments with extensive fringe, the beadwork, the jewelry—these strongly draw our thoughts toward the cultural traditions of the Plains. Has there been a mistake in the documentation? Or did the people of Taos really dress in so "non-Pueblo" a fashion during the nineteenth century, as compared to their contemporaries to the south and west, as well as to their descendants at the pueblo today?

A second print of figure 7.1b found in the NAA clarifies the matter. Its file attributes the photograph to Orloff R. Westmann and also assigns it an earlier date. The image's caption reads, "Girl Wearing Fringed Buckskin Dress, Beaded Buckskin Yoke and Ornaments 30 SEP 1871."

Apache, Tiwa, and Back Again

Figure 7.1 (a) "Woman and Child Near Adobe Wall, Both in Native Dress, One with Peace Medal, One with Ornaments 1877." National Anthropological Archives, Smithsonian Institution (BAE GN 01936 06330400); (b) "Girl in Native Dress with Ornaments Near Adobe Wall 1877." National Anthropological Archives, Smithsonian Institution (BAE GN 01934 06330200).

Moreover, the affiliated culture is no longer listed as Taos Pueblo but rather as Jicarilla Apache. And so the underlying story begins to emerge.

Westmann was a German immigrant and a photographer who, in 1871, was hired by William Blackmore, an Englishman, to accompany him to Taos Pueblo and capture a series of images of the "natives" (Taylor 1999:327). (These images later appeared in William Henry Jackson's 1877 *Catalogue of Photographs of Indians*, hence the misleading dates in the image captions of figure 7.1.) Blackmore and Westmann's 1871 visit coincided with the San Geronimo feast day, which is held every year at Taos Pueblo on September 30 and is filled with food, ceremony, trade, and visits between family and friends. This was also a time when the Jicarilla Apache, who lived a relatively mobile lifestyle in the surrounding landscape, came to Taos for an extended stay. Camping just outside the pueblo, Jicarilla women gathered willow shoots and spent the days leading up to September 30 weaving baskets for exchange. On San Geronimo Day itself, it was not uncommon for Jicarilla men to participate in the relay races at dawn or for Jicarilla girls to join the dances in the plaza. Certainly, everyone ate well, delighted in the antics of the ritual clowns, and socialized. Feast days were not just times when old interethnic relationships were rekindled, however; they were also opportunities for new relationships to begin. The maiden photographed by Westmann in figure 7.1b may have been keenly aware of this. In her feast dress with beaded buckskin cape and elaborate shell jewelry, she came to Taos looking her best—anticipating, perhaps, that she would meet her future husband at the event. In fact, young Jicarilla maidens often wore their hair Pueblo style at intertribal festivities like San Geronimo Day for this very reason (Veronica Tiller, personal communication 2018).

In this chapter, we explore the deep history of exchange and collaboration between the Jicarilla Apache and the two Northern Tiwa–speaking pueblos, Taos and Picuris (figure 7.2). Our point is not simply that this relationship was a close one. Prior scholarship has ably documented this fact (see Eiselt 2012; Gunnerson 1974; Opler 1936, 1944; Tiller 1992). Here, we seek to advance a somewhat different argument: that the Jicarilla Apache and Northern Tiwa are best understood as a single people or, more precisely, as a composite cultural adaptation in which movements across the village/nomad or Pueblo/Apache divide were strategically facilitated. These movements, as we will see, were physical insofar as they involved Plains Apache groups coming to live in the Taos region and Northern Tiwa groups going to live on the Plains. But they are also linked to fundamental questions of social identity, as such movements sometimes involved the adoption of new ethnicities as much as new residences. Certainly, they had a strongly political aspect as well. This was famously the case when escape to the Plains was part of a strategy adopted by the Northern Tiwa to evade Spanish control. As we will suggest, such lateral lines of flight between Pueblo and non-Pueblo groups during the colonial period appear to be extensions of a deeper precolonial history in the region. In this sense, the mistaken identities of the woman and her daughters in figure 7.1 may not be so mistaken after all, for the boundaries between the Jicarilla and Tiwa were often intentionally blurred.

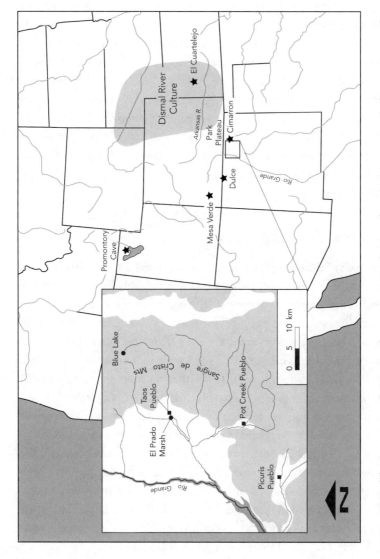

Figure 7.2 The locations of places and communities discussed in the chapter, including an inset of the Taos region.

There is, in other words, a rich history of Tiwa-Apache "shifting" that challenges archaeologists and historians to understand how ethnic groups develop in relation to one another—not just through trade, borrowing, or appropriation, as earlier ethnographic accounts suggested, but as social alternatives within a shared historical tradition over hundreds if not thousands of years. Drawing on archaeological and oral historical evidence, we entertain the possibility that regular interactions between the Tiwa and the Jicarilla may have commenced as early as the thirteenth century. We document how, by the eighteenth century, these interactions had resulted in a blended material expression shared by both the Jicarilla Apache on the Plains and the Tiwa in the Rio Grande valley. And we conclude with a consideration of how such ethnic shifting complicates the dominant philosophies of movement and becoming in the Indigenous Southwest.

JICARILLA-TIWA SOCIETY

Our analysis of the entanglement of Jicarilla Apache and Northern Tiwa identities takes its cue from repeated statements by Native commentators and their ethnographic chroniclers. The assertion that the Jicarilla and Northern Tiwa are "one people," for instance, was a recurrent theme during a recent gathering of tribal elders from the Jicarilla, Taos, and Picuris communities, convened to discuss their shared history. Individual attendees at that gathering who had either married across this ethnic divide, or whose parents or grandparents had done so, put forth their own family histories as implicit demonstrations. Indeed, a small but consistent level of Jicarilla and Northern Tiwa intermarriage goes back as far as we have written records in the region, and this pattern becomes all the more significant when we note that almost no intermarriage has been documented between Taos and Picuris, despite their proximity to one another and their shared language. The Jicarilla-Taos and Jicarilla-Picuris relationships seem always to have been more intimate and mutually constitutive than even the Taos-Picuris relationship.

But when tribal elders today speak of being "one people," it is clear that more is implied than just the movement of marriage partners back and forth. Many additional traditions, beliefs, and social organizations have been shared as well. The intertribal ceremonies at Taos Pueblo on

San Geronimo Day, for instance, are paralleled by the Jicarilla Goijiya gatherings, which involve very similar relay races (see Opler 1944), as well as dancing, feasting, and social exchanges. "It was no accident that the Jicarilla chose September 15th to celebrate Goijiya," adds Veronica Tiller (personal communication 2018): "Every year since the Jicarilla Apache were permanently settled on their northern NM reservation in 1887, they have celebrated Goijiya on September 15, two weeks prior to the San Geronimo Day. Two weeks was sufficient time to travel by horses and wagons from the Jicarilla Reservation, across the mountains and the Rio Grande, to Taos Pueblo for this special day that the Jicarilla attended for many centuries." Families from Taos and Picuris needed sufficient time to travel to Stone Lake and join in the Goijiya ceremonies as well, which many did on a regular basis. In fact, had Westmann traveled to photograph the Jicarilla after their removal to Dulce, he very well might have come home with photographs of visitors from Taos Pueblo, who would have been later misidentified in the archives as examples of Jicarilla Apache culture.

To be sure, tribal reflection on their shared historical experience as "one people" is itself an expression of deep-seated co-ethnic principles, evident in the intersecting narratives and practices of both groups. Like most Indigenous southwestern communities, the Jicarilla and Northern Tiwa make occasional reference to their emergence far to the north, but both also place greater emphasis on the local landscape features that mark their fundamental origin—as a people—in the Taos region. A great deal of Taos Pueblo's conceptual attention is directed toward Blue Lake, the stunning body of water that is the source of the community's principal river and is also the focus of the community's initiation ceremonies each August (see Bodine 1988). Situated high in the mountains to the east and at a far remove from the village, Blue Lake is in an area that, at least during the colonial period, was more closely associated with the Jicarilla people's upland adaptation (see Eiselt 2013). The Jicarilla, for their part, have traditionally anchored their cosmology in a spring located in the middle of El Prado marsh, a short distance west of Taos Pueblo. The spring is regarded as the heart of White Shell Woman, whose body extends out along the rivers and mountains of northern New Mexico to define the Jicarilla world (Eiselt 2009, 2012:153; Mooney 1898; Opler 1938:43). The center of the Jicarilla conceptual landscape, then, is located in the midst of what has been traditionally understood by anthropologists as the core Northern Tiwa territory. In this way, both Jicarilla and Taos Pueblo individuals historically had to travel into the lands of the other to visit the places that grounded their identities.

Jicarilla and Northern Tiwa cultures intersect at the level of social organization as well, notably in the shared importance of moieties. Pueblo moieties are best documented among the Tewa-speaking villages to the southwest of Taos, where they function as inherited ceremonial affiliations that facilitate community governance (rather than marriage, as in the classic anthropological understanding of moiety organization; see Ortiz 1969). But it is only due to the paucity of published ethnographic descriptions that Taos Pueblo is not regarded as its own wellspring of moiety expression. Indeed, recent revisionist studies now emphasize not only that dual organization is strongly present in the architecture, leadership, and ceremonial life of Taos Pueblo, but also that this pattern can be traced back to ancestral Northern Tiwa sites of the thirteenth century, well before moieties can be detected in the ancestral Tewa tradition (Fowles 2005, 2013).

It is significant, in this sense, that the Jicarilla also participate in a dual division. Whereas Taos is composed of northern and southern moieties, the Jicarilla are organized according to an east-west division between two bands: the Ollero, who traditionally dwelt in the mountainous territory of the northern Rio Grande region, and the Llanero, who traveled the Plains east of Taos and were more centrally adapted to bison hunting. (The Jicarilla also frequently refer to these bands as the White and Red clans, respectively, although they do not comprise "clans" in the strict anthropological sense.) In his discussion of the Ollero/Llanero division, Morris Opler points in particular to the annual Jicarilla footraces, which express moiety organization in a fashion that is remarkably similar to the Taos races. "The connections between this Jicarilla rite and Eastern Pueblo ritual are conspicuous," he writes.

> For the choosing of sides the two Jicarilla bands are utilized in place of the moieties of the Eastern Pueblos. The runners are dressed and painted in corrals which have the shape of kivas and which the Jicarilla freely compare to the Pueblo kiva. Before the race each side dances to the corral of its opponent carrying a tall standard

to which two ears of corn are tied. Without trying to enumerate all the Pueblo-like elements, it may be noted that this is the only Apache ceremony which has a calendrical touch, and that in the story of how the rite was obtained, it is affirmed that the Jicarilla, Taos, San Juan, and Picuris all were given the ceremony at the same time [Opler 1936:216].

The Jicarilla, in fact, maintain that the relay race was originally taught to them by the sun and moon, who were symbolically represented by a Taos and Jicarilla couple. Of course, most anthropological commentators have been inclined to simply view Jicarilla moieties as a recent borrowing from a much deeper Pueblo tradition (just as Northern Tiwa moieties were once regarded as a recent borrowing from a much deeper Tewa tradition). As we will argue shortly, however, there are good historical grounds for entertaining the possibility, directly expressed by Opler's consultants, that dual organization has a shared and quite early origin among *both* the Jicarilla and Northern Tiwa.

Historic similarities between these two groups seep down into many aspects of their material culture. Given the archaeological penchant for equating ceramic types with ethnic identities, it is perhaps especially significant that both Jicarilla potters and those at Taos and Picuris Pueblos took up the production of micaceous pottery at roughly the same time. Researchers continue to debate who taught whom (Eiselt 2006:337–341; see also Trabert et al. 2016), which at the very least points to the high levels of social coordination and mutually constitutive cultural exchange already present during the early colonial period.

Styles of dress and bodily decoration mark another point of historic convergence. Today, the members of Taos and Picuris tend to conform to a general Eastern Pueblo aesthetic whenever they are called upon to dress in traditional attire. Late nineteenth-century photographs, however, reveal much more enthusiasm for "Plains" styles shared with the Apache. Consider the appearance of Wa-So-To-Ya-Min (Small Feathers of the Eagle), the Taos governor photographed in figure 7.3a. He wears the traditional blanket of a Pueblo leader, and he is conforming to the Pueblo tradition of holding a Lincoln cane to assert his office. But with his hair in braids and his fringed hide shirt, one might well have guessed this was an Apache rather than a Pueblo individual. Indeed, the beaded

Figure 7.3. (a) "Portrait (Front) of Wa-So-To-Ya-Min (Small Feathers of the Eagle). Spanish Name, Juan Jesus Leo; in Native Dress with Shell Gorget? 1877," by Charles Milton Bell. National Anthropological Archives, Smithsonian Institution (BAE GN 01922 06328700); (b) "Portrait of Chief Jose Martine in Native Dress with Blanket n.d." National Anthropological Archives, Smithsonian Institution (Photo Lot 24 SPC Sw Apache NM ACC 20263 Cat 129781 #9–49 02040000).

choker and shell gorget or medallion hanging from his neck look effectively identical to those worn by the Jicarilla woman in figure 7.1a. As a further comparison, consider the contemporaneous appearance of the Jicarilla Apache chief Jose Martine (figure 7.3b). The overall aesthetic is very similar. In fact, if there is an ethnic ambiguity surrounding Wa-So-To-Ya-Min due to his braids and fringe, we might locate an equivalent ambiguity surrounding Chief Martine due to his Pueblo-style blanket.

The first serious ethnographic descriptions of both the Jicarilla and the Northern Tiwa came a generation or two after these early photographs. We have already noted Opler's assessment that the Jicarilla were significantly "Pueblo-ized." Parallel assessments of Taos were also frequently made. Here is how Elsie Clews Parsons described the pueblo in the 1930s:

> In Taos culture there are many Apache-Plains traits or characters . . . : Bilateral descent and clanlessness; exclusion of women from the ceremonial life; marked separations of women from warriors; comparatively simple ceremonialism; comparatively indifferent craftsmanship; buffalo hunting; details in dress and headdress of men and women; aggressive, self-assertive, comparatively individualistic temper or character. In physical characteristics also Taos people are said to approximate Plains type. Indeed, except for their houses, Taos people might well pass for Indians of the Plains [Parsons 1936:3].

Note that Parsons not only made reference to organizational and stylistic elements in this statement, she also included personality and even phenotypic parallels. Others made similar observations. A decade earlier, Edward Curtis (1926:1) had written about his arrival at Taos Pueblo this way: "A horseman approaches, swathed in a white cotton sheet. . . . Another plainsman? . . . Soon the road is dotted with figures similarly garbed, and nearly all, especially the men, have that typical Plains physiognomy. One realizes that this nevertheless is the Taos type, but harbors a feeling that there must be a group of tipis behind yonder clump of willows down by the stream." One should not put too much emphasis on the racial assessments of early ethnographers—although, as a widely traveled photographer of Native America, Curtis's impressions are perhaps worth special contemplation.

Suffice it to say that Jicarilla society and Northern Tiwa society developed alongside and in creative dialogue with one another during the colonial period. And in their efforts to account for this special history of cultural exchange, past scholarship has focused on two primary stimuli.

The first is economic. The Pueblo communities of the Rio Grande valley, after about AD 1300, were uniformly organized into large villages pursuing an agricultural way of life that required a relatively high degree of sedentism, at least for the majority of the workforce during most of the year. Taos and Picuris placed somewhat greater emphasis on hunting than their Pueblo neighbors to the south, but even they would have significantly benefitted, it is argued, from trade relationships with more nomadic groups who regularly procured resources from faraway locations—particularly bison hides, fat, salt, and meat from the southern

Plains to the east. The nomads of the Plains, for their part, needed the carbohydrates in Pueblo corn and were further attracted by the cotton blankets, ceramics, obsidian, and turquoise of the Rio Grande villages (Spielmann 1991). In this model, the close relationships between Pueblo villages and bison nomads (Athapaskan or otherwise) could have developed only at the end of the precolonial period, following the shift toward large villages, agricultural overproduction, and centralized markets in the Rio Grande valley.

In her detailed history of the Jicarilla, Dolores Gunnerson (1974:25–26) further suggests that Apache trade would have rapidly increased as soon as Athapaskan bands began to take up part-time residence in the mountainous territories surrounding Pueblo villages, a development she dates to approximately 1525 in the Rio Grande valley and to right around 1542 in the Western Pueblo region. By occupying the mountains, the Apache would have cut off the villagers' access to hunting territories, argued Gunnerson, rendering the Pueblos yet more dependent on the Apache for meat and hides. Combined with the continued contributions of bison meat from the Plains, this may have effectively permitted the Apache to corner the market. Whether or not this was the case, extended winter sojourns by Apache visitors at the edges of Pueblo villages clearly provided ample time for cultural exchange, just as the need to secure trusted trade partners presumably served as the rationale for the exchange of marriage partners.

The second stimulus driving Apache-Pueblo relations was militaristic. The high mobility and hunting prowess of the intrepid Athapaskan nomads seem to have led at least some of the precolonial Pueblos to regard them with hesitation and an underlying distrust. The Teyas or Apache "knew the [Pueblo] people in the settlements, and were friendly with them, and they went there to spend the winter under the wings of the settlements," wrote Pedro de Castañeda in his account of the Coronado expedition. But, he added, "the inhabitants do not dare to let them come inside, because they cannot trust them" (Winship 1896:524). In fact, Castañeda reports that the Pueblos even posted sentinels to keep watch over their potentially unruly guests. But this "ambivalent attitude," as Gunnerson (1974:26) put it, seems to have notably improved during the colonial period, as many Pueblos came to rely on the Apache for key military assistance against the Spanish, the Comanche, and other rising threats. In a recent conversation about such alliances, Richard Mermejo, the former Picuris governor and war chief, explained that the Jicarilla served as dependable lookouts for the village, strategically camping in the surrounding hills as a kind of advance warning system and a reserve of allied warriors. This was the military equivalent to economic mutualism, and it was dramatically on show in what Sunday Eiselt (2012:100) encourages us to think of as the "Pueblo-Athapaskan Revolt of 1680." Indeed, it is not only that the Apache came to the aid of the Pueblos in their great struggle against the Spanish; the Pueblos also fought on behalf of the Apache, who had, by that time, suffered from decades of Spanish slave raiding and had their own reasons for ousting the colonizers. In fact, one of the key demands made by the Pueblo leaders of the revolt to Governor Otermín involved the release of all Apache prisoners.

One can identify, then, a strong tradition of Apache-Pueblo alliance and exchange extending right through the colonial Southwest. But this tradition ran particularly deep in the Taos region, where the Jicarilla-Tiwa relationship involved more than just the movement of trade items and military service—more, even, than the movement of marriage partners back and forth between communities. Time and again, whole social groups moved across this ethnic divide.

The best known of these shifts took place during the colonial period, when many Tiwa families from both Taos and Picuris responded to the Spanish invasion by taking flight to the Plains, where they effectively "became" Apache (or "Dismal River Aspect" peoples, in archaeological terminology; see Beck and Trabert 2014). Nearly everyone at Taos Pueblo, for instance, traveled east over the Sangre de Cristos in 1664 to join the Cuartelejo Apache for an extended stay. Some, presumably, never returned. In 1696, in the wake of Diego de Vargas's reconquest of New Mexico, many at both Taos and Picuris were reported to have up and left for the Plains (Thomas 1935:53–74). And in 1704, Picuris was effectively vacated for the same reason, leading Juan de Ulibarri on an expedition out to the Apachean settlements in Cuartelejo to eventually retrieve and resettle at least some of these colonial defectors. As the eighteenth century unfolded, the direction of these movements reversed. Intensive Comanche raiding on the southern Plains led large numbers of Jicarilla Apache to settle in Taos, some taking up residence in the pueblos while others retained a more mobile lifestyle in the nearby mountains.

A DEEP HISTORY OF TIWA-APACHE ETHNIC SHIFTING

But what is the source of this tradition of ethnic exchange? How far back does it go? Is it purely a response to the Spanish invasion and to new needs for collaboration in opposition to a colonial society that sought to subjugate both Tiwa and Apache? Or might there be a deeper precolonial history to such Tiwa-Apache shifting that was adapted and redeployed in response to changing political fortunes?

This issue, of course, is embedded within a much larger debate over the timing of the migration of Athapaskan-speaking groups south into the Pueblo world. Opinion has varied a great deal. Back in the days of A. V. Kidder, it was thought that the Athapaskan or Ancestral Apache arrival took place early on, perhaps three centuries before Spanish colonialism. Many—Kidder among them—went so far as to speculate that Apache raiding was responsible for the demise of Mesa Verde and other Ancestral Pueblo centers. During the second half of the century, however, these sorts of arguments were widely discredited as consensus settled around a model of late arrival. The Apache, in the eyes of most late twentieth-century archaeologists, were assumed to have arrived in the Southwest just before the Spanish. Drawing on an anonymous Pueblo statement made via translators during Coronado's expedition and only chronicled twenty years later, Gunnerson (1974:21) concludes that the Apache did not arrive in New Mexico until 1525, at which point they tried but failed to conquer the Pueblos and then quickly pursued economic collaboration instead. Influential though they were to the unfolding of the colonial Southwest, then, the Apache came to be viewed as largely irrelevant to accounts of precolonial times.

Over the past decade, this consensus has begun to change once again as a spate of new research pushes back our estimates of Athapaskan entry. Some of the site interpretations involved in this reappraisal remain contentious. However, there is a growing willingness to entertain the possibility that Athapaskan migrants may have traveled along a plurality of routes and that some of these migrants may have arrived in the Southwest much earlier than the Spanish (see Eiselt 2012; Seymour 2012; Seymour, ed. 2012). New research on the Promontory Cave assemblage in Utah is playing a particularly significant role in this shift of opinion, with well-dated moccasin assemblages now suggesting the presence of intrusive Athapaskan traditions of northern derivation during the thirteenth century, if not earlier (Ives 2014; Ives et al. 2014). If indeed Ancestral Apache communities had arrived in Utah by this time, we are prompted not only to imagine routes through the Rocky Mountains and Great Basin alongside the more widely accepted western Plains and Front Range migration pathways; we are also prompted to reevaluate the role of Apache groups within the precolonial history of the northern Southwest, particularly in frontier settings like Taos.

Located at the southern end of the Rocky Mountains (locally referred to as the Sangre de Cristo Mountains), Taos was likely among the very earliest sites of Pueblo encounters with Athapaskan migrants traveling south along either a mountainous or a Front Range route. Moreover, the two major Northern Tiwa villages that survived into the Pueblo IV period were both positioned near major mountain passes connecting the buffalo plains of the east to the centers of agricultural production to the south and west. Spanish commentaries during the eighteenth century went so far as to describe the Taos region as the Apaches' gateway into the Pueblo world. Based purely on geography, then, we would expect the Northern Tiwa to have a longer history of interaction with the Apache than perhaps any other Pueblo group.

Limited evidence from neighboring regions supports this possibility. Looking just to the north of Taos, research along Colorado's Front Range is now documenting the presence of ancestral Athapaskan sites well prior to the fifteenth century (Gilmore and Larmore 2012; see also Hill and Trabert 2018). And in the Cimarron region of New Mexico, just over the mountains from Taos, plausibly Apache tipi hearths have produced radiocarbon dates in the fourteenth century (Winter 1988:60). Arguably, this could be taken as a terminus ante quem for at least the occasional encounter between Athapaskans and Northern Tiwa groups.

Provocative hints of what might be an early Apache—or at least early "Plains"—presence have also been found in the core Taos region itself. At the thirteenth- and early fourteenth-century site of T'aitöna (Pot Creek Pueblo), for instance, excavations have produced an array of Plains artifacts fashioned from nonlocal materials (figure 7.4). Beveled "diamond knives," "turkey tail" bifaces, large snub-nosed scrapers, serrated bone fleshers, bison humerus-head abraders, a red stone elbow pipe—all

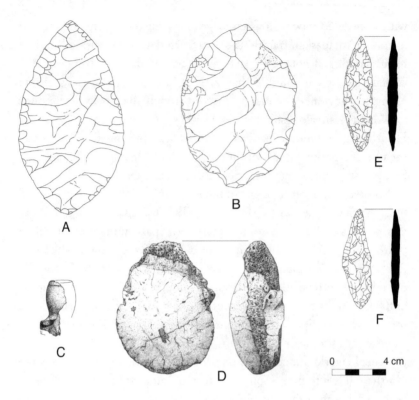

Figure 7.4 Plains-style artifacts from the ancestral Northern Tiwa village of T'aitöna (Pot Creek Pueblo).

these objects point to a transfer of technologies from Upper Republican and Panhandle cultures into the Taos region sometime around AD 1300 (Fowles 2018). Osteological research by Catrina Whitley (2011), in fact, may have demonstrated the presence of early non-Puebloan women by the end of the thirteenth century. As part of the preparation for the reburial of the site's human remains, Whitley identified two morphologically distinct populations of women at T'aitöna: one with the skeletal markers of long periods spent grinding corn and another without such markers. The latter are plausibly women who moved to Taos from the Rocky Mountains or Plains to join the growing Pueblo community.

In fact, there is no point during the past millennium when Taos archaeology does not reflect the creative entwining of Plains and Pueblo traditions. The earliest part-time farmers of the Developmental period

Apache, Tiwa, and Back Again

(locally, AD 950–1200), for instance, produced small numbers of Kwahe'e Black-on-white jars that look similar to contemporaneous Chaco vessels and betray a strong Ancestral Pueblo heritage. But they also produced plenty of unpainted jars with herringbone incised motifs and neck banding that have no Pueblo antecedents and instead link early Taos pottery to that of Cimarron and Trinidad, if not also to southern Plains ceramic traditions more generally (Fowles 2004; figure 7.5). Early Sopris phase communities at the start of the ninth century, for instance, are now known to have locally produced their own versions of "Taos Incised" pottery, while also importing vessels from the Taos region itself (see also Mitchell 1997). This evidence suggests an earlier Developmental period occupation of the Taos region that is yet to be found. More central to the

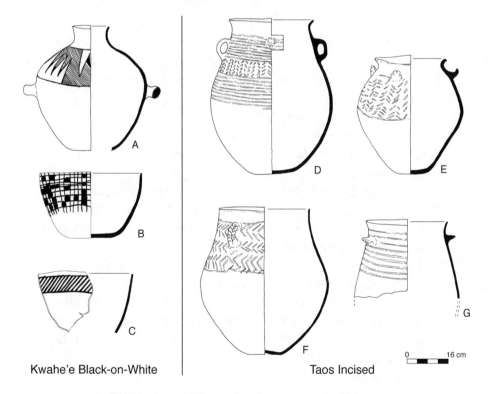

Figure 7.5 Valdez phase (AD 950–1200) pottery of the Taos region displaying a mixture of Pueblo-style black-on-white vessels (A–C) and Plains-influenced incised vessels (D–G).

Figure 7.6 Micaceous pottery of the Jicarilla and Northern Tiwa traditions. *Left*: Therese Tohtsoni-Prudencio (Picuris); *middle*: Virginia Romero (Taos); and *right*: Shelden Nunez-Velarde (Jicarilla). Image by Sunday Eiselt.

question at hand, however, it also establishes that the history of movements and cultural exchanges back and forth across the Sangre de Cristo Mountains—between "Pueblo" and "Plains" groups—predates Spanish colonialism by some eight hundred years.

This new evidence of a deep history of interregional ceramic exchange, which is now placing the source of the earliest incised pottery into question, is paralleled by similarly revisionist accounts of the origin of micaceous pottery (figure 7.6). Early interpretations typically assumed that ceramics (along with most other cultural innovations) first emerged among Pueblo communities and were only secondarily adopted by Athapaskan groups after their arrival in the Southwest. Opler (1938, 1944, 1971), for instance, explicitly proposed that Taos Pueblo taught pottery making to the Jicarilla. Based on his early excavations at Picuris Pueblo in 1965, Herb Dick (1990) also concluded that Picuris potters have been producing Peñasco Micaceous since AD 1600, just before what was then the accepted beginning date for Jicarilla ceramics. More recent research, however, is mounting a challenge to this Pueblo-centric model of the micaceous pottery tradition.

Indeed, studies in the Athapaskan migration corridor are now demonstrating a clear tradition of proto-Apache pottery production at least as early as the Dismal River Culture in Colorado (Trabert et al. 2016) and perhaps as far back as the Promontory Culture of thirteenth-century

Utah (Gabriel Yaniki, personal communication 2017; see also Ives et al. 2014). Athapaskan pottery making, in other words, may predate these peoples' arrival in the American Southwest, a possibility that emboldens the findings of James and Dolores Gunnerson (Gunnerson and Gunnerson 1970; Gunnerson 1969:37) in northeastern New Mexico, where they found evidence that the Jicarilla were actively producing Ocate Micaceous by 1600 at the latest. Moreover, reevaluations of excavated materials at both Taos and Picuris have suggested that Northern Tiwa production of micaceous pottery may be somewhat later than previously thought. Dick (1990:6), for instance, eventually revised his earlier position, suggesting that although Peñasco Micaceous and Vadito Micaceous (the two Picuris-produced types of micaceous pottery) may have originated as early as 1650, they "probably came into prominence about 1706 when a number of Picuris were returned from the eastern Plains by the Spanish." Reevaluation of the Taos Refuse Mound III deposits also suggested to Bart Olinger and Anne Woosley (1989; see also Woosley and Olinger 1990) that locally produced Taos Micaceous may not appear in the archaeological record until the early 1700s, thus dating to a time when the Jicarilla were actively settling the northern Rio Grande to escape Comanche raiding on the Plains.

Of course, the presence of only minor technical differences in lip form and surface finish often frustrate attempts to use Jicarilla, Taos, and Picuris vessels as ethnic markers, so the question of "who made what" at this or that site will no doubt continue to be debated. Women from each community even exploited the same mountain clay sources, leading to complex and overlapping geochemical signatures for ceramic types that are difficult to disentangle at the regional scale (Eiselt 2012). But it is precisely this interethnic convergence of pottery styles and resources that we regard as the more important point. Like the incised pottery tradition before it, micaceous pottery serves as a material signature of the continued movement of people, ideas, and material culture across the Pueblo-Plains divide.

How far back might the Apache have participated in this interregional history of cultural exchange? Again, until recently, the answer would have been, "Not much." Rather than a sign of early Athapaskans, for instance, the Plains-style artifacts at T'aitöna might be linked to, say, the Antelope Creek focus of the Texas Panhandle region (as defined by Lintz 1986) and, by virtue of this, to Caddoan traditions. Moreover, as Habicht-Mauche et al. (2018) have suggested, the provocative early evidence of Taos Incised pottery on the Park Plateau might be interpreted as a product of the mixing of early migrants from the upper San Juan Basin with local Plains Woodland groups who had been in the region long before the Athapaskan entry. To be sure, the Apache were neither the only nor the earliest group to engage in cultural exchanges between the Pueblo and Plains regions. Nevertheless, as archaeologists continue to push back the timing of the Athapaskan migrations, it becomes increasingly plausible that their participation in these exchanges is of greater rather than lesser antiquity.

STORIES OF SHARED HERITAGE

From our perspective, the most compelling reason for exploring this possibility stems from the way it dovetails with repeated Indigenous accounts of the shared Tiwa-Jicarilla history of the Taos region. Consider the narratives recorded at Taos Pueblo by Matilda Coxe Stevenson in 1906 (Fowles 2004, 2013). During that research, Stevenson learned that Taos people, like the neighboring Tewa, recounted their history as a coming together of Summer People and Winter People. But quite *unlike* the Tewa, the Summer People of Taos were presented as Pueblo-oriented farmers from the south while the Winter People were Apache-speaking hunters from the north. The narratives themselves are complex, and they acknowledge the historically contingent manner in which other groups, beyond these two core peoples, migrated in to join the growing ancestral Taos world. In fact, this historical complexity continued to be present in the social organization of twentieth-century Taos. Stevenson learned, for instance, that Taos individuals inherited clanlike identities from their fathers and that it was one's membership in these corporate kin groups—rather than in the kivas per se—that located individuals within the socioceremonial sphere.

Table 7.1 presents a list of the various kin groups that were active at the time of Stevenson's research, most of which are presumably still active at Taos today. Each group had its own migration history, and each had its own ceremonial responsibilities. Each also appears to have had special songs and prayers in its ancestral language, which partly explains why

Table 7.1 Languages Spoken by the Ancestors of the Taos Pueblo Community, as Related to Stevenson

Kiva	People Name	Language Spoken at Emergence
Big Earring	Abalone Shell	Keresan (Santo Domingo dialect)?
Big Earring	Corn	Keresan (Santo Domingo dialect)
Big Earring	Small White Shell Bead	Keresan (Santo Domingo dialect)
Big Earring	Turkey Plume of Kwathlowúna	Keresan (Santo Domingo dialect)
Day	Sun	Jicarilla Apache
Day	Day	Jicarilla Apache
Day	Very Small Olivella Shell	Jicarilla Apache
Knife	Stone Knife	Jicarilla Apache "with a slight difference"
Knife	Ratlike Animal	Tiwa (Taos variant)
Knife	Elk	Jicarilla Apache "with a slight difference"
Water	Water	Tiwa (Taos variant)
Water	Corncob	Tiwa (Taos variant)
Water	Red Shell	Apache
Water	Wolf	Tiwa (Taos variant)
Feather	Golden Warbler	Tiwa (Taos variant)
Feather	Macaw or Parrot	Tiwa (Taos variant)
Feather	Eagle	Tiwa (Taos variant)
Old Axe	"Named for the Creator"	Apache "but . . . only a very, very little like the Jicarilla Apache"
Old Axe	White Shell	Apache "but . . . only a very, very little like the Jicarilla Apache"
Old Axe	Green Leaf	Apache "but . . . only a very, very little like the Jicarilla Apache"

Source: Stevenson 1906–1910:File 3.1.

Stevenson's informants could relate quite specific linguistic affiliations for each group's ancestors. Note that more than half of the named kin groups at Taos in 1906 actually descended from Apache-speaking ancestors (Fowles 2018). Considered alongside the archaeological evidence, it seems entirely reasonable to conclude that local historical knowledge is here providing quite a faithful accounting of a past in which it was not at all uncommon for Apache families to migrate to Taos, adopt the lingua franca, and become "Northern Tiwa" as a result.

Suffice it to say that we seem to be looking at societies that co-emerged through the repeated movements of individuals and families back and forth. Occasionally, one even finds Indigenous commentary on how this process of ethnic shifting might have unfolded. Consider the following Jicarilla Apache story relating what used to happen when groups broke away and moved to the Pueblo region. First, "the children would begin playing games," the narrator observes. Then, "the children of one group would say, 'Let's play we are Pueblo people.' . . . The grownups paid no attention at first, but the children kept on using this strange language and carrying on in these strange ways. Soon everyone began to know this manner of talking and these ways, and before long this was the way everybody talked and acted" (Opler 1938:47). We might imagine that this story is specifically referring to the assimilation of Jicarilla groups into Taos society.

Given this historical backdrop, it should come as little surprise that the Jicarilla and Tiwa appear prominently in each other's creation narratives. Jicarilla stories feature repeated interethnic exchanges that situate their ties with Taos Pueblo in a mythical past. In some versions, for instance, the sun and moon are portrayed as a Taos boy and a Jicarilla girl who are married by the Holy Ones to ensure that they always work together, helping each other "shine and give light" (Opler 1938:22). Other versions introduce the story of two wandering girls who escape the underworld and become pregnant by the sun and moon. The act of conception with celestial beings transforms the girls into White Shell Woman and White Painted Woman, who soon give birth to the twin culture heroes, Killer-of-the-Enemies and Child-of-the-Water. The twins acquire powers from their father, the sun, to vanquish monsters that have been menacing their Tiwa neighbors. The saga of Killer-of-the-Enemies and his brother, Child-of-the-Water, forms a major part of the Jicarilla creation narrative, interweaving themes of mobility, alliance, and intermarriage between the Jicarilla and the Tiwa, as well as of the Jicarillas' heroic adventures to establish the northern Río Grande as a shared Apache-Pueblo space.

Creation narratives at Taos Pueblo are, if anything, even more inclusive in their treatment of the Jicarilla. As we have seen, many of the Taos kin groups are said to have actually spoken Apache at the time of emergence. But the order of emergence is equally telling. The most elaborate variant of the Taos creation narrative specifies, for instance, that it was the Apache who first received permission to ascend to the upper world. The Winter People—who spoke Apache at the time of emergence and subsequently adopted Tiwa when they joined Taos Pueblo—were the next Native group in line. And only then, after the Athapaskan emergence was complete, did the creator permit the Tiwa-speaking Water and Feather Peoples to make their ascent (Stevenson 1906–1910:File 2:19).

Other variants further underscore the centrality of the Apache to the Tiwa historical imaginary. Consultants at Taos Pueblo told Jean Jeançon (1930:7) that the first people sent to stabilize the upper world—prior to emergence—included one Taos and one Apache man. About the same time, Curtis (1926:28–29) was told that after their emergence far to the north in Colorado, the Taos people followed a culture hero know as Tai-faína (Person Red-That)[1] on a series of migrations: "In groups corresponding to the present ceremonial societies they traveled in an easterly direction to the plains, where they turned southward to a large river which the present traditionalists believe to have been near Arkansas. They long roamed the plains before recrossing the mountains to become a sedentary tribe in their present habitat." There is not a single authoritative creation narrative among the Northern Tiwa, of course. Both Taos and Picuris have traditionally been pluralistic societies composed of kin/ceremonial groups with pasts that extend outward into many parts of the continent. In this way, different narratives reflect the different perspectives of the varied subgroups within Tiwa communities (Fowles 2018). But close relations between the Tiwa and Apache are a persistent theme, and the Taos oral history recorded by Curtis helps us understand why this is so. Crossing and recrossing the mountains between Plains and Pueblo regions, shifting from nomadism "to become a sedentary tribe" (as well as the reverse)—these were historical experiences shared by many "Tiwa" people over time, just as it was part of the historical experience of many "Jicarilla Apache" people.

CONCLUSION: ETHNIC SHIFTING AND INDIGENOUS PHILOSOPHIES OF MOVEMENT

How are we to think about this situation, then? And how might we relate the long interweaving of Jicarilla and Tiwa histories to the broader philosophies of movement that stand at the heart of the present volume?

As our Pueblo colleagues have repeatedly emphasized, movement is ontological insofar as ways of moving are ways of being. "Movement is a part of us . . . without movement, there is no life," explains Tessie Naranjo

(1995:25), whose writings have been foundational to much contemporary thought on movement and mobility in Southwest archaeology. The Jicarilla Apache philosopher Viola Cordova—who, incidentally, grew up in Taos—draws on Hopi traditions to expand this core idea. "What exists has motion," she writes. "What has no motion does not continue to exist.... Thus, for the Hopi at least, there are not 'things' but rather ... 'events': *being, peopleing, mountaining*, and so on" (Cordova 2007:117). Indeed, one finds this materially expressed in everything from dances in which the *katsina* are made present through the specific arm, head, or torso motions of the katsina dances to shrines in which much attention is given to the different roads that guide supplicants toward the center, thereby underscoring particular social identities through particular ways of moving (Fowles 2011).

Athapaskan identities are equally shaped by movement; here, however, the emphasis is more strongly on movement within a landscape that is saturated with historical referents. Rather than thinking "about" the landscape, many Athapaskans refer to the way their thoughts dwell "in" storied places (Basso 1996; Nelson 1993). The Jicarilla creation narrative, for instance, tells us that Killer-of-the-Enemies made the northern Rio Grande in the image of his mother, White Shell Woman, locating her heart in El Prado marsh. Major rivers required for long-life and naming ceremonies flowed within and from her heart, and the most powerful Hactcin spirits were placed in the mountains making up her spine, arms, and legs. Other Hactcin were sent into the plants, animals, and substances of nature to animate them and to represent their core essences or powers (Mooney 1898; Opler 1938). To move through such a landscape—as the highly mobile Jicarilla bands of the pre-reservation era did constantly—was to revisit, rehearse, and reaffirm the stories that grounded one's identity.

Generally speaking, creation narratives among the Indigenous groups of the Southwest are structured around two types of movements. The first is traditionally referred to as a process of emergence by which the ancestors traveled up from the lower world into the present world. In the Pueblo tradition, this journey often involves climbing an immense tree to access a hole in the sky; indeed, a theatrical expression of this is on display each fall when ritual clowns at both Taos and Picuris climb a pole made from a giant ponderosa pine tree to retrieve packages of food tied at its apex. The Jicarilla equivalent of this original migration to the upper world is invoked in the Growing Mountains Emergence Rite. Here, the ascent is aided by the creation of a great mountain that the Hactcin sing to life from a sandpainting. The growth of the mountain is interrupted by two wayward girls who have wandered to the top ahead of the others and caused the mountain to stop growing, leading the Hactcin to create a ladder from the web of a spider and four rays of the sun. The people climb this ladder to the place of emergence (Opler 1938:20). Emergence narratives of this sort fundamentally link upward motion to personhood. As Leslie Marmon Silko (1995:162) put it, "the Emergence was an emergence into a precise cultural identity" as much as it was a pathway into a new landscape. Let us call this the "vertical" logic of movement in the Indigenous Southwest.

We can contrast it with a "longitudinal" logic that governs a second type of movement: the post-emergence migrations of ethnic groups as they searched for the middle or center place. In most Pueblo traditions, these narratives involve a series of geographic relocations, each of which is envisioned as a step toward one's present home. Alfonso Ortiz's (1969:13–17) description of the twelve steps taken by the Ancestral Tewa during their travels from the northern place of emergence is perhaps the most precisely specified example. Northern Tiwa accounts of their post-emergence migrations are less systematic and more like Hopi migration narratives, insofar as each *t'aina* or "people group" followed its own distinctive path before gathering with the others at the center place (see Bernardini and Fowles 2011; Fowles 2018). The Jicarilla narrative offers yet another twist on this theme, describing the center place as a metaphorical heart that is reached by traveling the earth in an ever-shrinking spiral (Opler 1938:47). Nevertheless, the post-emergence histories of all Indigenous communities in the Southwest are similarly structured by movements that we refer to as "longitudinal" insofar as they involve migrations in a generally southern direction from a northern place of emergence (however circuitous those migrations might have been in their details). What draws both vertical and longitudinal movements together is their collective embrace of teleology. Both chart out routes of becoming that lead—by design—toward contemporary ethnic communities, grounding identities by portraying them as predestined endpoints.

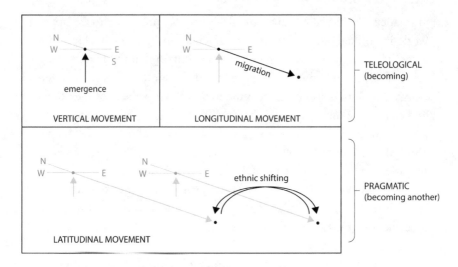

Figure 7.7 Three types of movement in the Indigenous Southwest: the "vertical" movement of emergence; the "longitudinal" movement of migrations; and the "latitudinal" movement of ethnic shifting.

The ethnic shifts we have highlighted in this chapter, however, are entirely distinct from the formal logics of movement expressed in both the classic emergence and migration narratives (figure 7.7). Indeed, there is nothing teleological or preordained about the back-and-forth demographic exchange between Northern Tiwa and Apache communities. Let us call this other type of movement "latitudinal," then, because it literally involved (in our case study, at least) an east-west set of exchanges between the southern Plains and the northern Rio Grande valley, but also because, at a conceptual level, it runs against the grain of formal creation narratives. Here, the underlying logic does not adhere to a telos of becoming at all. Rather, what we seem to encounter is a much more pragmatic set of historical responses to shifting political and environmental exigencies.

Many other examples of such "latitudinal" movements are likely to be found in the margins of Spanish colonial documents and Indigenous oral histories. One might look, for example, to the Tewa flight west to settle among the Hopi following Vargas's reconquest or to the Hopi tradition of sending families out to join the Navajo during times of hardship, both of which involved strategic shifts in ethnic identities. Our argument, however, is that such alternative movements are neither limited to the recent past nor solely a response to the violence of colonialism. Ethnic shifting, we suggest, was a vital aspect of Indigenous mobility throughout Southwest history. Alongside the story of ethnic "becoming"—which dominates archaeological no less than Indigenous accounts of the past—we are therefore obliged to seek out those more complicated histories whereby individuals and groups "became another," joining in with their neighbors and strategically shifting their ethnic identities in the process.

ACKNOWLEDGMENTS

The authors gratefully acknowledge the assistance of the Jicarilla historian Dr. Veronica Tiller. Dr. Tiller offered comments on an earlier draft of the manuscript and collaborated with the authors to host a roundtable of elders designed to explore the rich history of intertribal exchanges between the Jicarilla, Taos Pueblo, and Picuris Pueblo. This chapter was inspired by that gathering.

NOTES

1. *Tai-faína* likely refers to the same mythic figure later recorded as "Red Person" by Parsons (1936:112) based on her conversations at Taos Pueblo. Significantly, Parsons concluded that "Red Person . . . is to be identified with Red Boy of the Jicarilla Apache."

REFERENCES

Basso, Keith. 1996. *Wisdom Sits in Places: Landscape and Language Among the Western Apache*. University of New Mexico Press, Albuquerque.
Beck, Margaret E., and Sarah Trabert. 2014. Puebloan Occupation of the Scott County Pueblo, Western Kansas. *American Antiquity* 79:314–336.
Bernardini, Wesley, and Severin Fowles. 2011. Becoming Hopi, Becoming Tiwa: Two Pueblo Histories of Movement. In *Movement, Connectivity, and Landscape Change in the Ancient Southwest*, edited by Margaret Nelson and Colleen Strawhacker, pp. 253–274. University Press of Colorado, Boulder.
Bodine, John J. 1988. The Taos Blue Lake Ceremony. *American Indian Quarterly* 12(2):91–105.
Cordova, V. F., with Kathleen Dean Moore, Kurt Peters, Ted Jojola, and Amber Lacy (editors). 2007. *How It Is: The Native American Philosophy of V. F. Cordova*. University of Arizona Press, Tucson.

Curtis, Edward S. 1926. *The North American Indian*. Vol. 16. Plimpton Press, Norwood, Massachusetts.

Dick, Herbert W. 1990. Background Information for the Study of Micaceous Pottery. Handout at the Euro-American Ceramics Workshop. New Mexico Archaeological Council, Santa Fe.

Eiselt, B. Sunday. 2006. The Emergence of Jicarilla Apache Enclave Economy During the 19th Century in Northern New Mexico. PhD dissertation, University of Michigan, Ann Arbor.

Eiselt, B. Sunday. 2009. The Jicarilla Apaches and the Archaeology of the Taos Region. In *Beyond the Mountains: Papers in Honor of Paul R. Williams*, edited by Emily Brown, Karen Armstrong, David M. Brugge, and Carol Condie, pp. 57–69. Archaeological Society of New Mexico, Albuquerque.

Eiselt, B. Sunday. 2012. *Becoming White Clay: A History of Archaeology of Jicarilla Apache Enclavement*. University of Utah Press, Salt Lake City.

Eiselt, B. Sunday. 2013. Upland-Lowland Corridors and Historic Jicarilla Apache Settlement in the Northern Rio Grande. In *From Mountain Top to Valley Bottom: Understanding Past Land Use in the Northern Rio Grande Valley, New Mexico*, edited by Bradley Vierra, pp. 131–144. University of Utah Press, Salt Lake City.

Fowles, Severin M. 2004. The Making of Made People: The Prehistoric Evolution of Hierocracy Among the Northern Tiwa of New Mexico. PhD dissertation, University of Michigan, Ann Arbor.

Fowles, Severin M. 2005. Historical Contingency and the Prehistoric Foundations of Moiety Organization Among the Eastern Pueblos. *Journal of Anthropological Research* 61(1):25–52.

Fowles, Severin M. 2011. Movement and the Unsettling of the Pueblos. In *Rethinking Anthropological Perspectives on Migration*, edited by Graciela S. Cabana and Jeffery S. Clark, pp. 45–67. University Press of Florida, Gainesville.

Fowles, Severin M. 2013. *An Archaeology of Doings: Secularism and the Study of Pueblo Religion*. School for Advanced Research, Santa Fe, New Mexico.

Fowles, Severin M. 2018. Taos Social History: A Rhizomatic Account. In *Puebloan Societies: Homology and Heterogeneity in Time and Space*, edited by Peter Whiteley, pp. 75–102. School for Advanced Research, Santa Fe, New Mexico.

Gilmore, K. P., and S. Larmore. 2012. Looking for Lovitt in All the Wrong Places: Migration Models and the Athapaskan Diaspora as Viewed from Eastern Colorado. In *From the Land of Ever Winter to the American Southwest: Athapaskan Migrations, Mobility, and Ethnogenesis*, edited by Deni J. Seymour, pp. 37–77. University of Utah Press, Salt Lake City.

Gunnerson, Dolores. 1974. *The Jicarilla Apaches*. Northern Illinois University Press, DeKalb.

Gunnerson, James H. 1969. Apache Archaeology in Northeastern New Mexico. *American Antiquity* 34:23–39.

Gunnerson, James H., and Dolores A. Gunnerson. 1970. Evidence of Apaches at Pecos. *El Palacio* 76(3):1–6.
Habicht-Mauche, Judith A., Jun Ueno Sunseri, and Steven Mack. 2018. Early Dates for Taos Gray Pottery from the Southern Park Plateau, New Mexico and its Implications for Northern Tiwa Origins and Identity. Paper presented at the 2018 Southwest Symposium, Denver.
Hill, Matthew, and Sarah Trabert. 2018. Reconsidering the Dismal River Aspect: A Review of Current Evidence for an Apachean (Ndee) Cultural Affiliation. *Plains Anthropologist*. Electronic document, https://doi.org/10.1080/00320447.2018.1435606.
Ives, John W. 2014. Resolving the Promontory Culture Enigma. In *Archaeology in the Great Basin and Southwest: Papers in Honor of Don D. Fowler*, edited by Nancy J. Parezo and Joel C. Janetski, pp. 149–162. University of Utah Press, Salt Lake City.
Ives, John W., Joel C. Janetski, Duane Froese, Fiona Brock, and Christopher Bronk Ramsey. 2014. A High Resolution Chronology for Steward's Promontory Culture Collections, Promontory Point, Utah. *American Antiquity* 79(4):616–637.
Jeançon, Jean Allard. 1930. Taos Notes. *El Palacio* 18(1–4):3–11.
Lintz, Christopher. 1986. The Historical Development of a Culture Complex: The Basis for Understanding Architectural Misconceptions of the Antelope Creek Focus. *Plains Anthropologist* 31(114):111–128.
Mitchell, Mark. 1997. Interregional Perspectives on the Sopris Phase: An Examination of Prehistoric Frontiers in Southeastern Colorado and Northeastern New Mexico. MA thesis, Department of Anthropology, University of Colorado, Denver.
Mooney, James. 1898. The Jicarilla Genesis. *American Anthropologist* 11(7):197–209.
Naranjo, Tessie. 1995. Thoughts on Migration by Santa Clara Pueblo. *Journal of Anthropological Archaeology* 14:247–250.
Nelson, Richard K. 1983. *Make Prayers to the Raven: A Koyukon View of the Northern Forest*. University of Chicago Press, Chicago.
Olinger, Bart, and Anne I. Woosley. 1989. Pottery Studies Using X-Ray Fluorescence, Part 4: The Pottery of Taos Pueblo. *Pottery Southwest* 16(1):1–8.
Opler, Morris Edward. 1936. A Summary of Jicarilla Apache Culture. *American Anthropologist* 38(2):202–223.
Opler, Morris Edward. 1938. *Myths and Tales of the Jicarilla Apache Indians*. Memoirs of the American Folklore Society Vol. XXXI. American Folklore Society, New York.
Opler, Morris Edward. 1944. The Jicarilla Apache Ceremonial Relay Race and Its Relation to Pueblo Counterparts. *American Anthropologist* 46:75–97.
Opler, Morris E. 1971. Pots, Apache, and the Dismal River Culture Aspect. In *Apache Culture History and Ethnology*, edited by Keith H. Basso and Morris E.

Opler, pp. 29–33. Anthropological Papers of the University of Arizona, Vol. 21. University of Arizona Press, Tucson.

Ortiz, Alfonso. 1969. *The Tewa World*. Chicago University Press, Chicago.

Parsons, Elsie Clews. 1936. *Taos Pueblo*. George Banta, Menasha, Wisconsin.

Seymour, Deni J. 2012. Gateways for Athabascan Migration to the American Southwest. *Plains Anthropologist* 57(222):149–161.

Seymour, Deni J. (editor). 2012. *From the Land of Ever Winter to the American Southwest: Athapaskan Migrations, Mobility, and Ethnogenesis*. University of Utah Press, Salt Lake City.

Silko, Leslie Marmon. 1995. Interior and Exterior Landscapes: The Pueblo Migration Stories. In *Landscape in America*, edited by George F. Thompson, pp. 155–169. University of Texas Press, Austin.

Spielmann, Katherine. 1991. *Interdependence in the Prehistoric Southwest: An Ecological Analysis of Plains-Pueblo Interaction*. Garland, New York.

Stevenson, Matilda Coxe. 1906–1910. Unfinished manuscripts and notes on file. National Anthropological Archives, Washington, D.C.

Taylor, Colin. 1999. William Blackmore: A 19th Century Englishman's Contribution to American Indian Ethnology. In *Indians and Europe: An Interdisciplinary Collection of Essays*, edited by Christian F. Feest, pp. 321–336. University of Nebraska Press, Lincoln.

Thomas, Alfred B. 1935. *After Coronado: Spanish Exploration Northeast of New Mexico 1696–1727*. University of Oklahoma Press, Norman.

Tiller, Veronica. 1992. *The Jicarilla Apache Tribe: A History*. BowArrow, Albuquerque, New Mexico.

Trabert, Sarah, B. Sunday Eiselt, David V. Hill, Jeffrey Ferguson, and Margaret Beck. 2016. Following a Glittering Trail: Geo-chemical and Petrographic Characterization of Micaceous Sherds Recovered from Dismal River Sites. *American Antiquity* 81(2):364–374.

Whitley, Catrina Banks. 2009. Body Language: An Integrative Approach to the Bioarchaeology and Mortuary Practices of the Taos Valley. PhD dissertation, Department of Anthropology, Southern Methodist University, Dallas, Texas.

Winship, George Parker. 1896. The Coronado Expedition, 1540–1542. In *Bureau of Ethnology, Fourteenth Annual Report*, pp. 329–637. Government Printing Office, Washington, D.C.

Winter, Joe. 1988. *Stone Circles, Ancient Forts, and Other Antiquities of the Dry Cimarron Valley: A Study of the Cimarron Seco Indians*. Historic Preservation Division, Santa Fe, New Mexico.

Woosley, Anne I., and Bart Olinger. 1990. Ethnicity and Production of Micaceous Ware in the Taos Valley. In *Clues to the Past: Papers in Honor of William M. Sundt*, edited by M. S. Duran and D. T. Kirkpatrick, pp. 351–373. Papers of the Archaeological Society of New Mexico No. 16. Archaeological Society of New Mexico, Albuquerque.

Moving Ideas, Staying at Home
Change and Continuity in Mid-Eighteenth-Century Tewa Pottery

Bruce Bernstein, Erik Fender, and Russell Sanchez

Sometimes staying in place requires movement. To stay in their pre-Spanish settlements required Tewa people to shift their loci of cultural practice, as well as reorder their intellectual and material culture. In the mid-1700s the Tewa adopted wheat farming, which, in turn, meant receiving Spanish culture and ideas into their villages and homes (Frank 2000; Trigg 2013:221). This shifting of ideas and world views is cultural movement: movement strategically conceived and used to remain in their villages, ending the diaspora begun with Spanish settlement and accelerated through the Pueblo Revolt and reconquest. Although a precept of Tewa culture is movement, unlike in other epochs of Tewa history, evidence suggests that seventeenth- and eighteenth-century Pueblo leadership believed that moving from established villages might permanently and irrevocably disrupt cultural continuity because Tewa culture is based on the idea of movement creating continuum rather than change.

Metaphoric and physical movement has been used throughout Tewa history to create culture because movement allows for the "act of becoming" (Ortiz 1969, 1994; Swentzell 1988). However, at this moment in Tewa history, physical movement became increasingly fraught because of the combination of population loss and ever-increasing Spanish encroachments on Tewa lands. No doubt, too, the living memory in grandparents and parents—generations of physical relocation and harsh treatment by the Spanish—probably indicated to the Tewa that leaving and surviving away from their villages would require absorption into other Native communities or repudiating their Native heritage to become Spanish or *vecino* (Cattanach and Agostini, this volume).

This chapter approaches migration and movement in a decidedly nonarchaeological way. Nonetheless, it describes a methodology that can be used by archaeologists. The methodology is one that suggests anthropologists and other academics work alongside and in partnership with communities to begin to contribute to Pueblo history in place, in addition to writing for our academic peers. Writing with Pueblo people will help to create Pueblo history in place of archaeology. This chapter may be the most explicit of the volume in suggesting that working in partnership might be not only the best way, but also a method for collecting more information, increasing the context of that data, and building more accuracy.

In looking at eighteenth-century Tewa pottery, we can see that there is a break with pottery of the previous fifty years. But what to make of these changes? Past work has considered these changes as stylistic and part of the naturally evolving art world, each new form dependent on the last (Batkin 1987a; Harlow 1973; Harlow and Frank 1974). While there is value in this approach, it lacks contextual information. In what follows are two contextual sets of data with which to understand pottery change: first, the descendant community and its historical memory and the continuing functionality of the Tewa world view; and second, Spanish historical documents. Both of these sources have been used in past work, but Native ethnogenesis has generally not been used to establish the narrative around which history, anthropology, archaeology, ethnology, and ethnohistory are arranged.

Our chapter looks first at cultural fissures and the motivations for change, then determines that no physical migration was made and, moreover, that cultural change ensured no migration would be made. Without change the Tewa could not stay in place, but by staying in place, they would resist further diaspora and its potential destabilizing effects on Tewa culture. Staying in place can result in cultural change just as migration inevitably requires some cultural adjustments (Clark 2001:85–86).

Tewa oral narratives about movement and migration are geographically directional.[1] Archaeology (with notable exceptions, including this volume) of necessity draws from Western understandings of cultural response and action—indeed, this is why it is archaeology and not Pueblo history. As academics we can put forward the same types of theses, for example, that movement is often a response to spatially uneven change in social and economic conditions. There is value in both approaches, as well as in becoming wholly multidisciplinary by using multiple perspectives. Here, then, we put forward a new methodology, model new approaches, and provide views and interpretations that intrinsically resonate with the Pueblo community. We privilege the Tewa world view and ethnogenesis.[2]

Pottery making over the long arc of Tewa history is episodic; social changes brought small- and large-scale modifications and sometimes transformation to pottery forms and iconography. Pottery, or more precisely its aesthetics and production, is ritualistic, serving as a critical material and conceptual ideal of the Tewa world. And significantly, pottery is a social tool, whether mediating Tewa people's settlement on new lands during the fourteenth century, their adaptation to Spanish colonization, or the onset of a cash economy and the twentieth-century market for Pueblo art pottery. As Tewa people remind us, "Our history is recorded in pottery" (plate 7). Pottery is the collective agency of Tewa people, simultaneously a record of, portent of, and participant in change. A reading of the older pottery reveals that it is history and ceremony, painted by men as a permanent record of a moment and, more importantly, the simultaneity of cultural continuity and change. In sum, people used pottery to create meaning, as a cultural account of the circulation of new goods (wheat) and the new economic processes shaping its use within and outside of the Tewa village.

Eighteenth-century pottery might be viewed as an ardent example of that record. Tewa pottery is a highly structured and direct method of recording cultural change—the process of making pottery records history, and its designs recount origins and landscape and world view. A ceremony or ritual marking the acceptance of wheat was unnecessary because wheat was incorporated into an existing system, rather than requiring a new system for its growth and use.

Our work seeks to identify the cultural and historical contexts of Tewa pottery production and to explore pottery's capacities to identify general and specific Tewa processes of culture continuity and change. "With few exceptions, ethnographers too have neglected the implications of the manufacture and distribution of pottery in the Pueblo economy" (Snow 1973:55). Our approach replaces a reliance on stylistic analysis that describes the object but not the cause for change, an assumptive and well-worn viewpoint that gazes onto and into a culture. Moreover, this methodology assumes that Tewa culture and art are more similar to Western culture and accepts aesthetics as a universal category of human behavior that works similarly across cultural boundaries rather than within a society's own distinctive materialization of social interaction.

The use of the Tewa world's "inner workings" is intended to provide greater insights into understanding, writing about, and interpreting Tewa history and culture (Sando and Agoyo 2005:83–84).

In locating cultural change and adaptation, our methodology combines ethnohistory, object study, and fresh ethnographic inquiry with living potters and descendant community members. Working with today's potters and descendants is a pleasure; they are intellectually engaged and challenge flaccid ideas and concepts. But collaboration requires care, too. As outsiders we tend to ask too many questions and take concepts beyond the comfort range of individuals or the community. As Pueblo people, we are well taught to share very little with the non-Pueblo world. But what if we desire to set the record straight, to begin to untie the knots of anthropological description and interpretation and replace them with an interpretation based on ethnogenesis? In all of this there is room for ideas that have never been explored in pottery scholarship because people have mostly engaged potters and community members on non-Pueblo terms, forcing Puebloan concepts into places they may not belong. Our approach in this chapter illuminates two significant moments in pottery production: first, a new style of pottery specifically for wheat agriculture was created in the mid-1700s; and second, men had a primary role in the creation of this new pottery style, particularly in determining the novel iconography, as well as painting the pottery.

The new style of pottery was designed to imbue wheat with Tewa meanings at the same time that it kept wheat separate from the sacredness of Tewa plant-life ideologies. Tewa leadership viewed wheat as a potential negotiating strategy because it made the Tewa appear to be in better alignment with their non-Tewa neighbors, a necessary evil for eighteenth-century Tewa people if they were to remain in their villages. The bringing of wheat agriculture into a Tewa village was a complicated endeavor, particularly during the highly nativistic period that followed the harsh treatment of Tewa people during and following the reconquest. Growing wheat meant that Spanish culture and ideas would take up residence in homes and villages. Pottery thus served a dual role of separating and including; the specialized pottery kept wheat separate in the cosmology of Tewa plant life, while additionally and simultaneously allowing wheat to be included in Tewa cosmology by enclosing it in a ceramic container made of fertile Tewa substances and covered with designs that are Tewa prayers for fertility and moisture.

Men—more specifically, men with ritual knowledge, privilege, and responsibility in the community—were charged with bringing wheat into the village. Their knowledge allowed them to see the whole of Tewa society, compared to other village members who might have only a partial view.

The Spanish viewed themselves as dominant in transactions with the Tewa, particularly those involving wheat because of its association with Spain and Catholicism. In their interactions with the Spanish about wheat, however, the Tewa viewed themselves as sovereign, apart from the Spanish and their viewpoints (Lee and LiPuma 2002:200). Pottery served as an explicit and unyielding representation of Tewa opposition to the Spanish world. Instead of adaptation, the adoption of wheat was an act of sovereignty. The placing of wheat into the established system of summer/winter and wild/cultivated was the Tewa way of maintaining separate worlds, a sovereign Tewa world. We see this in the construction of new pottery styles; nonetheless, the new styles, no matter how different, are Tewa.

Alfonso Ortiz (1969:77) describes this Tewa way of being as "division and unity," taking the foreign and sometimes unwanted and placing it into the orderly world of the two Tewa moieties, Summer and Winter. The most basic Tewa social organization of Summer and Winter Moieties is "a system of checks and balances . . . a symbolic inter-transposability of the whole (society) and its two major constituent parts (the moieties)" (Ortiz 1969:77). This duality is inherent in all things Tewa.

WHEAT AND THE TEWA WORLD

As a strategy, taking wheat into a Tewa village demonstrated a willingness to change, to become "Hispanicized," which essentially provided a means to stay in place. Taking on wheat agriculture during the eighteenth century was difficult and involved choosing from a Spanish repertoire that Tewa people had paid for through genocide, the Spaniards' profound disregard of Pueblo culture and religion, and their encroachments on land and water, as well as their serving as encomenderos and on repartimientos. Moreover, wheat adaptation was fraught because Pueblo Revolt leader Popé directed people "to burn the seed which the Spaniards sowed and to plant only maize and beans, which were the crops of their ancestors" (Hackett and Shelby 1942:2:235; see also Sando and Agoyo 2005).

The drawing together of post-1700 Pueblo and Spanish populations was made necessary by the continued loss of Pueblo population and the growth of vecino residents; by 1780 Hispanic residents outnumbered Pueblo people (Brown 2013:79). This meant pressure from intruding Spanish settlements due to vecino population growth and non-Tewa control of water and the hinterlands necessary for wood gathering, hunting, and wild-food harvest. But it was an outside threat that imperiled both. The Apache and Navajo, who had bedeviled the New Mexican frontier from 1640 onward, grew progressively troublesome, and even more foreboding was the appearance along the northern border of two enemies: the Ute and Comanche.

Importantly, moving might well mean oblivion. As Tewa and other Pueblo people returned to their villages in the early 1700s, they needed to swallow the bitter pill of obtaining permission from their Spanish colonizers. Moreover, nearby Tewa villages Jacona, K'uuyemugeh, and P'osuwaegeh all demonstrated that the Spanish had quickly filled the void left by departing Tewa people. Ortiz's (2005:90) observations of actions leading to the Pueblo Revolt—"Pueblo religious leadership lead by prayer retreat and sacrifice, not by anger or confrontation"—are applicable to understanding eighteenth-century Tewa survival as well. No doubt, too, memories were still very fresh of grandparents and parents being forced to leave the Rio Grande valley in the 1690s to survive the harsh retaliatory treatment of the Spanish during their resettlement.

While we cannot know, we have little doubt that the inner workings of Tewa communities shifted significantly following the reconquest and operated with increased caution and deliberation. People nominally practiced Catholicism but clearly under their own terms. Nonetheless, Pueblo people requested of Diego de Vargas in 1693 that they no longer serve as Spanish labor (Sando 2005:43). The religious leaders responsible for deciding to adopt wheat agriculture were likely also sons and grandsons of the religious leaders active during the reconquest. This meant that wheat agriculture was more fraught and required that the community proceed with caution because wheat agriculture would also serve the larger ideal of restoration of balance in the community.

There are two basic ways to view wheat agriculture adaptation by Tewa people: one of science and sentience and the other of emotion and cosmology. While climatic change, population pressures, and raiding by the Comanche and other Plains tribes may have been factors in the decision to change, Tewa decision-making cannot be attributed solely to external forces. Rather, the potentialities of change served as important ontological markers of Tewa society and of its sentience as outwardly expressed through religious and ceremonial life. The decision to adapt wheat was not simply focused on change—growing wheat or not growing wheat—but on how it could be incorporated into the Tewa world and social organization.

At Tunyo (Black Mesa) in 1694, Tewa people used a strategy of deception to reach a relative stasis with Spanish aggressors by organizing and minimizing fighting with the Spanish, potentially avoiding the devastation of communities (Aguilar and Preucel, this volume). The adoption of wheat agriculture might best be understood as a similar type of strategy: escaping the scrutiny of the colonizers by setting up a front to shield ongoing Tewa societies and religious practice.

As a means of negotiating with the Spanish, the adaptation of wheat agriculture was a strategy that would appear to have drawn the Tewa villages closer to Spanish settlement. In actuality, their adaptation was like a taut line simultaneously pulling closer and delineating Tewa versus Spanish practices. The decision was a means of survival and perseverance. While wheat became a staple of Pueblo farming in the mid-1700s, once the villages began recovering, as evidenced by population gain in the mid-twentieth century, wheat agriculture diminished and today is no longer part of Tewa farming. As one Pueblo friend described it to us: "[Wheat] has no relevance . . . no songs, no prayers, no ceremonies ever existed for wheat in the Tewa communities and there is no use for wheat today. I don't know anyone that grows or thinks about wheat."[3] In contrast, even within the declining numbers of acres farmed by the Tewa today, people grow corn because they must fulfill their ceremonial and religious obligations and corn represents life in Tewa narratives spoken, danced, and sung. Contemporary harvest dances, where an arbor is built and filled with plant life, contain no wheat and no references to wheat.

WHEAT AGRICULTURE AS FOOD/SCIENCE AND CULTURE

We thought we would ask some female Pueblo friends about wheat agriculture and pottery. After all, both the agricultural products and the responsibilities for preparing food belong to women. One woman thought wheat farming was something that arrived with U.S. government farm agents, indicating her displeasure and the foreignness of wheat to her, her family, and perhaps her village. How much flour is needed to make an oven's worth of bread, we asked. Flour comes today in 25 lb sacks of flour (Blue Bird brand is the favorite). This sack will make about twenty to twenty-two loaves. "My grandmother used to say, 'Don't count your chickens before they're hatched,' as a warning that the creator takes what is needed and necessary."

There is no doubt that people enjoy oven bread; it is on every feast-day table. Making bread is a communal activity, a way to reintegrate women who live outside the village back into Pueblo life. Oven bread shapes symbolize fertility, too. Our friends further suggested that wheat keeps better and makes more varieties of food. Corn is tiresome—corn stew, cornbread. But wheat can be made into tortillas. Wheat is more versatile. But we must be careful with believing, for example, that oven bread is traditional; other traditional feast-day foods such as Jell-O and potato salad might provide us with needed guidance in this area.

However, we are reminded again and again that "corn is life" and that the Corn Mothers are the original Tewa mothers in the Lake Origin Place; as a result, corn is incorporated into Tewa prayers, songs, ceremonies, and cosmologies. Although the Tewa no longer live in agrarian societies, they rely on a planting and harvest cycle to guide their lives. In addition, they still grow corn for food and as a form of prayer, symbolizing the good, fertile world and nourishing people for everyday and ritual activities. Today's rituals could not continue without corn, but wheat has not played a role in ritual. Corn represents life because of its long relationship with Tewa people in this world and the before worlds. Wheat was not there.

TEWA SOCIAL ORGANIZATION AND WHEAT AGRICULTURE

The Spanish arrived in New Mexico eating corn, as evidenced by every seventeenth-century Spanish colonial site that includes sandstone comals. But the Spanish may have preferred European grains and meats, as well as the ethnic boundary and status they represented. Moreover, wheat was necessary to make the Eucharist wafers for use in the churches and missions. Spanish crops required considerably more care and effort than Indigenous crops like maize, beans, and pumpkins. Eastern hemisphere grains required plowing, sowing, harvesting, threshing, winnowing, and hand sorting; moreover, in New Mexico wheat and barley could be grown only with irrigation (Trigg 2013:126–127).

In the Tewa communities, religious authorities carefully regulated the growing of the aboriginal corn, bean, and squash crops, when the ditches were cleaned and the first water of the season brought into the village, following a cornmeal path laid down by religious leaders. Authorities decided when planting began. But wheat agriculture required an adjustment of the Winter and Summer Moieties' authority over the annual yearly cycle of planting, irrigation, and harvest because the planting, irrigation, and harvest of wheat fell outside of the norms of Tewa agriculture (Ortiz 1969).

Wheat is unorganized and unwieldy, falling outside the world of Tewa direction and knowledge. But as with other incorporated Spanish cultural traits, the consequences of change are corralled by the dynamic duality of the Tewa (Ortiz 1994). Importantly, the new pottery style, Ogapoge, was designed to help put order to these circumstances by contextualizing wheat through its iconography, which are specific prayers and offerings for its good growth and incorporation into Tewa life.

Wheat, Ortiz (1969:175–176n22) suggests, is "of the middle," of the world of man and the spirits, a mediating category. Wheat is in a liminal space, betwixt and between, not one or the other, but in a state of transformation and becoming. Unlike other cultigens it can be planted in autumn, winter, or spring, crossing the lines of the Summer and Winter Moieties. He identifies crops as either "hot" or "cold," each plant having a moiety association, but wheat as being neither hot nor cold. Summer plants include corn, beans, and squash, referring to their ripened, domesticated qualities, while the cold category corresponds to unripened, green domesticates and wild plants, as well as watermelons and green chile.

Wheat is planted in March because it requires longer germination and growing periods than Indigenous crops and must be harvested by August to avoid insects that endanger the crop. This means, too, that it must be irrigated before the ceremonial cleanings of ditches and the bringing of the first water into the fields. Seemingly to avoid disorder and rupture of the moiety structure, the governor was put in charge of wheat (Ortiz 1969:115). The governor is a secular position, created by the Spanish in 1620, providing more evidence of the outsider status of wheat agriculture. Wheat planted in March and harvested in August is outside of the Tewa annual cycle, resulting in an inequity between Summer and Winter Moiety chiefs. Ortiz suggests wheat as principal reason for the unequal amount of time spent on village leadership by the Summer and Winter Moieties and concludes that by dropping wheat farming, balance would be immediately restored. Pueblo friends confirm that dropping wheat has helped restore balance between the winter and summer sides.

Tewa people continue to eat wheat-based foods, as noted. Outdoor-oven-baked bread is held in high regard as a special and traditional food. But over the last one hundred years store-bought commodities have replaced Tewa-produced wheat. In contrast, corn and cornmeal for traditional purposes are not purchased from a store. The quick and uneventful demise of wheat agriculture is further evidence that wheat worked outside the annual societal and agricultural organization. Burdensome and perhaps unwelcome, once wheat as a tool of survival and perseverance was no longer necessary, it became, as friends suggest today, "irrelevant . . . something no one grows today. And I can't think of a reason why they would grow wheat."

HISTORIC PERIOD TEWA POTTERY, 1540–1880

Spanish explorers were impressed by Pueblo pottery, and in 1581 Piro and Tiwa pottery was praised as "better quality than the pottery of New Spain . . . and Portugal" (Hammond and Rey 1966:82, 85, quoted in Snow 1973:61). Spanish settlers became dependent on Pueblo wares for household and other needs, as amply demonstrated in the archaeological record (Snow 1973:61). During the first period of Spanish settlement (1598–1680), some pueblos made ceramic pieces for Spanish consumption, particularly pieces such as censers, chalices, bowls for holy water, candlesticks, and other items for religious function, at the behest of the Franciscan missionaries. The most numerous forms are soup bowls, which are found in greater numbers around Santa Fe and K'uuyemugeh. For the most part, Pueblo people did not adopt these shapes into their permanent ceramic repertoire. The Spanish produced little if any pottery during the colonial period, relying on Pueblo people for all of their domestic needs and acquiring the pottery through repartimiento, sale, barter, or trade (Brown 2013:79; Trigg 2013:130–133).

During the seventeenth century, three pottery types dominated Tewa and Spanish households: Biscuit C or Cuyamungue Black-on-tan wares, Tsankawi Black-on-cream (1525–1650; Harlow 1973; Snow 1982:90), and Tewa Polychrome (1600–1740). Tewa Polychrome manufacture increased through the seventeenth century (figure 8.1). During the historic period there was a considerable increase in the use of micaceous wares and polished black pottery, also known as Kapo Black. Both have been suggested as the introductions of Mexican Indigenous populations who came to New Mexico with the Spanish (Hurt and Dick 1946; Warren 1979:90). We recently asked a Tewa potter about this and received the reply, "That seems logical."

The Pueblo Revolt and the ensuing twelve years of freedom from the influence of the Spanish was a watershed in pottery development. Following the reconquest, potters abandoned glaze-paint pottery for matte-paint pottery with vegetal painted designs and used red paint to create polychrome vessels. In addition, tall-neck and indented-bottom jars replaced the round-bottomed bulbous disk jar shape. The change to vegetal and mineral paints from the runny, imprecise glaze paint may have represented a desire by potters to control the clarity and complexity of their designs (Frank 1991:283). They saw exactly these elements in the wares that the Spanish imported into New Mexico from Mexico and Europe.

In 1803 we have the first documented use of animal dung to fire pottery (Carrillo 1997:170), which reduced the firing temperature and ultimately the serviceability of the vessels. The change in fire fuel might also have been a result of mid-eighteenth century Spanish consolidation of authority and subsequent changes in land use and ownership; under new systems, once large open tracts of land became highly regulated, and community owned and controlled, reducing access for the collection of wood.

Museums did not begin collecting whole-vessel historic pottery until the latter third of the nineteenth century. But none of it was collected systematically, and older pottery, purchased in Pueblo villages, has collection rather than manufacture dates. For historic pottery, the Indian Arts Fund housed at the School for Advanced Research is used as the type collection. However, all but two Ogapoge examples were collected from dealers and Indian arts and crafts stores primarily during the late

Figure 8.1 Following Spanish settlement, or perhaps as a reaction to Spanish settlement, a new style of pottery was created: Tewa Polychrome. While the beginning date is generally agreed upon, the ending date corresponds with the invention of Ogapoge pottery. Tewa Polychrome is a stylistic evolution with elements of biscuitware bowls and Tsankawi jars. This jar was excavated at Cuyamungue in 1952. Cuyamungue has an abundance of Tewa Polychrome, particularly Spanish-style soup plates. The red body distinguishes the pottery; at the bulge or widest portion black organic paint is applied onto an often-chalky slip surface. The bottom of the pot is indented, and the shape is highly efficient for carrying water as the narrow neck minimizes the amount of water sloshing back and forth. The jar is engineered to be balanced when lifted and carried, and the bulge serves as a handle for lifting and steadying the jar. Cat. 21864/11. San Ildefonso polychrome jar, ca. 1690. Blair Clark, Photographer. Museum of Indian Arts & Culture, Laboratory of Anthropology, Santa Fe.

1920s (see also Bernstein 1994).[4] Dating pottery is taxing because of the considerable overlap in styles, which may take generations to morph into the next recognizable form because of the vicissitudes of individual and family pottery-making habits and aesthetics.

While anthropologists have written scores of volumes on archaeological pottery, they have written relatively little about historic pottery (see Bernstein 1994, 2009). The aversion to such studies might reflect anthropology's own self-defined interest in the past and the constructed authenticity it continues to represent to the discipline. Pueblo pottery scholar Kenneth Chapman described the circumstances:

> Doubtless it was the lure of the unknown that has prompted so much digging, but if the archaeologists had only realized that the rarest of all Pueblo pottery is that of the two centuries following the Conquest, they might have diverted at least a part of their energy to ferreting out the remnants of the antique ceramics of each pueblo. A mistaken belief that pottery making was influenced by contact with the invaders was long current among those who based their conviction on nothing more tangible than the wide variance between the pre-Spanish and the later wares of each pueblo [Chapman 1936:xi].

POTTERY AS METONYM

Pottery—its aesthetics and production—is ritualistic. Pottery making is a prayer; pottery making is creating life. Moreover, pottery has profound significance in Tewa culture: the creation of pottery is the combining of two sacred and fertile substances—water and earth—to make a new life. Designs on pottery are neither iconographic, metaphoric, nor symbolic but rather become the form that is painted—a leaf form is a leaf, a painted feather is prayer or breath. Painting infuses pottery with sacredness. Pottery is visual prayer.

Ogapoge pottery pieces are cosmological containers, serving as a critical and conceptual ideal of the Tewa world (figure 8.2). Ogapoge pottery was created to mediate the Spanish and Tewa worlds by dislodging and transforming the Tewa people's historic and contemporary relationships with the non-Tewa world, as well as the travails of farming. By

Figure 8.2 Large jars were used for storing wheat and other foods and clothes. These large jars are unique; jars like these did not exist before the mid-eighteenth century and Pueblo adaptation of wheat agriculture. Pueblo people were familiar with wheat and grew wheat for their Spanish oppressors. But with the acceptance of growing wheat in Pueblo fields, new tools were needed, including large jars for wheat storage. Similar jar size and capacity indicates that the jars were also used for measurement. Alternating panels contain the newly invented iconography for large wheat-storage jars, variations of constellation or star designs. The designs are associated with prayers for moisture and crops. Courtesy of the School for Advanced Research, cat. no. IAF 1547. Photograph by Addison Doty.

combining precontact and new iconography, the potters indicated a new circumstance and reminded Tewa users—and other viewers, too—of the strength and continuity of Tewa culture: "We are still here," or perhaps, "Stay strong."

Wheat stored, prepared, and served in the Ogapoge pottery would be enveloped in the fertile womb of Tewa life. The iconography continually produced prayers for the well-being of the crop and plant life, as well as surrounding it with Tewa thought to separate Tewa wheat from what once was Spanish. In this way, pottery functioned as interplay of ideas and symbols, serving a dynamic and fundamental role in the cultural makeover of wheat. Non-Tewa people are privileged to witness some of this same methodology—Tewa ceremonial life in the form of public dances that might be utilized to align the natural messiness of daily life and the non-Tewa world with the Tewa world view.

Aesthetics shape social relations to a tremendous extent, ritual making new life every time it is used (Ortiz 1969:130). Pottery as materialization of the Tewa world view possesses the same duality as other parts of the Tewa world: male and female, corn and wheat, Spanish and Tewa, outside and inside. Men working on pottery, made of materials from the soft womb of the earth, is yet another dualism. Duality is the natural order of the world; incorporating wheat within that structure and maintaining it as outside would further encode wheat with Tewa-specific ideology, as well as place it within the dual subsistence system (moieties, Summer and Winter) of the Tewa world (Ortiz 1969:132). Importantly, the moiety system of the Tewa is dynamic and flexible, "the dual organization as the only way . . . [to] operate meaningfully in social relations, and the only way they could impose order on their world" (Ortiz 1969:135). Finally, this duality does not need to be uniformly reciprocal but might also express the reciprocity of subordination.

New pottery forms facilitated wheat in its becoming Tewa—from the chaos of newness to acceptability and usability in the Tewa world— and in becoming part of a well-ordered cosmos and social organization. Although all Tewa people engage in prayers and dances for rain and fertility, it is usually men's role to compose and produce public and private ceremonies. Therefore, it stands to reason that men painted the deeply orthodox, pious designs used on Ogapoge vessels.[5] Moreover, men's ritually obligated prayer and sacrifice extend into pottery making—creating

Figure 8.3 The Ogapoge pottery style includes designs that are clearly part of the male domain. Men are responsible for bringing change into the village, and these types of designs were used to create prayers for the integration of wheat into Tewa plant life, as well as to protect Tewa life from the Spanish crop. (a) Courtesy of the School for Advanced Research, cat. no. IAF 2134. Photograph by Addison Doty. (b) Cat. 16116/12. San Ildefonso storage jar, ca. 1790–1820. Blair Clark, Photographer. Museum of Indian Arts & Culture, Laboratory of Anthropology, Santa Fe.

containers to simultaneously incorporate and protect the village from the Spanish intrusion. Moreover, as we detail, the designs are exclusively from the male world. Fray Juan Bernal noted in 1794, "Particularly in the Tewa nation, the women labor harder than the men, and their common work is to make things of pottery by hand and without any instruments whatever" (quoted in Brown 2013:80). A closer examination of this comment reveals that a Spanish priest would protest against men laboring less than women because Tewa men's religious obligations would keep them from public view and, not unimportantly in the eyes of Fray Bernal, away from Catholicism.

Ogapoge pottery is part of a larger transformative period of Tewa culture, the type of epochal change that males are sometimes responsible for. The male painting is male subject matter, altars with clouds, rain, and lighting, while female-painted pottery more generally depicts the results of rain, plant life and harvests. As in matters religious and ceremonial, the misunderstood role of men in pottery making has been allowed to stand as a deflection or defensive mechanism, much as well-regarded secrecy has helped sustain Pueblo religions since the reconquest. Talking with Pueblo people today, we find that their answers are straightforward and without hesitation: certain designs are men's responsibilities and therefore could not and would not be painted by women (figure 8.3).

OGAPOGE POTTERY

Ogapoge Polychrome pottery was invented for the new bowls and storage jars that would be needed to store, process, and prepare wheat-based foods. The surviving examples include large, thick-walled bowls for mixing and letting rise bread dough and jars for storing threshed and winnowed wheat (figure 8.4). Additionally, the fact that storage jars have the same basic capacity suggests they doubled as measurement devices. Some scholars have used the location of the bulge, or widest portion in the lower third of the vessel, to identify Ogapoge pottery (Harlow 1973). The bulge is considered to be a continuation of a Tsankawi jar shape. But once this bulge moves toward the middle of the pot body, pottery scholars name this new style Powhoge. We suggest, however, that there is no new style or type of pottery, only a continuation of the Ogapoge style; an evolution and maturation of the pottery's manufacture as a naturalization of wheat took place and the necessity of men potting and painting subsided.

The painting on the jars is organized as a body design and neckband. Some jars have double neckbands, most have a single neckband, and a relative few have no neckband. There are also some jars with a narrow band at the base of the bulge preceding the body design. Differences in the placement of bands and the absence of a neckband may indicate an earlier date of manufacture. Surviving whole bowls are fewer in number. Bowls have a design below the rim on the outer face and might include designs on the inside as well. An argument can be made for the varieties of painted areas being part of the development of the style, which eventually settled on a canon of neckband and body designs. The location of the bulge may be an indication of relative age of the pottery. But we suggest caution in making too much of variety; these types of variations may also be pottery-making families' and potters' preferences.

Figure 8.4 Large bowls were created for mixing bread dough and letting it rise. Before the advent of wheat agriculture there were no bowls of this dimension and sturdiness in the villages because no one used bowls so roughly. The single band of white slip and double framing lines mimic seventeenth-century Tewa Polychrome bowls, but the design and construction of the bowl are unique. Courtesy of the School for Advanced Research, cat. no. IAF 770. Photograph by Addison Doty.

The jars are painted with an organic paint on a white-slipped and often stone-polished surface. Ogapoge designs are decidedly less geometrical than the previous century's Tewa pottery iconography, and they show more variety in iconography. But we also have evidence that Ogapoge designs and their organization are sometimes reformulations and recontextualizations of older designs. By combining pre-1598 and new iconography, the potters were indicating a new circumstance and reminding both Tewa users and other viewers, presumably, of the strength and continuity of Tewa culture. Tewa people understand this as original and *creating newness*, while scholars might see revitalization. The iconography is primarily abstracted flowers and feathers, often organized like altars, with an emphasis on abstraction of esoteric and religious iconography. As noted, the subject matter of the iconography and style suggests that men painted these pots. This is significant because of men's participation in the Tewa community's political, social, and religious leadership. Slipshod finishes and poor firing, while seeming to indicate a carelessness of manufacture, may be due to the relative inexperience of men painting three-dimensionally what they usually painted in two dimensions on flat surfaces like hides and walls. Men's painted jars also appear to have less iconographic organization, which could be either deliberate or the result of their inexperience in painting three-dimensional surfaces.

Some of the Ogapoge jars' design fields are divided into panels like Tsankawi (1500–1650) and Tewa Polychrome (1600–1750) ceramics. This may be part of maintaining a nativistic ideology in the midst of vast and rapid change. The use of panels is an observable continuation of an older design organization that harkens back to pre–Spanish colonization days. But additionally, the panels might well represent a sacred space, much like the broad, seemingly empty space of a Pueblo plaza (Swentzell 1988) or the unpainted areas of paper used by emerging San Ildefonso watercolorists to represent the dance plaza. These spaces are sacred spaces where Tewa creation continues. Because the dance figures, and by extension these pottery designs, appear in these sacred "soft" spaces—a beforetime of creation—the painted figures or designs are part of the continuing creation of the world. "Their sense of 'home' is the space between the earth and clouds and not within specific human constructions" (Swentzell 1993:145). This space, whether found in early watercolorists' works or on pottery walls, is also equivalent to the episodic kiva murals. In this way, a similar open and nondifferentiated space with the additions of dance figures, clouds, rain, parrots, and pottery is imbued with sacredness and purpose to participate in the ongoing creation and continuance of Tewa life.

ETHNOGENESIS

Pottery scholars have spent considerable time performing stylistic analyses—distinguishing and typing pottery to develop a dating sequence and, in non-Tewa eyes, a logical progression of stylistic development (see Batkin 1987a; Harlow 1973; Harlow and Frank 1974). The stylistic approach, whether used for sherds, whole vessels, or historic or contemporary pottery, constitutes an assumptive and well-worn viewpoint that looks into the culture, methodologically assuming that Tewa culture and society are more similar to Western culture and society than not and accepting art and aesthetics as universal categories of human behavior that work similarly across cultural boundaries. There are assorted problems with this viewpoint because it is laden with culture-centric perspectives and assumptions. This limited approach assumes a linear sequence and shared practice by all potters rather than idiosyncratic differences that are the result of individual preference, skill, and age. Stylistic analysis in a matter of thinking is anti-movement and suggests that pottery manufacture depends only on preceding pottery manufacture to replicate and change. Pottery, as we have discussed, is pure movement: the demarcation of ethnic boundaries with Spanish neighbors, the alteration and integration of Tewa ideals and practices, and the adoption of wholly new pottery styles arriving in the villages with the movement of people and commerce in eighteenth-century New Mexico.

Understandably, our knowledge of Tewa pottery from 1680 to 1700 is constrained because of the small sample size (Trigg 2013), and little excavation work is allowed in the Tewa villages. Expanding the utility of the data set is proving challenging because it is primarily focused on typologies of archaeological sites rather than finding the explanatory principles of Tewa society. Historic whole-vessel museum collections and scholarship suffer from the same myopic methodologies of description and typology. Studied as typology, one pottery type depends on the last, but human cultures do not always operate in straight lines. And, in particular, we are apt to privilege Western knowledge over that of Tewa people, a long habit of colonial powers and academic disciplines. Investigating change helps us to understand Tewa pottery history and provides models for better understanding the time horizons and rationale for making the changes.

Museum collections suggest that the production of large jars and bowls began slowing in the mid-nineteenth century. Further evidence of this is that the vast majority of storage jars and bowls in museum collections were already used rather than newly made in the post-1850 period. While during the 1880–1900 Tewa revival potters made large jars again, some revisiting Ogapoge forms, they created these jars largely for sale rather than home use. The movement of manufactured goods and foods along with the change from a barter to a cash economy may have pushed this change. On the other hand, Ogapoge jars and bowls are, because of their thick-walled manufacture, durable; with dropping populations there may have been a lesser need for wheat-processing, storage, and cooking pottery.

Museum collecting of large Tewa jars appears to confirm this change. In each decade following 1880 people increasingly needed money to purchase the pottery's replacements—manufactured dressers and bureaus and store-bought foods. So although James and Matilda Coxe Stevenson during the last two decades of the nineteenth century collected hundreds of pieces of Tewa pottery, the number of large vessels in the Smithsonian's anthropology collections is small. However, the post-1900 museum collections at the American Museum of Natural History, Heye Foundation (now National Museum of the American Indian), San Diego Museum of Man, Indian Arts Fund, and the Museum of New Mexico have proportionally and numerically far greater numbers of large jars.[6] San Ildefonso potter Maria Martinez recalled opening her grandmother's storage room in about 1909 and each female relative choosing one jar to keep, while museum curator Herbert Spinden purchased the remaining storage jars not wanted by the family. She remembered Spinden needing four wagons to transport them to Santa Fe to be shipped to New York City's American Museum of Natural History (Martinez 1946).[7] Wages, farm and ranch products, and wage labor helped Tewa people earn needed cash to purchase flour, further diminishing their need to grow wheat. The ease with which wheat agriculture was replaced with purchased wheat is further evidence of wheat's existence outside of the Tewa cosmology. The success of Tewa people's own reorientation begun in the mid-eighteenth century is evident today in the strength of the communities that we might witness during public dance ceremonies, with agency and authority over their own histories and culture as a result of both collaboration and state and federal laws.

Treatments of seventeenth- and eighteenth-century New Mexico present the Rio Grande Pueblos as people whose primary accomplishment involved resisting Spanish acculturation and persisting as "pure" Native peoples. This view provides no basis for thinking about why certain elements of Spanish culture were incorporated into the Pueblo tradition while others were not or the manner in which these elements were incorporated; Pueblo perspectives on Spanish beliefs, practices, and technologies; and how this process varied across communities and adhered to Tewa ideologies. This hermetic and tired viewpoint also sets up contemporary Pueblo culture as the result of a long history of willful isolation and nonmovement. It is reinforced by the anthropological literature on the Pueblos, which focuses on reconstructing "pre-Hispanic" Pueblo culture (see Eggan 1950; Longacre 1970; Ware 2014), and promotes a view of the Pueblo tradition as involving isolated, internally focused communities. In the current framing, the most "traditional" pueblos are the ones who have isolated themselves most thoroughly from the outside world and have been "impacted" least by Spanish and American culture. Ortiz's (1969, 1994) seminal work makes clear that internal systems must be investigated and cultural movement—change—taken into account.

Some of the long-term results of the Columbian exchange for Rio Grande Tewa communities are obvious today. Nearly every Pueblo community has a church as well as a kiva; Tewa life-cycle rituals might incorporate Comanche-, Spanish-, and Tewa-derived elements; and most Tewa people have no problem viewing themselves as simultaneously Catholic and Pueblo. Traditional Pueblo foods include wheat bread, chicken and mutton stew, and corn, beans, and squash. For Pueblo people today, this collection of things and practices is Pueblo tradition, regardless of the historical origin of each element. Tradition is movement because without movement generated through cultural and societal change, tradition becomes stagnant and nonfunctional.

Tewa scholars like Alfonso Ortiz never worry about the source or the origination of change or that cultural change comes from the absorption of new ideas and material objects. As Tewa people find balance—"seeking life"—they find dynamic instruments and actions in always continuing to become Tewa people (Swentzell 1993). "Pueblos have traveled and traded widely among one another since far back into prehistoric times and . . . they have traded not only material objects but, far more subtly, social institutions and religious knowledge and meanings as well. This pattern of extensive trading and exchange was not so much altered by the Spanish and Americans as it was augmented" (Ortiz 1994:302).

Tewa people frame their culture in terms such as *continuity*, *persistence*, and *insistence*, strongly indicating their own view of how new ideas are considered and accepted, adapted, or rejected. Tewa culture is movement, perhaps at times hidden from an outsider's vantage point, but at other times fully recognizable, such as with Ogapoge pottery.

Older structures and world views stand at the core of Tewa culture, with its ideals of balance and duality, each element weighed for and against maintaining this balance. As outsiders we are privileged to see Tewa culture doing some of its hardest work when numbers of people come home from nearby and distant cities to participate in a feast day and visitors descend on the community. Tewa people living away from their community enjoy an independence and individuality that may be challenging to duplicate at home, particularly in a long line of choreographed dancers. Public dances are shared displays of the internal set of principles and the mechanisms that have sustained Tewa cultures over the centuries.

The movement of culture is as fraught as any migration. While movement creates the necessary changes needed for survival, it may also obliterate what has come before. Oral traditions are one means of recording what has come before, chronicling didactic and metaphoric histories. Pottery is movement's materialization. That Ogapoge pottery is new and inventive is movement and can be read today as eighteenth-century movement. As we have illustrated, cultural data are encoded into each pot and decipherable, as we learn not only the language of pottery but also the historic contexts of the cultural data.

Beautiful and unique, Ogapoge pottery documents the immense historical changes that Tewa people and culture were subjected to. Moreover, the Ogapoge pottery tradition is fixed between two enormous historic circumstances: the revolt and reconquest and Americanization. Both epochs required of Tewa people resourcefulness and resiliency to persevere through far-reaching economic and social upheavals. Worrying about the source of change, or that there is change, ignores the necessary movement of Tewa culture.

Pottery over the long arc of Tewa history is episodic; social changes bringing large-scale, even complete, changes to pottery forms and iconography. Wheat agriculture is one of those episodes. We cannot go back and know what was in people's minds when wheat was brought into the community. But Ogapoge pottery provides provocative clues to those inner workings and decisions. When postrevolt and reconquest period pottery is spoken or written about, the discussion usually includes the observation that glaze-wares production was abruptly and permanent stopped. To this discussion Ogapoge pottery and wheat agriculture might be added.

NOTES

1. A historic example of the meddling in Tewa ceremonial practice and understanding of oral narrative is recounted in Hewett 1930:81–82.

2. Some readers might take exception to this methodology, perhaps suggesting that Tewa culture as practiced today is too new and without cultural memory, is not scientifically verifiable, and is of diminishing utility for archaeology. But consider the epistemology of names and naming. Recently, a potter told coauthor Bernstein about knowing the source for a prized pottery material thought to be lost to time and memory. But because the location of this pottery-making clay was named in Tewa, the potter could easily locate it. As a cultural practitioner, the potter knew the place by Tewa name and narrative rather than by a description of the modern overlay of roads and place-names. The Tewa presence is ancient and permanent.

3. Here and elsewhere in the chapter, quotations indicate formal and informal interviews performed in preparation for writing this chapter. Their names are not used to protect interviewees' confidentiality.

4. The other two jars were purchased from San Ildefonso potter Julian Martinez. Both jars are far older than the 1920s IAF collection date. The purchase price of the two jars is the highest paid for any of the large storage jars in the IAF collection.

5. A number of archaeologists argue that women exclusively produced ceramics in the pre-Hispanic period (Brown 2013:65–106; Mills and Crown 1995; see also Frank 2000). These observations are no doubt built on solid but limited data not expanded by conversations with living community members. Others make the case for a late nineteenth-century man, Florentino Montoya, being the first male potter (Batkin 1987b; Chapman 1970). There is no doubt that the dramatic societal changes of the early twentieth century again necessitated men taking a lead role in developing and painting new iconographies as pottery was for the first time principally made to sell to non-Native people.

6. There are approximately ninety-six Tewa pots identified in the Smithsonian's anthropology collections; of these about three are large storage jars and bowls. The American Museum of Natural History collections include 209 Tewa pots of which 11 are large jars and bowls. Frederick Hodge in 1899 and Herbert Spinden in 1909–1912 principally collected the Tewa pottery. Wesley Bradfield and Thomas Dozier in 1912–1913 made a highly significant collection for the San Diego Exposition, notable because they collected in the villages rather than from arts and crafts stores. Jesse Nusbaum appears to have been a

partner in the collecting as well. The bulk of the collection is the San Diego of Man collections (Hedges and Dittert 1984), but Nusbaum sold a significant portion of the collection (perhaps on behalf of his friend Bradfield) to George Heye in 1916. These pots are part of the National Museum of the American Indian collections.

7. As noted, while Nusbaum collected in the villages, purchasing from Pueblo people, the Indian Arts Fund collection is overwhelmingly purchased from traders and Indian arts and crafts shops.

REFERENCES

Batkin, Jonathan. 1987a. *Pottery of the Pueblos of New Mexico, 1700–1940*. Taylor Museum and Colorado Springs Fine Arts Center, Colorado Springs, Colorado.

Batkin, Jonathan. 1987b. Martina Vigil and Florentino Montoya: Master Potters of San Ildefonso and Cochiti Pueblos. *American Indian Art Magazine* 12(4):56–69.

Bernstein, Bruce. 1994. Potters and Patrons: The Creation of Pueblo Art Pottery. *American Indian Art Magazine* 20(1):70–79.

Bernstein, Bruce. 2009. Review of *Born of Fire: The Life and Pottery of Margaret Tafoya*, Charles S. King. *American Indian Culture and Research Journal* 33(2):117–121.

Brown, Tracy L. 2013. *Pueblo Indians and Spanish Colonial Authority in Eighteenth-Century New Mexico*. University of Arizona Press, Tucson.

Carrillo, Charles. 1997. *Hispanic New Mexican Pottery: Evidence of Craft Specialization 1790–1890*. LPD Press, Albuquerque, New Mexico.

Chapman, Kenneth. 1936. *The Pottery of Santo Domingo Pueblo: A Detailed Study of Its Decoration*. Laboratory of Anthropology, Santa Fe, New Mexico.

Chapman, Kenneth. 1970. *The Pottery of San Ildefonso Pueblo, Albuquerque*. Published for the School of American Research by the Museum of New Mexico Press, Santa Fe.

Clark, Jeffery S. 2001. Disappearance and Diaspora: Contrasting Two Migrations in the Southern U.S. Southwest. In *Rethinking Anthropological Perspectives on Migration*, edited by Graciela S. Cabana and Jeffery J. Clark, pp. 84–110. University Press of Florida, Tallahassee.

Eggan, Fred. 1950. *Social Organization of the Western Pueblos*. University of Chicago Press, Chicago.

Frank, Ross. 1991. The Changing Pueblo Indian Pottery Tradition: The Underside of Economic Development in Late Colonial New Mexico, 1750–1820. *Journal of the Southwest* 33(3):282–321.

Frank, Ross. 2000. *From Settler to Citizen: New Mexican Economic Development and the Creation of Vecino Society, 1750–1820*. University of California Press, Berkeley.

Hackett, Charles, and Charmion Shelby. 1942. *Revolt of the Pueblo Indians of New Mexico and Otermín's Attempted Reconquest, 1680–1682.* 2 pts. University of New Mexico Press, Albuquerque.

Hammond, George, and Agapito Rey (editors and translators). 1966. *The Rediscovery of New Mexico, 1580–1594: The Explorations of Chamuscado, Espejo, Castaño de Sosa, Morlete, and Leyva de Bonilla and Humaña.* University of New Mexico Press, Albuquerque.

Harlow, Francis. 1973. *Matte-Paint Pottery of the Tewa, Keres, and Zuni Pueblos.* Museum of New Mexico Press, Santa Fe.

Harlow, Francis, and Larry Frank. 1974. *Historic Pottery of the Pueblo Indians, 1600–1880.* New York Graphic Society, Boston.

Hedges, Ken, and Alfred Edward Dittert. 1984. *Heritage in Clay: The 1912 Pueblo Pottery Collections of Wesley Bradfield and Thomas Dozier.* San Diego Museum of Man, San Diego, California.

Hewett, Edgar L. 1930. *Ancient Life in the Southwest.* Bobbs-Merrill, Indianapolis, Indiana.

Hurt, Wesley, and Herbert Dick. 1946. Spanish American Pottery from New Mexico. *El Palacio* 53:280–288, 307–312.

Lee, Benjamin, and Edward LiPuma. 2002. Cultures of Circulation: The Imaginations of Modernity. *Public Culture* 14(1):191–213.

Longacre, William (editor). 1970. *Reconstructing Prehistoric Pueblo Societies.* University of New Mexico Press, Albuquerque.

Martinez, Maria. 1946. Interview with Alice Marriott. Archives of Western History Collections, University of Oklahoma Libraries, Norman.

Mills, Barbara, and Patricia Crown (editors). 1995. *Ceramic Production in the American Southwest.* University of Arizona, Tucson.

Ortiz, Alfonso. 1969. *The Tewa World: Space, Time, Being, and Becoming in a Pueblo Society.* University of Chicago, Chicago.

Ortiz, Alfonso. 1994. The Dynamics of Pueblo Cultural Survival. In *North American Indian Anthropology: Essays on Society and Culture*, edited by Raymond DeMallie and Alfonso Ortiz, pp. 296–306. University of Oklahoma Press, Norman.

Ortiz, Alfonso. 2005. Po'pay's Leadership: A Pueblo Perspective. In *Po'pay: Leader of the First American Revolution*, edited by Joseph Sando and Herman Agoyo, pp. 82–92. Clear Light, Santa Fe, New Mexico.

Sando, Joseph. 2005. The Pueblo Revolt. In *Po'pay: Leader of the First American Revolution*, edited by Joseph Sando and Herman Agoyo, pp. 5–53. Clear Light, Santa Fe, New Mexico.

Sando, Joe, and Herman Agoyo (editors). 2005. *Po'Pay: Leader of the First American Revolution.* Clear Light, Santa Fe, New Mexico.

Snow, David. 1973. Some Economic Considerations of Historic Rio Grande Pueblo Pottery. In *The Changing Ways of Southwestern Indians: A Historic*

Perspective, edited by Albert Schroeder, pp. 55–72. El Corral de Santa Fe Westerners Brand Book, Santa Fe, New Mexico.

Snow, David. 1982. Spanish American Pottery Manufacture in New Mexico: A Critical Review. *Ethnohistory* 31(2):93–113.

Swentzell, Rina. 1988. Buingeh: The Pueblo Plaza. *El Palacio* 94(2):14–19.

Swentzell, Rina. 1993. Mountain Form, Village Form: Unity in the Pueblo World. In *Ancient Land, Ancestral Places: Paul Logsdon in the Pueblo Southwest*, edited by Stephen H. Lekson, pp. 139–147. Museum of New Mexico Press, Santa Fe.

Trigg, Heather. 2013. *From Household to Empire: Society and Economy in Early Colonial New Mexico*. University of Arizona, Tucson.

Ware, John A. 2014. *A Pueblo Social History: Kinship, Sodality, and Community in the Northern Southwest*. School for Advanced Research, Santa Fe, New Mexico.

Warren, A. H. 1979. Historic Pottery of the Cochiti Reservoir ARA. In *Archaeological Investigations in Cochiti Reservoir, New Mexico, vol.4: Adaptive Change in the Northern Rio Grande Valley*, edited by Jan Biella and Richard Chapman, pp. 235–245. Office of Contract Archeology, Albuquerque, New Mexico.

9

Toward the Center
Movement and Becoming at the Pueblo of Pojoaque

Samuel Villarreal Catanach and Mark R. Agostini

At the Pueblo of Pojoaque, stories and memories of movement from within and outside the community make up much of its history and continue to influence the daily lives of its people. In the face of severe adversity, mobility has been the pueblo's ally, facilitating forms of resistance, survivance, and revitalization that have shaped it into what it is today and what it will be in the future. However, events set in motion by different processes of movement at Pojoaque have historically been left decontextualized by anthropologists and archaeologists, those whose perspectives on Pueblo communities and personhood, in many respects, diverged early on from the values and viewpoints held by community members. The paucity of Pueblo perspectives on movement and migration events in scholarly research, which this volume seeks to ameliorate, stretches across all scales of Pueblo social history—from the regional-scale mass migration of Ancestral Puebloans who once inhabited what is now the Four Corners region (as migration anthropologists and anthropologists continue to debate today; see Duwe and Cruz, this volume) to the subregional movement of Pueblo populations to and from villages in what is now the northern Rio Grande of New Mexico.

Historically, static ideas of Pueblo social being have been perpetuated by a Western world view. Concerning Pojoaque, instances of movement away from "normal" village-based agricultural lifestyles have therefore called into question the community's "Pueblo-ness." Ironically, this notion overlooks how a Tewa ethnic identity first came about in the past—through the continuous movement and coalescence of disparate ancestral peoples with diverse culture histories. Further, the consequences of forced movement and resettlement over numerous periods marked by colonialism in New Mexican history have constructed cultural imaginaries, constraining the fluidity of Pueblo identity and limiting how it is negotiated within and between communities.

At the Pueblo of Pojoaque, physical movement away from the community due to a host of socioeconomic factors brought on by colonialism and missionization resulted in the movement away from Pueblo cultural identity, one tied to place. Not only has the movement of Pojoaque people played a major role in the evolution of their identity, so too has the movement of outsiders into the community. Loss of land and culture, diminished through violence, disease, and economic imposition, has simultaneously set in motion histories that inform who the people of Pojoaque are today. The Pueblo of Pojoaque is a community of mixed cultural and historical backgrounds, something embraced by its people, but it is their shared Pojoaque and Tewa identity that sustains them.

Movement is a common theme of Pueblo origin traditions. The Tewa emerged into the world above from a lake to the north. As they traveled southward, they sought the center place wherever they settled, until they began moving once again to find a new center. These stories continue to show the people how vital movement is in the human and nonhuman Tewa world. And yet, as a response to the myriad socionatural forces acting on communities throughout Pueblo history, movement simultaneously disrupts, challenges, and changes this world. In this chapter, we discuss movement within the context of becoming at the Pueblo of Pojoaque. We define this process as one in which the community is constantly moving toward its *center place*, that state in which it and its people are most in balance and complete. In the case of Pojoaque, social identities persist in flux as varying combinations of shared beliefs, practices, and material culture continuously undergo periods of rest and renewal.

We begin by examining and contextualizing the emergence and development of a civic identity status called *vecino* at the Pueblo of Pojoaque dating to the late colonial period (1692–1821). We argue that the use of the term *vecino* in this context reflects a time when Pojoaque people were maintaining increasingly fluid identities in the face of adversity, paralleling the later reestablishment of the pueblo beginning in the 1930s and its subsequent revitalization as a Tewa community. We also aim to further problematize the idea of the Pueblo of Pojoaque as ever having been abandoned by expounding upon the contingent historical significance of movement within the Tewa philosophy of becoming.

VECINO ETHNOGENESIS AND THE PUEBLO OF POJOAQUE

Being of mixed background is not unique to contemporary Pojoaque, as transitions in identity through multiethnic residential practices and beliefs have been taking place since time immemorial. The establishment of the first Spanish colony in New Mexico at San Gabriel de Yunque Owingeh near present-day Ohkay Owingeh (formerly San Juan Pueblo) brought about new interactions and relations between colonists of mixed cultural heritage and an array of Indigenous groups (Brooks 2002; Jenks 2017; Snow 1996; Swadesh 1979; Trigg 2005). During the mid-eighteenth century, colonial New Mexican populations began to shift away from the early colonial *regimen de castas*, a system of racialized and status-based identity categories tied to social and economic capital (Frank 2000), by adopting vecino, a civic status–based identity defined by individuals with mixed cultural heritage. Literally translated as "neighbors," vecino constituted an increasingly fluid identity category. The term gave precedence to one's residence and membership in new multiethnic colonial communities over any one distinct ethnic heritage, effectively reconfiguring colonial citizenship into what Kelly Jenks (2017:215) calls "something a little less 'Spanish.'"

The expansion of these civic identities under a new communal name or ethnonym marked ethnogenesis, a process whereby new ethnic identities resulted from conscious transformations made to preexisting social classification schemes (Cipolla 2013; Sturtevant 1971; Voss 2008). While our forthcoming analysis relies upon primary-source documents to examine vecino ethnogenesis, a comparative case study on identity formation conducted by Barbara Voss (2008) at El Presidio de Francisco (1776–1821) relies on historical archaeology to explore how life in colonial California was transformed by the construction of the "Californio" identity. Defined by the affiliation of a diverse group of individuals with mixed Mexican, African, Indian, and European heritage with an eighteenth- and nineteenth-century Spanish military outpost, Californio identity comprised both a common set of practices and relations among a diverse population and the imposition of social boundaries between the colony and Indigenous populations (Voss 2005, 2008). Like Voss's innovative study, any examination of vecino ethnogenesis must not overlook how the participation of New Mexico's Indigenous population shaped vecino identity, as they maintained their own social identities and lifeways over time. We therefore consider how this new identity category was in tension with Pueblo practices, beliefs, and ontological principles while also serving as a tool in the survivance and expression of Pueblo-specific ways of life within multiethnic colonial communities.

Although Hispano culture in New Mexico has received much scholarly attention and been the subject of considerable debate (Frank 1996, 2000; Nostrand 1970, 1975, 1980, 1992; Rodríguez 1986; Van Ness 1987), an examination of the historical relations between Pueblo people and the emergent vecinos has only recently been initiated (Darling and Eiselt 2017; Eiselt 2005, 2006; Eiselt and Darling 2012, 2016; Jenks 2017). To bridge this gap, we begin by integrating census and baptismal data on vecino and Pueblo populations from the late colonial period at the Pueblo of Pojoaque (1779–1839) with previous research conducted on vecino ethnogenesis in the northern Rio Grande.

A study of the movement to and settlement of the Pojoaque Valley by vecino populations helps to shed light on how vecino and Pueblo populations became interconnected in a markedly unequal socioeconomic system. Following the Pueblo Revolt of 1680 and second revolt of 1696, the Pueblo of Pojoaque was uninhabited; it was resettled in 1706 by five families as the new mission of Nuestra Señora de Guadalupe (Hodge 1910:274). By 1750 the census for the communities including Pojoaque, Cuyamungue, and San Ildefonso counted twenty-two families and 186 individuals, *excluding* the Pueblo population, which was not recorded (Christmas 2010). In 1760 the Pueblo of Pojoaque was reduced to the status of a satellite mission community as a *visita* of Nambe. By 1776 a census for the area yielded a total population of 512 individuals for the valley proper. The near tripling of the population from 1750 to 1776 reflects an earlier pattern of growth for vecinos moving into the Pojoaque Valley, relative to the doubling of populations recorded for the entire Rio Grande region much later in the early 1790s. This population influx may be attributed to Indigenous groups forced to move away from settlements as a result of Comanche and Athapaskan raids during the 1760s and 1770s (Darling and Eiselt 2017:192) and a general increase in land requests over that same period (Snow 1979).

The Pueblo of Pojoaque was elevated to the status of a full mission in 1782, with the pueblos of Nambe and Tesuque now serving as its visitas, and this administrative change likely corresponded to an influx of vecino communities to the Pueblo of Pojoaque beginning in the late 1770s. From 1780 to 1786 individuals baptized at Pojoaque began to travel from missions at Santa Clara, Tesuque, and Nambe (figure 9.1). Toward the end of this six-year span, the mission church at Pojoaque was concentrating local social networks with vecino populations at the Pueblo of Pojoaque and becoming more ethnically and geographically diverse as families of Navajo, Ute, and Apache heritage traveled from Abiquiu, Chimayo, Cundiyo, and Rio Tesuque to baptize their family members. The 1790 census for the Pojoaque Valley recorded 359 persons, marking a 30 percent decrease in vecino population over a fourteen-year period. This decreased growth rate may be attributed to a smallpox outbreak in the region from 1781 to 1782 and vecino populations moving from villages via active participation in local and regional trade networks extending into the New Mexican borderlands.

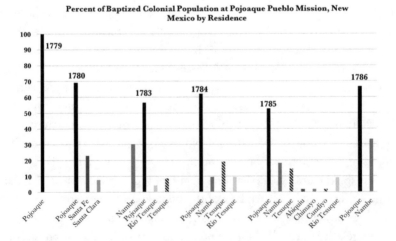

Figure 9.1 Colonial populations baptized at Pojoaque Pueblo by residential jurisdiction, 1779–86.

As vecino populations rapidly expanded into areas of the northern Rio Grande by the close of the eighteenth century, census data suggest a prioritization of settlement at the Pueblo of Pojoaque over other Spanish mission communities in the Pojoaque Valley. In 1798 Fray Diego Martinez recorded that 195 Pueblo people and 20 vecinos were serviced out of adjacent Nambe Pueblo. In contrast, at the Pueblo of Pojoaque only 79 individuals were recorded as Pueblo while vecinos were triple that amount, totaling 243 individuals. The inverse proportions of Pueblos and vecinos living at Nambe and Pojoaque are intriguing and suggest an administrative focus for settlement by vecino populations within the mission community.

What almost certainly drew vecinos to the Pueblo of Pojoaque in particular were its fertile and well-irrigated lands on an ideal confluence of the Pojoaque Creek and Tesuque River. The Pueblo of Pojoaque is traditionally known in the Tewa language as P'osuwaegeh Owingeh, meaning "Water Drinking Place Village," a reference to this confluence. Neighboring Nambe Pueblo's term for the Pueblo of Pojoaque, Pojege, translates as "Down Where the Waters or Creeks Meet," more directly referencing this geographical feature (Harrington 1916:334). The significance of Pojoaque for its water, arable land for stock raising and farming, and trade cannot be understated as a driving force for its initial Tewa occupation and for the encroachment of expanding vecino populations onto Pueblo lands.

While distinctions between Pueblo and vecino, marked by unequal access to labor, land, and technological knowledge, contributed to divisions between the colonial populations, vecino material culture incorporated many Indigenous influences, including Pueblo farming practices (Quintana 1974), household stone tools, and other technologies (Eiselt 2005; Moore 1992). However, what perhaps increased ethnic distinctions between Pueblo and vecino identities were beliefs within crosscutting socioeconomic networks in which the cosmographic concept of center place in Pueblo communities framed the communalism of village life and centrality of the household during a time when increased movement away from the village became a necessary way of life for vecinos.

For the growing population of vecinos dependent on the land through a highly mobile trade economy, the village became increasingly ancillary, although it remained central for Pueblo people—not only for subsistence, but also as a center place within the world view of becoming, where traditions are performed and negotiated in an interconnected and continuous flow of relations among humans, supernatural beings, nonhumans, things, and places. However, vecino identity should not be taken as a monolithic identity category comprising heterogeneous groups. Rather, being vecino suggests that social, economic, and political tensions existed between a civic status defined by membership in a Spanish colonial settlement and an ethnic status defined from within and outside of a community.

While vecino identity was conceptualized as self-inscribed, records of baptized male and female populations from the Pueblo of Pojoaque sampled in approximately twenty-year intervals from 1779 to 1839 reveal how the vecino label retained preexisting racial categories of *casta* and other distinct ethnic identities. In 1779 baptismal records conferred both a racial and civic status upon individuals, including terminology such as Spanish vecinos and *coiota* vecino/vecina (figure 9.2). In the latter case, a distinction between colonized and colonizer persisted, combining the earlier institutionalized Spanish casta term of *coiota* with the vecino civic status. In that same year at the Pueblo of Pojoaque, claims to particular Indigenous ethnic identities alongside the term *vecino* began and recurred through time. This is evidenced by the baptisms of Comanche vecinas, a Pueblo vecino in 1786, and a Navajo vecino during the middle of the nineteenth century.

While studies on vecino communities in colonial New Mexico emphasize how the emergence of vecino identity led to common practices and social identification with their Indigenous neighbors, it is important to continue questioning how and why individuals of mixed heritage decided to affiliate with particular ethnic groups. At the colonial administrative level, it would appear that conferring earlier forms of racial and ethnic markers alongside a vecino status continued well into the eighteenth century. Ongoing studies of vecino culture are well positioned to explore not only how vecinos claiming Pueblo and other Indigenous ethnic identities were united by a common material culture through trade and exchange networks, but more importantly how colonial populations mediated differences in their beliefs, community histories, and ideations of social being and becoming.

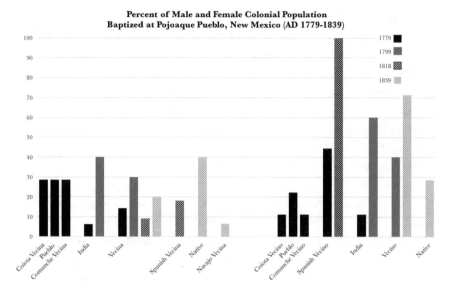

Figure 9.2 Colonial vecino and Pueblo populations at Pojoaque Pueblo by sex (e.g., vecino/vecina) and ethnic identity, 1779–1839.

SEEKING THE CENTER PLACE

The term *abandonment* is often associated with the Pueblo of Pojoaque. An article published on October 11, 1970, in the *Albuquerque Journal* refers to Pojoaque as "the mythological phoenix of New Mexico pueblos, the village that died and was reborn again in this century" (Hume 1970). While the narrative of abandonment coupled with a miraculous return makes good copy for newspapers, it undermines a continuous and unbroken effort by Pojoaque people to reclaim and renew the land. When taking into consideration the historical role of movement at Pojoaque, we realize that terms like *abandonment*, *extinction*, or *death* are misnomers precisely because leaving, over the course of Pueblo history, has been essential to sustaining the way of life of the community, as well as preventing the loss of population and culture.

Archaeological, ethnographic, or historical accounts of the Native peoples of what is now New Mexico classify Pueblo people as having traditionally been sedentary, living in their same communities for millennia. In addition to being categorized as agriculturalists, they were considered by Spanish and subsequent colonizers to be "more civilized" than the other Indigenous groups in the area and were given the name "Pueblos," meaning "towns" in Spanish. While it is true that Pueblo people have resided in their respective communities for many centuries, the process of movement has always been an essential aspect of who they are and how they live, and a central reason for their ability to continue to survive on their ancestral lands. Whether carried out geographically or through community-based practices like traditional dances, movement is the continuous and transformative path that is fundamental to the process of becoming within Pueblo life.

When the ethnographer John Peabody Harrington conducted his ethnographic fieldwork at the extant historic Tewa Pueblos in 1907, he recorded an ancestral village adjacent to the Pueblo of Pojoaque called Tekhe Owingeh, which had been independently referred to as a "middle" or center place by Pueblo collaborators from San Ildefonso, Nambe, and Ohkay Owingeh Pueblos. A place where the first group of Tewa people, as recounted in their origin stories (Ortiz 1969), came together and later split into two groups in the distant past. This same account was likewise recorded by Adolph Bandelier (1892[1890]:84) years prior, and he documented the Tewa claim that this ancestral site was the center of the range of their people and the place where the division into two branches (the Tewas of the north and Tano of the south) took place in ancient times. Explicating these oral histories alongside archaeological and linguistic data is an intriguing process in its own right; however, taken at face value such stories demonstrate a cosmographic continuity at Pojoaque shared among many other Tewa communities, whereby the process of becoming is shaped by people coming together and moving apart in search of new center places over time.

As Rina Swentzell, a Native scholar from Santa Clara Pueblo, explains, "We talk about traveling and searching for the center place alongside lightning, sacred clouds, rainbows and water spiders . . . as clouds shift and seasons change, so do human thoughts and human-made processes" (Naranjo 2009:4). The center place or middle place, as it relates to identity formation and those greater socionatural forces represented by movement, holds considerable time depth and variability as a physical and ontological reference point for ancestral and contemporary Tewa communities. The ontology of becoming among the Tewa is therefore inseparable from ideations of movement, identity, and the land itself as a repository of enduring community memory. Concepts of rest and renewal that refer to the necessity of living in and leaving places come to encompass population movements, so-called village abandonments, the fallow cycles of agricultural land (Anschuetz 2007, 2013), and what we argue for here: the persistence of Tewa people at the Pueblo of Pojoaque in the wake of Spanish, vecino, and modern-day colonialism.

During his fieldwork at Pojoaque, Harrington (1916:337) described how he could "not find an Indian at Pojoaque, although a girl was found who said she was partly Indian but did not know the Indian language." He did, however, note that three men with the surname Tapia were purported to be from Pojoaque but at that time resided at Nambe and Santa Fe. On this basis, following observations made previously by Bandelier (1892[1890]:84), Harrington, along with anthropologists F. W. Hodge (1910:274) and Elsie Clews Parsons (1996[1939]:1), categorized the Pueblo of Pojoaque as having become "extinct" as a Tewa community.

As we have attempted to chart out in this chapter, such conclusions stem from the dichotomous distinctions between Western and non-Western ideas of movement and becoming within the history of the Tewa world view. To debunk the notion of the Pueblo of Pojoaque as ever having been abandoned or become extinct requires further investigations into vecino ethnogenesis as a process that both distanced distinct ethnic identities and simultaneously cultivated a new framework with which individuals could retain and claim Pueblo identity within multiethnic Hispanic communities of the late colonial period and into the present day.

While Harrington and others privileged the criteria of linguistic competency, a perceived degree of purity, and the fixity of Pueblo identities for identifying Tewa people at the Pueblo of Pojoaque, the fluidity of Pueblo identities through time and the dynamic role of becoming as a continuous and transformative process within Tewa history have, until quite recently, been beyond the critical purview of anthropological and archaeological inquiries. Movement away from Pojoaque as a process of becoming within the context of vecino ethnogenesis suggests that even when villages are no longer inhabited, they are not necessarily abandoned. As Tewa people are always in a state of becoming, so too are the places they call home and the ways in which they identify as a people, which are subject to periods of rest and renewal before they may be reoccupied and revitalized.

MOVEMENT AND THE PROCESS OF BECOMING

Naturally, movement toward one direction results in movement away from another. At the Pueblo of Pojoaque, evidence of this, external and internal to the community, can be traced to before and after the emergence of vecino identity. Unfortunately, beginning with the Spanish invasion of what is currently New Mexico in the sixteenth century, much of that movement has been driven by the unrelenting process of colonization, resulting in Pojoaque people's departure from formerly established ways of life. According to an account in the journal of Gaspar Castaño de Sosa, who documented his travels through the Rio Grande between 1590 and 1591, on January 10, 1591, the appointment of the first governor at the Pueblo of Pojoaque was "done with the proper ceremonies to the sound of trumpets and arquebuses" (Schroeder and Matson 1965:116). This imposed form of leadership at Pojoaque marked one of the first internal movements away from traditional structures within the community, like that of the moiety system, in which the Winter and Summer sides are led by their respective caciques. At this point in time, Pojoaque was beginning to move along a path toward foreign ways of life, movement that would only grow stronger as the Spanish demanded more of the people and their land.

But while accounts provided by non-Natives concerning the Pueblos reflect ongoing processes of colonization, they also provide insights into what early postcontact life was like at the Pueblo of Pojoaque. In an account by Antonio de Espejo during a 1582 visit to the pueblo, he describes the basic architectural elements of the community, stating that it was "composed of two- to four-story room blocks that enclose[d] two small plazas, each with [its] own kiva" (Hammond and Rey 1966:21). This suggests that, like the other pueblos during this period, Pojoaque's moiety system was fully in place, with each side having its own plaza and kiva. Today, Pojoaque has one plaza and kiva, each shared by the entire community.

Following the formalized colonization of northern New Mexico, beginning with Juan de Oñate's occupation of Yungue Owingeh in 1598 and the further mistreatment of Pueblo people, the people of Pojoaque took action against their oppressors. Pojoaque people participated in the Pueblo Revolt of 1680, taking the lives of several Spanish individuals living among them (Hackett 1942:xxxiv). This resulted in the migration of Pojoaque people from their lands due to fear of a Spanish reprisal, a decision that was undoubtedly a difficult one to make (Sturtevant 1979:325).

Twelve years later, in 1692, the Spanish made a so-called peaceful reentry into Santa Fe and the greater Tewa region. In 1693 don Diego de Vargas and his men turned to brute violence as a means of reoccupying the area. Pojoaque, once again, resisted. Along with peoples from the Pueblos of San Ildefonso, Santa Clara, Tesuque, Jacona, and Cuyamungue, they climbed atop Black Mesa, staving off Vargas's attempts at regaining control (Preucel 2007:186). However, while successful in certain instances, such acts of resistance could not fully prevent the overall effects of Spanish and subsequent American colonization. Over time, the population of Pojoaque dwindled as families moved away in order to sustain themselves, resulting in the community's inability to fully maintain its various cultural practices (figure 9.3).

The effects of this diaspora are well captured in an 1881 interview conducted by John Gregory Bourke, a captain of the U.S. Army who visited the Pueblo of Pojoaque, among several other pueblos and towns, during a trip to the Southwest. At Pojoaque, he spoke with a man named Juan Pablo Tapia who told him of the condition of the clan system in the pueblo at the time, as well as a story describing one of the many struggles Pojoaque people had to endure: "The Alcalde gave me his name as Juan Pablo Tapia—Ojuo-poanya—Nube (cloud) of the Sacate gens (Grass people.) 'My wife is dead; her name was Lorenzo [Laurencita] Chirina.' I read him the list of gentes [clans] obtained in San Ildefonso and San Juan; he commented upon it by saying 'we have the same clans here represented, but not so many of course as there are so few of us. But we are all one people with those of the pueblos you name'" (Bloom 1937:69–70).

Bourke continues, describing an account shared by Juan Pablo Tapia of a time when the people of Pojoaque fled to "San Juan Country" in order to escape the "Spaniards who tried to impose grievous work upon them." After a significant amount of time there and following promises made by the Spanish to no longer mistreat them, they returned, only to

Figure 9.3 "General View, Showing Church, Pueblo of Pojoaque, New Mexico, 1899," by Adam Clark Vroman. National Anthropological Archives, Smithsonian Institution (BAE GN 02090 B).

find themselves in the same situation as before. Further, Juan Pablo Tapia told Bourke of how the Navajo had long been "at war" with Pojoaque, attempting to "carry off the women as slaves," but how, through such interactions, a plan was made that would allow the Pojoaques to once again escape their Spanish oppressors, this time to Navajo country. Following four days and nights of discussion, it was planned that the entire community would make their way northwest by way of Tierra Amarilla. However, the plan was apparently spoiled and subsequently called off (Bloom 1937:70).

Juan Pablo Tapia's comments regarding the status of the clan system at Pojoaque and his explanation for its decline speaks volumes on the cultural trajectory of Pojoaque. His account of the people fleeing from the Spanish and their interactions with the Navajo further demonstrates the degree to which the social memory of Spanish colonization remained in the minds of its people, even some sixty years after New Spain had lost control of the area. Unfortunately, Bourke does not appear to contextualize Juan Pablo Tapia's comments and account when he makes the statement, "The inhabitants of Pojuaque [Pojoaque] differ in no essential [way] from the Mexicans surrounding them" (Bloom 1937:71). Even after encountering several other individuals within the community and learning of the clans they represented, he seemed to doubt their "Pueblo-ness," contributing to the narrative that Pojoaque was no longer a "proper" pueblo. In the year before Bourke's visit, an 1880 federal census recorded that only twenty-six people were living at the pueblo.

In 1906, one year prior to Harrington's visit to Pojoaque, the census reported that twelve individuals resided there, three of whom were Tapias and would play a key role in the later reestablishment of the pueblo in 1932. As a result of encroachment on their lands and in order to seek out work and better opportunity for themselves, members of the last remaining family at the Pueblo of Pojoaque—Jose Antonio Tapia, son of Juan Pablo Tapia; his former wife, Senovia Montoya; and their daughter, Feliciana Tapia (Samuel's great-grandmother)—moved away.

During this time, Feliciana met Fermin Viarrial, a man of Hispanic and Indian blood from the village of Chimayo, New Mexico, whom she later married. In the 1920s, after coming across a government-placed ad in the newspaper searching for Pojoaque Indians to reclaim their lands, Fermin, Feliciana, and their daughter, Cordelia, made the trek by horse and buggy back to the pueblo. Jose Antonio Tapia subsequently followed suit and the renewal of the community had begun. With the return of other Pojoaque people from the surrounding pueblos and area, as well as a reintroduction of traditional practices through the guidance of Tewa elders and religious leaders from the other villages, Pueblo life was renewed at Pojoaque. By seeking their center place through the process of becoming, the people came together to reestablish Pojoaque and renew Tewa social life within the community, as had been done since time immemorial.

An article from the *Journal North* (Sharpe 1991) entitled "Family Honors Hispanic Who Saved Pueblo" recounts the story of the role Fermin Viarrial played in the revitalization of the pueblo. In it, his son, Governor Jacob Viarrial, speaks to his own mixed Hispanic and Pueblo heritage, stating, "Despite being half Hispanic, [I have] always identified as Indian." He, like the girl in Harrington's early account, identified as Pueblo while retaining a mixed heritage. This, along with the cultural transformations beginning with the emergence of vecino identities in the eighteenth century, is illustrative of Pueblo identity within the Pueblo of Pojoaque as a whole.

Regarding my own sense of identity, I, Samuel, recognize and am proud of my mixed Spanish and Indigenous roots, though I consider myself Pojoaque and Tewa before anything else. For me, it is our experiences and, more importantly, our intentions as Pojoaque people that inform who we are as members of the community. I have found this to be a sentiment shared by others. Coming from families of mixed Native and non-Native heritages, they too recognize all aspects of who they are. But because of their upbringing within the community, their Pueblo culture is at the forefront of their experience. As a result, their sense of Native identity is strong, though not at the expense of those other backgrounds that also inform their sense of personhood. I especially see this in the younger generation of Pojoaque people as they reflect contemporary movement and the ongoing process of becoming within the community.

Within my own family, geographical movement away from the community has been commonplace since the pueblo's reestablishment. During the 1950s, my grandfather Jimmy Villarreal (son of Feliciana and Fermin) took part in the Indian Relocation program, moving his family to Chicago to pursue vocational training offered to him by the federal government. It was because of this that my mother was born there and that she and her siblings did not begin permanently living in the pueblo until she was nearly a teenager. Before returning to Pojoaque, they lived in Oakland, California, for over a decade while my grandfather worked as a truck mechanic. What finally drew them back was a request by Feliciana to return (Jimmy Villarreal, personal communication 2011).

Today, the pursuit of education remains a major factor in why Pojoaque people move within and outside the community. The transference of roles at Pojoaque requires the people to prepare and grow. The youth, as they willingly and with conviction accept new roles, recognize this and seek out formal and community-based education. The former often takes individuals away from the community, sometimes out of state, while the latter results in individuals taking on positions within the community that best suit their interests and the contributions they would like to make.

Another way the younger generation initiates movement within the community is through the ongoing process of cultural revitalization. At Pojoaque, this has meant not only movement toward new ways of being and doing, but a return to those the community has not been able to carry out for some time. In September of 2012, the Pueblo of Pojoaque Tribal Council voted to replace Columbus Day with T'owa vi Thaa (Peoples' Day), a day to celebrate the survival of Indigenous peoples in the face of colonization. During its nascent years, community members gathered to bake bread beginning in the early morning, hold a potluck, watch the Pueblo of Pojoaque youth hoop dancers perform (plate 8), and take part in a Pueblo throw. Soon after, it expanded, and from that October holiday came a new summer feast day by the same name. It is through such community growth and movement that the process of becoming at Pojoaque is continuously advanced.

CONCLUSION

Physical movement within and away from ancestral lands and the community, as well as how people come to identify and become recognized as Pueblo during periods of social, economic, and religious change, is inherent to the process of becoming. During the late colonial period, the process of becoming and the emergence of vecino identities played a fascinating and complicated role in mediating ideas of mixed heritage at the Pueblo of Pojoaque, one that merits further study. However, conceptions of movement need not be relegated to those periods of history marked by colonialism. Rather, movement and the process of becoming have taken place since the people's emergence, always bringing them closer to their center place, where social relationships, individuals, and the community as a whole are most in balance and complete.

Since the advent of Spanish colonization, the process of becoming has been stalled and maybe even thrown off course, but it has never stopped. Today, the process of decolonization has taken its place as the community realigns itself with the ways of its ancestors, those who laid the foundation on which the modern Pueblo of Pojoaque was reestablished. It is on this foundation that parents, grandparents, and great-grandparents have worked to rebuild the community.

With the guidance of the other Tewa pueblos, they have revived traditional dances at Pojoaque, bringing the community together during the feast day of its patron saint, Our Lady of Guadalupe. By electing Pojoaque's first female governor (the first of any pueblo), they have reinstalled women as prominent leaders within the community, setting a precedent for others to follow. And in the face of threats by the state, they have stood up for their sovereign right to provide for their people through financial means. From culture to economy, instances such as these demonstrate how Pojoaque has renewed movement and advanced the process of becoming, providing the younger generation with the means to move forward and grow in their own right. In the words of Tom Romero, the late governor of Pojoaque, "We built up, built up, and now we're really back up."

ACKNOWLEDGMENTS

We would like to dedicate this chapter to the memory of the late Cordelia Gomez (1929–2017), the daughter of Feliciana Tapia Viarrial and Fermin Viarrial and the last surviving member of P'osuwaegeh Owingeh to have come to the pueblo by horse-drawn wagon in 1932.

REFERENCES

Anschuetz, Kurt F. 2007. Room to Grow with, Rooms to Spare: Agriculture and Big Site Settlement Systematics in the Late Pre-Columbian Tewa Basin Pueblo Landscape. *Kiva* 73(2):173–194.

Anschuetz, Kurt F. 2013. Water Is Life: Anthropological Perspectives in the Study of Movement as an Ancestral Puebloan Lifeway. Paper presented at the 2013 New Mexico Archaeological Council Fall Conference, November 16, Hibben Center, University of New Mexico, Albuquerque.

Bandelier, Adolph F. 1892[1890]. *Final Report: Investigations Among the Indians of the Southwestern United States, Carried on Mainly in the Years from 1880 to 1885, Part II.* John Wilson and Son, Cambridge.

Bloom, Lansing B. (editor). 1937. Bourke on the Southwest, XI. *New Mexico Historical Review* 12(1):41–77.

Brooks, James F. 2002. *Captives and Cousins: Slavery, Kinship, and Community in the Southern Borderlands.* University of North Carolina Press, Chapel Hill.

Christmas, Henrietta M. (editor). 2010. *New Mexico Baptisms: Nambé, 1707–1837, and Pojoaque, 1779–1839.* Extracted by Members of the New Mexico Genealogical Society. New Mexico Genealogical Society Press, Albuquerque.

Cipolla, Craig N. 2013. *Becoming Brothertown.* University of Arizona Press, Tucson.

Darling, Andrew J., and Sunday B. Eiselt. 2017. Vecino Origins and the Settlement Archaeology of the Rio del Oso Grant, New Mexico. In *New Mexico* and the Pimería Alta: The Colonial Period in the American Southwest, edited by John G. Douglass and William M. Graves, pp. 187–212. University Press of Colorado, Boulder.

Eiselt, Sunday B. 2005. A Brief Guide to the Identification of Historic Micaceous Ceramics of the Northern Rio Grande; Including Types Attributed to Hispanic, Northern Tewa, Northern Tiwa, and Jicarilla Apache Potters. Manuscript on file, Museum of Indian Arts and Culture, Laboratory of Anthropology Library, Santa Fe, New Mexico.

Eiselt, Sunday B. 2006. The Emergence of Jicarilla Apache Enclave Economy During the Nineteenth Century in Northern New Mexico. PhD dissertation, Department of Anthropology, University of Michigan, Ann Arbor.

Eiselt, B. Sunday, and J. Andrew Darling. 2012. Vecino Economics: Gendered Economy and Micaceous Pottery Consumption in Nineteenth-Century Northern New Mexico. *American Antiquity* 77(3):424–448.

Eiselt, B. Sunday, and J. Andrew Darling. 2016. Ethnogenesis and Archaeological Demography in Southwest Vecino Society. In *Exploring Cause and Explanation: Historical Ecology, Demography, and Movement in the American Southwest*, edited by Cynthia L. Herhahn and Ann F. Ramenofsky, pp. 155–176. University Press of Colorado, Boulder.

Frank, Ross. 1996. Economic Growth and the Creation of the Vecino Homeland in New Mexico, 1780–1820. *Revistas de Indias* 56(208):743–782.

Frank, Ross. 2000. *From Settler to Citizen: New Mexican Economic Development and the Creation of Vecino Society, 1750–1820*. University of California Press, Berkeley.

Hackett, Charles Wilson. 1942. *Revolt of the Pueblo Indians of New Mexico and Otermin's Attempted Reconquest, 1680–1682*. University of New Mexico, Albuquerque.

Hammond, George P., and Agapito Rey. 1966. *The Rediscovery of New Mexico, 1580–1594: The Explorations of Chamuscado, Espejo, Castaño de Sosa, Morlete, and Leyva de Bonilla and Humaña*. University of New Mexico Press, Albuquerque.

Harrington, John P. 1916. *Ethnogeography of the Tewa*. 29th Annual Report of the Bureau of American Ethnology. Government Printing Office, Washington D.C.

Hodge, Frederick W. 1910. Pojoaque. In *Handbook of American Indians North of Mexico*, Vol. 2, edited by Frederick W. Hodge, p. 274. 2 vols. Bureau of American Ethnology Bulletin 30. Government Printing Office, Washington, D.C.

Hume, Bill. 1970. Pojoaque Pueblo Smallest in State. *Albuquerque Journal*, October 11, G-1.

Jenks, Kelly L. 2017. Becoming Vecinos: Civic Identities in Late Colonial New Mexico. In *New Mexico and the Pimería Alta: The Colonial Period in the American Southwest*, edited by John G. Douglass and William M. Graves, pp. 213–238. University Press of Colorado, Boulder.

Moore, James L. 1992. Spanish Colonial Stone Tool Use. In *Current Research on the Late Prehistory and Early History of New Mexico*, edited by Bradley J. Vierra and Clara Gualtieri, pp. 239–244. New Mexico Archaeological Council, Albuquerque.

Naranjo, Tessie. 2009. Some Recent Thoughts About Tewa Ancestral Movement. Paper presented at the 2009 New Mexico Archaeological Council Fall Conference, November 14, Hibben Center, University of New Mexico, Albuquerque.

Nostrand, Richard L. 1970. The Hispanic-American Borderland: Delimitation of an American Culture Region. *Annals of the Association of American Geographers* 60(4):638–661.

Nostrand, Richard L. 1975. Mexican Americans Circa 1850. *Annals of the Association of American Geographers* 65(3):382–396.

Nostrand, Richard L. 1980. The Hispano Homeland in 1900. *Annals of the Association of American Geographers* 70(3):378–390.

Nostrand, Richard L. 1992. *The Hispano Homeland*. University of Oklahoma Press, Norman.

Ortiz, Alfonso. 1969. *The Tewa World: Space, Time, Being, and Becoming in a Pueblo Society*. University of Chicago Press, Chicago.

Parsons, Elsie Clews. 1996 [1939]. *Pueblo Indian Religion*. 2 Vols. University of Nebraska Press, Lincoln.

Preucel, Robert W. (editor). 2007. *Archaeologies of the Pueblo Revolt: Identity, Meaning, and Renewal in the Pueblo World*. University of New Mexico Press, Albuquerque.

Quintana, Frances L. 1974. *Pobladores: Hispanic Americans of the Ute Frontier*. University of Notre Dame Press, South Bend, Indiana.

Rodríguez, Sylvia. 1986. *The Hispano Homeland Debate*. Working Paper Series No. 17. Stanford Center for Chicano Research, Stanford University, Palo Alto, California.

Schroeder, Albert H., and Dan S. Matson. 1965. *A Colony on the Move: Gaspar Castaño de Sosa's Journal, 1590–1591*. School of American Research, Santa Fe, New Mexico.

Sharpe, Tom. 1991. "Family Honors Hispanic Who Saved Pueblo." *Journal North*, July 31, A-1.

Snow, David H. 1979. Rural Hispanic Community Organization in Northern New Mexico: An Historical Perspective. In *The Survival of Spanish American Villages*, edited by Paul Kutsche, pp. 45–52. Colorado College Studies 15. Colorado College, Colorado Springs.

Snow, David H. 1996. *New Mexico's First Colonists: The 1597–1600 Enlistments for New Mexico under Juan de Oñate, Adelante and Gobernador*. Hispanic Genealogical Research Center of New Mexico, Albuquerque.

Sturtevant, William C. 1971. Creek into Seminole. In *North American Indians in Historical Perspective*, edited by Eleanor Burke Leacock and Nancy Oestreich Lurie, pp. 92–128. Random House, New York.

Swadesh, Frances L. 1979. Structure of Hispanic-Indian Relations in New Mexico. In *The Survival of Spanish American Villages*, edited by Paul Kutsche, pp. 53–61. Colorado College Studies 15. Colorado College, Colorado Springs.

Trigg, Heather B. 2005. *From Household to Empire: Society and Economy in Early Colonial New Mexico*. University of Arizona Press, Tucson.

Van Ness, John R. 1987. *Hispanos: Ethnic Identity in Cañones*. Working Paper Series No. 20. Stanford Center for Chicano Research, Stanford University, Palo Alto, California.

Voss, Barbara. 2005. From Casta to Californio: Social Identity and the Archaeology of Culture Contact. *American Anthropologist* 107(3):461–474.

Voss, Barbara. 2008. *The Archaeology of Ethnogenesis: Race and Sexuality in Colonial San Francisco*. University of California Press, Berkeley.

10

Getting Accustomed to the Light

Joseph H. Suina

Pueblo Indians have successfully managed our social and environmental situations for thousands of years by moving from village to village. Difficulties were never insurmountable no matter how bleak the conditions. In times of severe drought or when the local resources were no longer enough to support us, we found a more suitable location. If some irresolvable difference divided the community, even with all the sorrow that it entailed, a part of the village broke off and started anew. However, after the Spanish invasion and the Anglo imposition, we were no longer free to move about. Pueblo people have had to engage with foreign ideas and things at our home villages, in some cases very rapidly. This "migration in the mind," a migration primarily in the form of new ideas and technologies, took place for us with breathless rapidity.

By 1950, with the end of World War II, the pumped-up optimism of America was spilling over into our pueblo. The walls of isolation that let us be who we were collapsed under the pressures of many innovative ideas and things coming in from the outside world. These modernizations were already routine in American life, and each occurred over a stretch of seventy-five years; they were discovered, refined, and incorporated into the dominant society at a reasonable pace. However, these changes were incorporated into Pueblo life in a mere ten years, giving us no time for careful consideration as to what impacts these glamorous ideas and gadgets might have. Unlike the rest of the citizenry, we did not come to America; America came to us in the form of ideas and things supposedly designed for our welfare. Some changes arrived seemingly overnight, like electricity: one flip of a switch and there was light. Others were more subtle, such as the shift from a barter system to a cash economy. In the process, our Native life lost its old groove. Our lives transformed from those of simple subsistence in the form of farming and togetherness to those of hectic struggle for survival in the material world.

Our people have experienced major changes in the past with the imposition of critical Spanish life elements including Catholicism, domesticated animals, and new crops. Maybe because the Spanish brand of change also came with a heavy hand, we responded with a determined resistance to never permit the complete takeover of our daily livelihood and traditional beliefs. During this period, every man, woman, and child was committed to keeping our religion private and pretending we were becoming devout Catholics. This was especially true for the people living in the villages in the Rio Grande area, where the Spaniards were concentrated. We used their saints to support the continuance of our dances and ceremonies and to appease our invaders at the same time. We embraced their foods and beasts of burden with little or no compromise of our values. While Christianity took hold with some, it never overpowered our own beliefs.

The changes following the Spanish period were gradual extensions of what had come earlier. But this all took a turn in the 1950s. We became immediately attracted to and consumed by popular culture and the material benefits of modern American life. I am certain that mass media and faster transportation expedited the American influences. Some of these changes were encouraged by our own people to a certain degree. Thirty-three men came home to us from World War II with a greater appreciation for life after seeing the horror of humanity at its worst. They were eager to share and work for the "good things" they learned about in American life. Many of these things had to be bought and paid for, and the sale of handmade crafts was the immediate solution to getting our slice of the American pie. Our mothers labored late into the night on beadwork and pottery to buy things from the store. Children strung corn necklaces to take to Santa Fe or to the Domingo Trading Post, where they received credit, not cash, for the immediate purchase of the necessities we came to rely on.

Paving the twelve miles of dirt road from our pueblo to the interstate intensified selling and buying. Our leaders purchased a "community truck" to make a weekly run into Santa Fe, where tourists in need of souvenirs congregated. Farming declined, and horses, our beasts of burden and proud possessions, were put out to pasture. The wagons they once pulled sat silent and rusted. By 1954 at least a half dozen personal vehicles were tooling around the village. For families without one, fifty cents to travel to and from town was a fair fee. It bought the owner three gallons of gas. With a paved road and more automobiles, some people began commuting to Santa Fe and Albuquerque to jobs. The majority went to sell their crafts at the "Long Porch" (at the Palace of the Governors) or to a shop owner at a much-reduced profit. Members of other pueblos were also out and about selling—the shift in subsistence pattern was not unique to us.

The word *groceries* became firmly fixed in our conversations. It did not make sense to break your back hoeing a garden under a scorching sun and taking a chance at being outdone by weeds and critters when you could just buy food off the shelf. But it took hard cash to live modern, and the more crafts sold, the greater the purchasing power. If one had a job, a steady flow of cash was possible. Since few were available at home, our people looked to town for jobs, too. Town, cash, and groceries went hand in hand, and our farming heritage and associated activities seemed irrelevant, but no one seemed too concerned.

It was unthinkable for a Pueblo woman to work outside the home, but some found housekeeping jobs in town. An Indian housemaid soon became fashionable for some Anglo families in Santa Fe, much like an African American maid was elsewhere. The job ceiling for our men was janitorial and grounds-keeping work. There, they saw others with a better education enjoy better work conditions and higher wages. This led to their strong encouragement of Pueblo youth, like me, to acquire as much education as possible for better employment opportunities.

While modern things made life easier, they also cut into interdependence, a cornerstone of Pueblo culture. Interdependence meant supporting, caring, sharing, taking part, and all the ways that one could give to others. It was our obligation to give a hand when called upon for a village cleanup or ditch work. Before our annual feast, we refurbished our kivas, the church, and other public buildings with a new coat of mud plaster. The youth hauled and poured water, and men mixed mud and delivered it to the women, who applied a fine finish. We were proud to show off our well-kept village to the hundreds who came to visit us on feast day.

One year, our leaders decided to try stucco, a plaster used all over Santa Fe to give buildings that "Pueblo ambience" for the tourists. Supposedly, it looked better than our mud mix and was much more durable. We hired someone to apply this wonderful material. It looked great and it saved us time and labor, but there was a side effect. Graffiti appeared on a public building for the very first time. It seemed the sense of ownership and pride in work well done was now lacking. And then, ugly white streaks stained the synthetic plastered wall up to three feet from the base on the interior side. The stucco trapped moisture and did not allow the adobe to breathe naturally, causing the encased bricks to crumble to dirt that poured through cracks that developed. We learned that some things just do not mix naturally, no matter how attractive or easy they made life.

Typically, not much went on at night except resting and relaxing after a hard day of work. Night was a time to visit with friends and family. Almost everyone in the village lived within a short walk from the plaza area. Grandmother, whom I lived with, always brought along something good to eat on a visit. During our visits, the children played busily by themselves and the adults talked and laughed and just plain enjoyed each other's company. The men were very much a part of the scene if not in a ceremonial house preparing for a dance. Storytelling was a form of entertainment we all enjoyed, and it was an important teaching tool. Some stories were explained to convey the full meaning they carried, while others were left to our interpretation. English was nowhere to be heard except in school, where any utterance of our language led to shaming and discipline by our non-Indian teachers. After an hour or two of visiting, guests bid farewell and went home to sleep for the night.

Before electricity, we had kerosene lighting, and during the winter the fireplace gave ample light and heat for all our needs. The village night turned soft with the warm illumination of kerosene lamps. The comforting glow was a symbol of security and family togetherness. With hardly any light pollution, the night sky dazzled with stars, and the Milky Way cut a brilliant swath from north to south, like a symbol of our migration. Our walk home from a night visit was something to behold. Midway home, Grandmother would pull out a cornmeal offering, and we would stop to pray (figure 10.1).

One afternoon, I went to my mother's house and found a stranger gouging and scraping a snakelike path right across her beautiful white adobe wall. This stranger with one good eye, defacing the wall, frightened me. Sensing my fear, my mom hugged me and explained that it was the

Figure 10.1 Joseph Suina, with his mother and grandmother, in the 1950s.

path of the electric wire soon to bring us lights so bright that we would see every nook and cranny on the darkest night and make our lives much better.

Before long, electricity came into our homes like a thief in the night and stole two very special things we have never been able to recover: our nighttime home gatherings and the incredible night sky. I was surrounded by my parents, grandmother, and little brother when it came time for me to officially pull the cord in a light-welcoming ceremony. I was not quite sure what was about to happen; I hesitated. Encouraged by Mom, I yanked the chain and there it was! It was so very bright all around us, but still I could not see how it was going to improve our lives.

Our modern all-electric home had a single lightbulb suspended from a small chain in the middle of the ceiling. At first, there were no electrical appliances. In a matter of a few weeks, appliances and electrical gadgets began to find their way into many of our homes. Table lamps, clocks, and radios were among the first things purchased. English took over our homes, blaring constantly in music, news, and programs like *Fibber McGee and Molly*. Soon we were singing, "Davy, Davy Crockett, king of the wild frontier," and other tunes of the day. As for Grandmother, electricity was somewhere in the future. She did not trust it and did not think we needed it anyway.

Electricity brought yet another experience, a monthly bill. It was always on time and without fail pressing us to keep up a steady flow of cash. With this we took a giant leap away from the village barter system that always had a degree of flexibility built in if one could not make a payment right then. Mom worried that her electricity would get cut off if she did not pay on time. I worried, too, as I imagined electric wires snipped right over her house and dangling from the pole so the whole world could see that we were poor and irresponsible.

Once villagers discovered the time-payment plan, they began charging refrigerators, washing machines, and other major appliances. Before long, we were up to our ears in bills with no clue about the tricky fine print that laid out the interest charges. Among the many appliances and gadgets was a turtlelike metal device at the end of an electric cord that plugged in and heated water right in a pail. I dipped my finger in to test if the warnings I had received about the consequence of doing that were true. I learned about the power of electricity with a nasty jolt that went right to my bones.

With regard to our acquisitions, more than once I overheard elders saying that we were playing the game of keeping up with the neighbors. To them, this behavior was appalling in a communal culture heavily focused on the welfare of everyone. Individual wants and needs steered us away from this important concept. Money was clearly harder to share than the melons we used to grow. Melons would rot if you did not share them, and sharing always got you something in return—if not immediately, then in the future. But money did not rot; one could horde it or spend it on yet another thing that looked good until you got tired of it. This type of happiness was fleeting, and some villagers recognized this early on.

Much to our dismay, many had purchases repossessed and some had electricity cut off, which was something different from the dangling wires I had envisioned. We learned firsthand that a payment on time mattered a whole lot more than any personal circumstance. Again, we had to compromise in order to fit into the white man's world.

All of these new needs and wants in modern life made cash an absolute necessity, and our reliance on tourism became even greater. With electricity in the home, both husband and wife worked late into the night creating crafts to pay the bills and buy the groceries we never had before. Night visiting was now done mostly by those who could afford it. Ironically, these were people like my grandma and other seniors who had the vision and the sense to see what was happening. Grandmother and I still went to Mom's, but not as regularly. Our night guests and those we visited dwindled down to other grandmothers and grandkids like me who still needed each other. This was all before a certain little box made its appearance.

Television entered the pueblo several months after the first light switch was pulled. Before that, adults must have known about TV from trips into town, but its expense must have made it prohibitive, or maybe acquiring it was yet too bold in our culture at that point. It first came to the Tafoyas, an elderly Hispanic couple living across the canal near the fields. One afternoon a friend dashed up to make a historic report to a group of us playing in the plaza. He blurted about this magic box with little people and little cars and little houses in it that all were real! It took us no time to scoot down the road and across the bridge to the Tafoyas'. With great caution we approached to peek into their window. To our surprise, their living room was filled wall to wall with young and old villagers who had beat us there! They were staring straight ahead and totally unaware of us. They all had a gray ghostlike reflection on their faces and seemed to be in a state of trance. They were captivated by some strange power emanating from that box.

Soon, I found myself among the gray faces enthralled by the images and the foreign tongue that was not so foreign in a short while. We took over the poor Tafoyas' living room at four every afternoon when Roy Rogers rode into town. Happily, we adhered to the nickel fee or the request to bring in firewood to earn TV time, which they unsuccessfully imposed to keep us away. Television cast its spell on adults, too, especially on Monday nights. It showed Mike London's Monday night wrestling! We all got emotionally charged reacting to the body slams, choke holds, and the referee banging the count on the mat.

We learned more English and more about the world from TV than we ever did at school. We compared the fast-paced and carefree lifestyle of the white world to what felt like our mundane way of life. We learned defiance and independence and got confused about our identity. Weren't the cowboys always beating up on the Indians? We all wanted to be a cowboy and never an Indian in our hero-imitation games. Indians were nameless losers we did not wish to identify with. Never before did we have another group with whom we could so easily compare ourselves. Because of the magic of TV, we could see so many glaring deficiencies in our life and we felt shame.

More TVs came into our community as buyers were enabled by creditors. New owners could not keep their purchases a secret, and villagers flocked to their doorsteps, ready to help watch the TV. At least the crowd was getting distributed around the village, much to the relief of the Tafoyas. Then came a surge in TV ownership in the summer of 1954. A major forest fire broke out in Idaho, and our dads and grandfathers flew out to fight it. Villagers teased those who were terrified about flying for risking their lives just to have a TV and about prolonging the fire to make just enough money for a set. Sure enough, we saw many more households glowing gray soon after their return.

Eventually every home had bright lights and a gray glow. These replaced the warm evening glow of kerosene lamps, as well as the laughter and storytelling. In their place were programs in a foreign language from a foreign culture. We were still together but no longer focused on one another. It was all on the black-and-white TV in front of us. Within a few years, we saw that our children could no longer carry on a conversation in our own tongue.

This period of rapid changes was more than anyone ever anticipated. Changes were not always made with careful thought, but our parents meant well and tried their best to give us things they never had. The life before was hard, and no one today would wish to go back to the days of outhouses and a steady diet of tortillas and beans. We can see, however, that many healthy community attributes fell to the wayside. Our evening gatherings, farming, and language were just some of the practices that were sacrificed to fulfill the American dream in the pueblo, and we migrated in a whole other direction without moving over the hill.

It has been more than a half a century since that rapid-fire change descended upon our pueblo. We have "migrated over to the next hill" in our minds and lifeways without leaving our village. Fortunately, we must have taken along the essential elements of our heritage, allowing our traditional life to not only survive but to thrive in the midst of today's hectic lifestyles. We have adopted and adapted American modernizations to fit our culture, much as we did with the Spanish influences of four hundred years ago. We have not compartmentalized meaning; we have not kept traditional and modern ways distinct and separate from one another as we did with Spanish Catholicism. Instead, we blended the more superficial, material culture of America with our own. Once again, we kept our deeper belief systems out of harm's way.

At times we replaced the old, like outdoor toilets with modern indoor bathrooms, and at others we combined the old with the new, as with our diet. Beliefs and religion form the foundation and, at a deeper level of culture, necessitated the compartmentalization of the two belief systems for us to retain the distinct nature of each, as in the Spanish era, for our benefit. But we accommodated the time and space of the imposed religion and synchronized it with our traditional calendar of dances and ceremonies. In time, our ancestors accepted the Catholic religion as another expression of our worship alongside our Indigenous beliefs. Since almost all of the American infusion has been at the material level, our core beliefs were not a central matter of concern.

Today, we are classified as one of the more conservative pueblos with a traditional government and a rich Native calendar of dances and ceremonies. Our council meetings are conducted in our Native tongue, and the welfare of our people is still a sacred responsibility. Expressions of interdependence abound in both the private sector of community life and the more formal public acts of support for our pueblo. The expectation still is that we share with the community in some way the knowledge and skills we have been blessed with over the years. To dance is a spiritual expression to gain blessings for all our people, and therefore participation is an obligation for everyone. More young people take part in dances and ceremonies today than in the days of fast change two generations ago.

The comparisons we made between ourselves and those in the American world in the early years of its arrival revealed many material deficiencies and led us to feel ashamed of our own culture. We did not have modern things, and the mass media portrayed Indians very negatively. We have learned much about the white material world since then and have access to that part of life, as much as any other group of people within the lower- to middle-class social-economic strata in America. Our values and expressions that we thought were backward and old fashioned in our culture, like storytelling, Native language, and gardening, are now being promoted as healthy and much needed in American life. More importantly, we find that practices centered on community and interdependence are sorely needed in the larger world. The lack of concern for others less fortunate is evident everywhere in the larger society, beginning with the number of homeless and those with mental illness who walk the streets of our cities without attention until another tragedy occurs. People do not seem to want to get involved unless it is for personal gain. The advancements in technology and materialism seem to far exceed those regarding the social welfare of all members of the dominant world. These glaring differences in values make us appreciate what we have, reversing our past negative perceptions of ourselves.

We still see many stereotypes and ignorance about Indian culture, such as sports team mascots, beginning with our nation's capital. A movement to point out the dangers of such portrayals has met with a mainstream pushback argued from a for-profit marketing perspective. We want more of our perspectives to be included in the curriculum of our schools for the benefit of all children. Through education, changes can come about, as we, too, have to take care that the negative aspects of America do not override the many wonderful things it has for all citizens to enjoy.

To live in both worlds and not be marginal in either one is a challenge. Sometimes, frustration comes about from simply trying to get employers to understand that we will be needed at the pueblo at a certain time. This has even led to firings of individuals who were called upon to serve in our traditional government, when they took time away from work to attend to duties at home. However, just to be present each and every night for several weeks leading up to a dance when you also have to be out the door at six thirty every morning and drive fifty-five miles to work fully awake and prepared for the challenges of the day can be wearing. To be a fully participating member of both worlds is demanding, and yet many individuals manage this schedule in order to meet obligations all the way around. At work, I would hear my colleagues planning a skiing trip or some leisurely getaway during the winter holidays at semester's end. As for me, I had to be at home preparing for the predawn Christmas buffalo dances inside the church followed by those on plaza until sunset. But that is our gift and our prayer of thanksgiving and petition for peace on earth for our people and all who are our guests on that day. Tiring though it may be, it leads to an incredibly rewarding and loving feeling at day's end. Christmas Day's dance is followed by four more days and nights of preparation and dancing during the holidays. With just one night's break, we're off and into the New Year's installation and celebration of new officials.

In spite of all that, we have not shied away from participating in the contemporary world of education and politics. Our pueblo has been recognized by the New Mexico Department of Indian Education as having more formally educated people with advanced degrees per capita than any other tribe in the Southwest. We have engaged the federal government in its own court of law and sued big corporations that have severely damaged our lands, and succeeded. Our relationship with the outside world is not always adversarial. We have created relationships with individuals and organizations willing to see us as equal partners in the true spirit of Indian self-determination. The wisdom and courage of our ancestors continue to be demonstrated by our people in defending and promoting our rights as a sovereign Native nation in the larger world. But tribal sovereignty is only as strong as the exercise of self-government and traditions and, even more fundamentally, our respect for one another and traditional authority. There are those in our village who have committed a lifetime to serving the physical and spiritual well-being of our people and all people everywhere. While their education may not be considered formal by outside standards, their esoteric knowledge exercised in prayer and fasting gives integrity to our beliefs and balance to our contemporary dual form of life.

Our actions to stave off language shift among our young children are more widespread than ever. We have language-revival programs based in both the community and school for adults and youth. We now have an early childhood full-immersion Native-language Montessori school that has become a beacon of this revival. It is visited regularly by tribes wishing to learn from our experiences. Our elders remind us to speak our language at every large gathering, and we now see many young people making a sincere effort to speak our Keres language.

As in the early days of TV and the opening up of America, we now have the world literally at our fingertips through the Internet. We see very agile, active fingers and focused faces on yet another, even smaller, device that can be taken everywhere: our personal cell phones. New and disturbing behaviors of people isolated and ignoring those around them in crowded public settings, and even in the intimacy of their homes, have us concerned. Our dances and even some of our most sacred and private ceremonies are posted on YouTube, sometimes by our own people, without tribal permission for all the world to see. Boy Scouts and other similar organizations are taking note, replicating what is sacred to us, and making a cheap sideshow of it for their personal amusement. It was secrecy that protected our ownership of what is sacred and brought us solidarity and unity within our communities when we were up against a foreign system that threatened to dissolve our culture. It is also our protection against scholars eager to appropriate our knowledge as their own expertise and authority on the subject.

How will our community-oriented people fare with the new migration that is already in motion? An old kiva leader once said to us, "No one will ever take our language and culture away from us, not the church, the school or anybody. If we lose it, it will be because we gave it up ourselves."

Commentary

Pueblo Perspectives on Movement and Becoming

Paul Tosa and Octavius Seowtewa

We opened the Amerind Foundation seminar with a Jemez prayer for a good meeting with knowledgeable people and a beautiful return home after the conference. Although this was a scholarly conference, it was important to set the proper spiritual context for discussing movement and becoming because these are important in the lives of Pueblo people.

It was through migration that the Pueblo peoples found their places in the homelands they were destined to occupy. The Jemez people, for example, had been instructed to "find the mountain," and when they saw the image of the eagle on the side of Wâavêmâ, they knew they had found their place in the world. Zuni, too, has a long history of migrations that sought the Middle Place, which they found at Halona:wa (Zuni Pueblo). Other Pueblos have similar accounts of migration to the center. But once settled in their homelands, Pueblo people continued to move throughout their land to honor the spirits and ancestors and harvest the bounty needed to sustain life. Movement still continues with the present generations.

We came together at the Amerind Foundation to talk with archaeologists and ethnographers about migration and movement because we think this will benefit future generations of Pueblo communities. It is a never-ending process. We were guided in our discussions by the Pueblo philosophy of gentle teaching, which seeks to provide people with the knowledge they need to understand the world and their place within it. This can be done by using a rock or a view or some other thing to quietly teach people important concepts, just like the corn grows when you sing during irrigation, planting, and harvesting. Strength and power come from the ancient people and time, and we continue our cultural practices with our language, in song and dance. We think combining traditional values with scientific facts, as we strove to do in the seminar, is a powerful method for understanding where we've been and where we are going.

The archaeologists we talked with at the conference framed their understanding of the past using time periods and archaeological classifications that are alien to Pueblo thought. We heard a lot about Basketmakers and a series of Pueblo periods designated with roman numerals. The terms archaeologists use for past people make it sound like they were a different people than who we are today. We think that while our clothing and pottery have changed over time, our culture remains the same. There is a common history shared by different Pueblo tribes. As Pueblo men, we know that the people have been the same since migration. The ancient sites are the same as our modern villages, with kivas, houses, and medicine lodges. We still have the same way of life that our ancestors did. Archaeologists see surface rubble and artifacts, but as Pueblo people we hear the spiritual ancestors who still reside in the places non-Indians call "archaeological sites." We are instructed to speak to the ancestors at our old villages, to sing and listen to the elders, to learn. "The spirits are waiting, they are waiting for you to come," we say.

Woody Aguilar, an archaeologist from San Ildefonso Pueblo, explained to the seminar how it is a challenge to make non-Indian archaeologists and anthropologists appreciate the Pueblo viewpoint. We come at this from two different perspectives. Pueblo people learn Western concepts in schools and by learning to speak English, but it doesn't work the other way around. Dwight Honyouti from Hopi agreed that this is an important issue and asked, how do you explain to someone the values and beliefs that are instilled from birth in a cultural setting? Non-Native archaeologists need to understand they might not fully grasp concepts that are framed in Native languages. Some concepts are not easily translated into English. Nonetheless it's good to talk together about concepts such as movement.

The heart and soul of our modern villages lie in the center of our pueblos. People come back for that. The connection is the movement out and the coming back. You always come home to take part in ceremonies. Spiritual umbilical cords connect our current villages with the places where our ancestors dwelled and made their lives. The connection between mother and child is like the connection between our shrines and us. Female cords are buried in the house; male cords are buried in fields because that is where men will work. There is a connection to the earth. Trails lead to shrines, so shrines are connected to the middle places of our villages. Pilgrimages to shrines give Pueblo people a strong hold on the land.

We still revere the places our ancestors traveled through during their migrations, which cover an area from Chimney Rock in southern Colorado to Paquimé in Chihuahua and beyond. Our ancestors traded with people over a wide area, exchanging piñon nuts for buckskins, and traded lots of other things needed to sustain a good life. Through travel, we maintained social relations between communities that were far apart. The land was open; there were no boundaries in the ancient time. Today, the places on the land that have Pueblo names remind us of our history. When we encounter these places during hunting or other land-use activities, we stop and discuss the stories associated with the land. The places we visit call to the cosmos. From our shrines, you can see "home" in all directions.

We learn about places from our tribal elders. Damian Garcia from Acoma Pueblo described how if we lose the interpretation, if we don't know the places, it looks like it is just a story rather than the history that it is. Knowing the places gives you a connection, a feeling of belonging. Each tribe has special places. We never "abandoned" those areas, we just moved. We may have forgotten that we lived in a place, but archaeological evidence is there. We are concerned with the deep meaning—the footprints and handprints—of our history.

Pueblo people share a deep history, but they also have distinct tribal histories that make it difficult to write a single, monolithic narrative. There must have been social and environmental upheavals that led to migration to new areas. There were probably multiple middle places along the way. As Aguilar discussed, movement needs to be conceptualized as both spatial and temporal. Ideas move over time, as well as things and people. The processes of movement are important in identifying who people are, and there will be variation in this between different villages. At the seminar, we touched on the Pueblo history of interacting with other groups. We need more discussion of this, and we think that all the Pueblo people need to get together and make a statement about who we are and our shared history. We have a closeness from the connections we share; we are the same people even if we come from different places. These things need more consideration.

Pueblo people work hard to maintain their traditions. Historically, we survived the atrocities associated with the Spanish colonization of New Mexico. Many Pueblos had to leave their homelands for a period during the Pueblo Revolt of 1680, but most of them returned. The Spaniards, and later the Americans, took much of our land, and even our children. Our ancestors went through hardships to save our history and culture for our present and future generations.

We still need to protect ancestral places and shrines from damage resulting from human-caused fires or the adverse effects of federal projects. The Zuni pilgrimage to Fort Wingate that had to be led by a bomb squad into an area impacted by unexploded ordnance is a jarring reminder that we live in a modern world. To respect our ancestors, we must respect the land and help clear it of explosives and other indignities. At Fort Wingate, the work will be worth it when the land is returned to the Zuni Tribe. How do we protect the homeland? By inducting new members into religious societies, taking them to these areas, and teaching them the songs and prayers. The involvement and participation of tribal members, season by season, renews ritual objects installed at shrines.

There are restrictions on Pueblo movement, some imposed by cultural rules about who is authorized to go to certain places, others imposed by the non-Indian world that privatizes property and puts up fences and gates that cannot be opened without trespassing. Knowledge about places that are restricted is maintained through oral history, and today cultural resource management projects often take us into those areas. When we are restricted by private property, we sometimes use a nearby shrine to connect with the area. We hope that projects like this seminar and book will help people understand the importance of maintaining connections to our ancestral places.

We spent some time in the seminar discussing the legacy of early anthropology in the pueblos, which too often entailed collecting esoteric information not meant to be shared with outsiders. As Damian Garcia from Acoma Pueblo said, "There are bad feelings about archaeologists and anthropologists. We are very private people. Our community still holds on to pieces of our culture and history and religion because that is our self-identity." Not all information should be disclosed; some information needs to be protected. We often speak in our Native languages to protect information from disclosure. We ask anthropologists to be cautious in their use of early anthropological publications. There are nuggets of useful information to be found in those early publications, but use of that information needs to be managed in collaborative research with Pueblo people. Early anthropology can be useful in documenting the longevity and continuity of Pueblo cultural beliefs and practices, but indiscriminate use of some publications is harmful. Each Pueblo community needs to decide for itself how early anthropology can be used to benefit the tribe, and anthropologists need to be sensitive to community concerns.

During our discussion, Aguilar observed that Pueblo people don't argue about the past in the same way that some archaeologists do when criticizing theoretical models. Pueblo people have a more civil way of understanding and talking about the past. They know that archaeology is "messy" because current knowledge is imperfect. This was not an issue in our seminar, but in writing about Pueblo archaeology, archaeologists need to keep in mind that they are talking about our ancestors and use a respectful tone.

We discussed what archaeologists call "Indigenous archaeology," or archaeology conducted by, for, and with Indigenous people, and thought about its utility in reframing Indigenous concepts. Aguilar commented on how Indigenous archaeology is often seen as inherently political, but it doesn't have to be. Maybe the work itself is a political statement. Whatever you call it, we think archaeology can be a tool for Indigenous communities to use in securing land and water rights and in documenting heritage. We think it's good that some archaeologists are beginning to use Native categories and theories in archaeological research.

Joseph Suina's touching description of the electrification of Cochiti Pueblo in the 1950s made us think about the many other changes that occurred as Pueblo culture moved into the modern world. Even though we both lived through this period, Suina's reminiscence makes us remember many things that we had forgotten. It's a powerful statement of where we've been, where we are, and where we're going. In our seminar discussion, it inspired Aguilar to talk about the cultural resiliency of the Pueblos today.

All of the Pueblo participants in the seminar felt it was rare to have the sort of discussions we had at the Amerind Foundation, with Pueblo and archaeological points of view being considered with equal respect. We are glad to see our non-Indian colleagues understand that an important change has taken place in the discipline of anthropology that makes room for this type of discussion. The information in this book is important in an academic sense, but it is also important to our finding ways to learn about and protect our places. Native people are adamant about preservation because the places go back to our ancestors.

We closed the seminar with a Zuni prayer for blessings for the land and people. The themes of emergence, rest, renewal, and use permeated our discussions at the Amerind Foundation. We cherished the opportunity to sit with archaeologists for four days to talk about the method, theory, and data they use in interpreting our past. As Aguilar commented, it's good to see Pueblo history discussed from a Pueblo perspective. We want to give the information in this book to the public. We all went home from the seminar feeling strong and good. This will be a great gift to our people. So, thank you.

CONTRIBUTORS

E. CHARLES ADAMS is a curator of archaeology at the Arizona State Museum and a professor in the School of Anthropology at the University of Arizona. Since arriving at UA in 1985, he has directed the Homol'ovi Research Program for the museum. Homol'ovi was a gathering place for many Hopi clans prior to their migration to the present villages around 1400. Adams received his PhD from the University of Colorado, Boulder, in 1975 and has previously held positions as senior archaeologist at the Museum of Northern Arizona and director of research at Crow Canyon Archaeological Center. He has published nearly one hundred articles and book chapters and single authored or edited ten monographs and other books. His most recent is the edited volume *Chevelon: Pueblo at Blue Running Water*, published as volume 211 in the Arizona State Museum Archaeological Series.

MARK R. AGOSTINI is a PhD student in anthropological archaeology at Brown University. He received his BA from the University of Vermont and his MA from Brown University. He has conducted archaeological research in Australia, Mexico, New England, and the US Southwest. Most recently, he has supervised fieldwork as an intern at Crow Canyon Archaeological Center. His current research applies geochemical and mineralogical techniques to Ancestral Puebloan pottery to study village formation and coalescence, ethnogenesis, and cosmological transformations in what is now the Rio Grande region of New Mexico. Among his honors are the Society for American Archaeology Student Poster Award, the James B. Petersen Archaeology Award for excellence in undergraduate research at the University of Vermont, and National Science Foundation Research Experience for Undergraduates Fellowship.

JOSEPH (WOODY) AGUILAR is an enrolled member of San Ildefonso Pueblo, New Mexico, and is a PhD candidate in the Department of Anthropology at the University of Pennsylvania. His primary research focuses on the archaeology of Spanish-Pueblo relations during the late seventeenth century, following the arrival of Spaniards into the northern Rio Grande region. His dissertation research examines Indigenous Pueblo resistance to the Spanish reconquest efforts in the latter part of the Pueblo Revolt era (1680–96) at Tunyo, San Ildefonso. He currently serves on the Advisory Board of San Ildefonso's Tribal Historic Preservation Office.

KURT F. ANSCHUETZ (PhD, University of Michigan, 1998) is an anthropologist and archaeologist based in Albuquerque, New Mexico. His research specialties in archaeology include late pre-Hispanic and early Historic period Pueblo agricultural land use, cultural landscapes, and social organization. The scope of his everyday work is to provide technical assistance to traditional and historic Native American, Hispanic, and Anglo communities working to sustain their relationships with the land, the water, and their cultural heritage resources as development proceeds throughout the region. Currently he is assisting the Pueblo of Acoma, as its tribal archaeologist, in preparing a traditional cultural properties study of the San Juan Basin. He previously worked with Acoma as a contributor to the Mount Taylor Traditional Cultural Property Nomination to the New Mexico State Register of Cultural Properties. Anschuetz has completed comprehensive cultural landscape studies of Native American, Hispanic, and Anglo communities' relationships with the Valles Caldera National Preserve. He also prepares expert testimony for land and water cases in north-central and west-central New Mexico either directly for various Pueblos, or on their behalf, as part of their government-to-government relationships with the U.S. Department of Justice.

CLAIRE S. BARKER serves as the state repatriation coordinator and the assistant NAGPRA coordinator for the Arizona State Museum. She received her PhD from the University of Arizona in 2017. Her research emphasizes the value of less visible artifact forms—such as utilitarian pottery or miniature vessels—in exploring the social lives of communities. Barker's most recent research interrogates the relationship between social identity, artifact style, and communities of practice, focusing on how the process of aggregation affected the differential expression of social identity on a public and private scale within the Pueblo IV communities of the Homol'ovi Settlement Cluster.

GRAYDON LENNIS (LENN) BERLIN is Emeritus Regents' Professor of Geography at Northern Arizona University. He holds degrees from Clarion State College (BS), Arizona State University (MA), and the University of Tennessee (PhD). His research interests center on the application of remote sensing to geoscience and archaeological investigations. In archaeology, most of his research focuses on identifying and mapping prehistoric and historic trail systems and prehistoric agricultural complexes. He has published extensively on his research and has authored and co-authored several books and numerous journal articles.

BRUCE BERNSTEIN is a trained ethnologist and has worked as a curator and museum director in Santa Fe and Washington, D.C. He presently serves as executive director of the Coe Center for the Arts and as historic preservation officer for the Pueblo of Pojoaque. His previous positions include director for collections and research at the National Museum of the American Indian, Smithsonian Institution; chief curator and director of Santa Fe's Museum of Indian Arts and Culture and Laboratory of Anthropology; and executive director of the Southwestern Association for Indian Arts. Bernstein has published broadly on Native arts and museums, as well as curated over a hundred exhibitions. His PhD in anthropology is from the University of New Mexico. He has dedicated his three decades of work in anthropology and museums to collaborative work and modelling new partnerships in research methodologies and curatorial principles and practices, contributing to today's working models of inclusive research, collections, and exhibition programs.

JACOB CAMPBELL is a cultural anthropologist with the Keller Science Action Center at the Field Museum, where he leads the social science team for the Chicago Region program. Campbell specializes in collaborative research that informs decision-making about biodiversity conservation, land management, and public space design. He co-directs the Urban Ecology Field Lab undergraduate summer course based at the Field Museum. In addition to his work in Chicago, Campbell has conducted ethnographic research with Native Americans in the U.S. Southwest, coastal Louisiana communities, and Trinidadian oil-field workers.

SAMUEL VILLARREAL CATANACH is from the Pueblo of Pojoaque. There, he most recently worked at the Poeh Cultural Center and Museum, learning and teaching the community's history and culture, as well as assisting with Tewa language revitalization efforts. In 2017 he received his MS in American Indian Studies from Arizona State University, where his research focused on federal Indian law, the history of the Pueblo of Pojoaque, and language revitalization methodologies. His positions have included internships with the Smithsonian's National Museum of the American Indian, Crow Canyon Archaeological Center, Where Are Your Keys? (a language revitalization organization), and the School for Advanced Research's Indian Arts Research Center. In 2018 Samuel was chosen as an inaugural Indigenous Digital Archive Fellow.

CHIP COLWELL is senior curator of anthropology at the Denver Museum of Nature and Science. He received his PhD from Indiana University and has held fellowships with Archaeology Southwest, the American Academy of Arts and Sciences, the National Endowment for the Humanities, and the U.S. Fulbright program. He has published more than fifty scholarly articles and book chapters and eleven books, many of which have received honors, including the National Council on Public History Book Award. He is the founding editor-in-chief of Sapiens.org, a digital magazine dedicated to sharing anthropological research, thinking, and discoveries with the public.

PATRICK J. CRUZ is from Ohkay Owingeh and is a master's-level archaeology student at the University of Colorado. His thesis work is an examination of thirteenth-century Pueblo migration processes, and particularly interactions between migrant and local populations in the northern Rio Grande. He is interested in migration, historical linguistics, material culture studies, phenomenological studies, and the topics of cosmograms, ceramic production and use, NAGPRA, and Indigenous archaeology.

SAMUEL DUWE is an assistant professor in the Department of Anthropology at the University of Oklahoma. His research focuses on Pueblo communities in northern New Mexico, and specifically on the deep and continuing histories of the Tewa pueblos. His current work addresses migration, ethnogenesis, colonial encounters, and the challenges and opportunities of contemporary collaborative archaeology.

B. SUNDAY EISELT is an associate professor of anthropology at Southern Methodist University. She is author and co-author of multiple articles and books on the Jicarilla and Hispanic societies of New Mexico, Hohokam and O'odham ceramic production, ceramic source geochemistry, and community-based and engaged approaches in archaeology. Specializing in the archaeology of southwestern Athapaskans, protohistoric to historic transitions, and archaeological ceramics, she has studied in numerous geographic regions including New Mexico, Arizona, California, and the Great Basin.

ERIK FENDER is descended from a distinguished line of San Ildefonso potters. He maintains a strict adherence to traditional pottery practices: he gathers and processes all of his own materials, he hand builds his wares, and he fires outdoors. The pottery he makes is used at home and sold at Indian Market and other venues, where he has won numerous awards. In addition, Fender teaches pottery making to Tewa people, sharing his broad knowledge of pottery making and pottery history. He is currently working with the Pueblo of Pojoaque's Poeh Center to return one hundred historic Tewa pots home from the Smithsonian Institution. Fender is an active member of his community.

T. J. FERGUSON is a professor in the School of Anthropology at the University of Arizona, where he edits the Anthropological Papers of the University of Arizona. He is also a managing member of Anthropological Research LLC, a research company in Tucson, Arizona, that specializes in archaeological and ethnographic research needed for historic preservation, repatriation, and litigation of land and water rights. His current research includes documenting how Native American heritage is grounded in place-names, cultural practices, and history.

SAMANTHA G. FLADD is a predoctoral research associate in the Anthropology Department at the University of Cincinnati and a PhD candidate in the School of Anthropology at the University of Arizona. Her current research focuses on the articulation of spatial and social organization throughout the life histories of the pueblos of the Homol'ovi Settlement Cluster in northeastern Arizona. She is also conducting research on patterns of discard and room closure in the great houses and small sites of Chaco Canyon, New Mexico, and works with an interdisciplinary team examining the potential for agricultural production within the canyon.

SEVERIN FOWLES is an associate professor at Barnard College, Columbia University. His research focuses on the histories of Indigenous and settler communities in northern New Mexico, where he has directed archaeological surveys, excavations, and oral history projects each year for the past two decades. His past publications include *An Archaeology of Doings: Secularism and the Study of Pueblo Religion* (School for Advanced Research, 2013) and *The Oxford Handbook of Southwest Archaeology* (co-edited with Barbara Mills, Oxford University Press, 2017), and he is currently at work on two new book projects: a wide-ranging history of image production in northern New Mexico from the Early Archaic to the present (co-authored with Benjamin Alberti, Lindsay Montgomery, and Darryl Wilkinson) and a more focused study of Comanche visual culture during the eighteenth and nineteenth centuries (developed in collaboration with colleagues in the Comanche Nation). His work has been supported by grants and fellowships from the National Science Foundation, the National Endowment for the Humanities, the Wenner-Gren Foundation, the School for Advanced Research, and the American Council of Learned Societies.

DAMIAN GARCIA (MS, Arizona State University, 2007) was the tribal historic preservation officer for the Pueblo of Acoma. He had over twenty years of experience working in the historic preservation field, including helping establish the Historic Preservation Office for the Pueblo of Acoma. Since his designation as Acoma's tribal historic preservation officer in 2017, Garcia worked with the Acoma Historic Preservation Advisory Board to come up with innovative ways to conduct archaeological inquiry that are sensitive to Acoma's traditions and values and cause less physical disturbance to cultural resources important to the pueblo's people. This includes brick-and-mortar projects to repair and restore parts of the San Estevan del Rey Mission and some of the oldest homes in Sky City; Section 106 consultation for a greenhouse project with the Bright Green Group of Companies; and coordination of the Navajo-Gallup Water Supply Project that identifies and makes recommendations for cultural resources important to Acoma. Lastly, he assisted the pueblo in all matters related to NAGPRA, ranging from repatriations and reburials of Acoma's ancestors whose remains were excavated by archaeologists to assisting other tribes in reburying their ancestors in accord with NAGPRA guidelines.

SAUL L. HEDQUIST was senior archaeologist and ethnographer with Logan Simpson. His research interests included Pueblo ethnography, landscape anthropology, and American Southwest archaeology, particularly that of northern Arizona. He worked with the Hopi Tribe on multiple projects since 2010.

DWIGHT C. HONYOUTI is from the village of Hotevilla, Arizona, and was raised on the Hopi Reservation, where he resided until adulthood. He received his BA from the School of Anthropology at the University of Arizona in 2016. Dwight currently works in the field of historic preservation, helping to protect important cultural heritage sites throughout Arizona.

MAREN P. HOPKINS is director of research for Anthropological Research, LLC, a company in Tucson, Arizona, that specializes in working with Indian tribes on historic preservation. Hopkins is a registered professional archaeologist with expertise in identifying traditional cultural places and evaluating their eligibility for the National Register of Historic Places. She has eighteen years of experience in conducting historic preservation research across the U.S. Southwest. Hopkins has authored and co-authored numerous technical reports, book chapters, and journal articles about archaeology, ethnography, and the relevance of collaboration in historic preservation research.

MATTHEW J. LIEBMANN is professor of anthropology at Harvard University. He received his BA from Boston College in 1996 and his PhD from the University of Pennsylvania in 2006. He is the author of *Revolt:*

An Archaeological History of Pueblo Resistance and Revitalization in 17th Century New Mexico (University of Arizona Press, 2012). Liebmann's research interests include historical archaeology and historical anthropology, collaborative archaeology, the archaeology of colonialism, NAGPRA, and postcolonialism. His recent research focuses on early Pueblo-Spanish interactions in the Jemez Valley, where he has conducted collaborative research with the Pueblo of Jemez since 2001. Currently, he is directing excavations of the San Diego de la Congregación Mission at Walatowa.

ROBERT W. PREUCEL is director of the Haffenreffer Museum of Anthropology and is the James Manning Professor of Anthropology at Brown University. He has conducted collaborative archaeology with the Pueblo of Cochiti in New Mexico since 1995, focusing on the meaning and cultural significance of Kotyiti Pueblo, their mesa-top village occupied just after the Pueblo Revolt of 1680. His major publications include *Contemporary Archaeology in Theory: The New Pragmatism* (with Stephen Mrozowski, Wiley-Blackwell, 2010), *Archaeological Semiotics* (Blackwell, 2006), *Native American Voices on Identity, Art, and Culture* (with Lucy Williams and William Wierzbowski, University of Pennsylvania Museum of Archaeology and Anthropology, 2005), *Archaeologies of the Pueblo Revolt: Identity, Meaning, and Renewal in the Pueblo World* (University of New Mexico, 2002), and *Processual and Postprocessual Archaeologies: Multiple Ways of Knowing the Past* (Southern Illinois University, 1991).

RUSSELL SANCHEZ is from San Ildefonso Pueblo and is a lifelong and active member of his community. His aunt Rose Gonzales taught him the basic skills of pottery making, instilling in him above all else, "Take what I do, but make it your own." Sanchez advocates making Pueblo pottery the Pueblo way, which requires harvesting clay, coil building his pots, and firing outside. Any other way is unacceptable. Sanchez understands these three parameters to be what separates Pueblo pottery from all other pottery and what, indeed, makes it Pueblo. He received the 2017 New Mexico Governor's Award for Excellence in the Arts.

OCTAVIUS SEOWTEWA is the leader of the Zuni Cultural Resource Advisory Team for the Pueblo of Zuni. Seowtewa is a member of the Eagle Plume Down Medicine Society, the leader of the Galaxy Fraternity, and a member of the Flat Wall Kiva group at Zuni Pueblo. He is a Corn Clan member and a child of the Crane Clan. Seowtewa has participated in projects related to the identification, interpretation, and protection of Zuni cultural resources for more than two decades, including national and international repatriation efforts for Zuni religious items.

JOSEPH H. SUINA is a professor emeritus in the College of Education at the University of New Mexico with twenty-five years of service. He directed the Institute for American Indian Education at UNM for tribes throughout the Southwest. Suina's publications on culture, education, and Native American issues are numerous. As a member of several boards and committees, he voices concerns for Native people in the areas of health, museums, language retention, sacred sites, economic development, and housing. Suina is an adjunct professor at Colgate University in New York and teaches courses in Native American Studies and education. Suina has maintained strong ties to Cochiti Pueblo throughout his academic career; he is a former governor and a current tribal council member. As an elder in the tribe, he provides guidance in the ways of tradition and culture for his people.

PAUL TOSA is enrolled in the Pueblo of Jemez, where he is a former governor and a current member of the tribal council. Tosa is an educator with a degree from the University of New Mexico. He has dedicated his life to sharing the teachings of his grandfather, Francisco Tosa, with tribal members and the public.

JOHN R. WELCH is a professor, jointly appointed in the Department of Archaeology and the School of Resource and Environmental Management at Simon Fraser University in British Columbia. He works with Native nations on projects at the interface of Indigenous peoples' sovereignty, or the rights and responsibilities derived from authority over people and territory, and stewardship, the sustainable and broadly beneficial uses of sociocultural and biophysical inheritances. Welch is also a founding member of the board of the Fort Apache Heritage Foundation and has published widely on Apache history and applied archaeology. He also directs SFU Archaeology's online Professional Graduate Program in Heritage Resource Management.

INDEX

abandonment, 2, 4, 5, 10, 50, 51, 87, 102, 115, 127, 139, 205, 224, 229, 231, 256
Abiquiu, 111, 226
acculturation, 215
Acoma: ancestors, 38, 42, 43, 46; Culture Province, 42 (*fig.*), 50, 51; emergence, 13, 20, 37, 38, 39, 40, 42, 47, 52, 53; First People, 37, 38, 39, 40, 41, 42, 43, 44, 45, 46, 47, 48, 50, 54, 55; identity, 49, 55; people, 18, 41, 44, 45, 52, 53; seasonal dispersal strategy, 50, 51; settlement system, 50, 51; traditions, 37, 51; values, 52
Acoma Pueblo (*Haak'u*), 2, 9, 12, 13, 17–20, 37–55, 68, 256, 257
aggregation, 5, 6, 22, 128–31
Aguilar, Joseph, 22, 161, 255, 256, 258, 259
Anschuetz, Kurt, 14
Antelope Mesa, 136, 137, 141
anthropology, 7, 8, 15, 196, 207, 215, 218, 257, 258
Anza, Governor Juan Bautista de, 69
Apache, 8, 9, 23, 74, 115, 152, 173, 176, 177, 178, 179, 184, 185, 190, 200, 226; Apache-Plains, 168, 173, 175; Apache-Pueblo relations, 175, 176, 177; Apache-Tiwa society, 170–77, *passim*; Cuartelejo, 177; Jicarilla, 23, 167, 168, 170–77, 185, 186, 187, 188; Mescalero Apache reservation, 66; Western, 18
archaeology, 4, 5, 11, 15, 53, 75, 101, 104, 161, 196, 218, 258; historical, 224; Indigenous, 9, 161, 258; Pueblo views of, 11, 257; sociopolitics of, 9; Southwestern, 1, 4, 5, 7, 11, 25, 96; symmetrical, 15

Arrow Mother (*Tyáakųzee*), 65, 66, 67, 69
assimilation, 10, 12, 186
Astialakwa (*Hâtyēlakwa*, Upright Wall Place), 68, 69, 153, 154, 157
Awatovi, 137
Aztec (*Séyû T'êæsh*, Bird People), 66

baptismal records, 225, 228
Bandelier, Adolph, 160, 230, 231
Bear Springs (*Anshe Ky'an'a*), 21, 80, 85, 92
becoming, 2, 13–16, 17, 19–25, 37, 38, 39, 41, 45, 47, 50, 52, 53, 55, 93, 98, 103, 115, 118, 128, 170, 189–91, 203, 209, 222, 223, 224, 226, 228, 231, 232–37, 238, 243, 254; another, 190 (*fig.*), 191; Apache, 177; and growth, ripening, 13, 37, 38, 39, 41, 203; Hopi, 22, 128; journey of, 2, 38; philosophy of, 224; process of, 13, 17, 22, 23, 39, 41, 115, 118, 191, 223, 230, 235, 236, 237, 238; Tewa, 118, 209. *See also* being
being, 2, 3, 13–16, 17, 20, 21, 25, 38, 55, 80, 93, 187, 188, 222, 235; Acoma, 20, 38, 55; Hispanic/Indian, 235; levels of, 97; "one people," 170; Pueblo way of, 2, 13, 17, 199; Tewa, 116, 149, 199; vecino, 228; Zuni, 21, 80. *See also* becoming
Bernal, Fray Juan, 210
Bernardini, Wesley, 138, 140
Binford, Lewis, 5
Blackmore, William, 167
Blue Lake, 171
Boletsakwa (*Bûlé tûukwa*, Shell Shrine Place), 68, 69, 70, 74, 154

272　　*Index*

Bourke, Gregory, 233, 234, 235
Bradfield, Wesley, 218
Bureau of Indian Affairs, 82

Cachini, Ronnie, 87, 91
Cajete, Gregory, 20, 150
Cañon de Valle, 158
castas, regimen de, 224
Castaño de Sosa, Gaspar, 68, 232
Castañeda, Pedro de, 176
Catholicism, 152, 199, 200, 210, 243, 250
Cebolleta Mesa, 51
Center Place, 189, 223, 227, 228, 229–232, 235, 237. *See also* Middle Place
Cerro Colorado Pueblo, 154
Cerro Colorado Mesa, 154
Cerro del Medio (*Ky'âagîwe Shı̨́ı̨́*, Shiny Rock Mountain), 71
Chaco Canyon, 43, 110
Chama Valley, 21, 97, 103, 104, 109, 110, 111, 112, 114, 115, 116, 117, 119
Chapman, Kenneth, 207
Chevelon Pueblo, 129 (*table*), 132, 133 (*fig.*), 135, 138
Child-of-the-Water, 186
Chimayo, 155, 226, 235
Chimney Rock, 256
Christmas dances, 251, 252
church, 67, 68, 69, 152, 153, 203, 216, 226, 234 (*fig.*), 244, 251, 253. *See also* mission
clan, 4, 18, 21, 22, 49, 61, 62, 64, 70, 78, 81, 124, 125, 127, 134, 138, 139, 140, 172, 175, 184, 233, 234, 235
Cochiti Pueblo, 19, 152, 157, 258
collaboration, 1, 2, 7–11, 13, 15, 18, 21, 23, 25, 26, 96, 160, 178, 198, 215, 257
Columbus Day, 237
colonialism, 6, 19, 21, 71, 73, 92, 150, 178, 182, 223, 231, 237
Colwell-Chanthaponh, Chip, 8, 14, 127
Comanche, 64, 69, 176, 177, 183, 200, 216, 226. *See also* vecino
congregación, 68
Corn Mothers, 202

Coronado, Francisco Vásquez de, 67
cosmology, 97, 116, 171, 198, 200, 215
Cottonwood Creek, 129 (*table*)
covenant, 15, 16, 20, 42; pact, 43, 124
Cordell, Linda, 5, 53,
Coronado, Francisco Vasquez de, 67, 68, 150, 178
Creator, 15, 62, 185 (*table*), 187, 202
Curtis, Edward, S., 175, 187
Cushing, Frank Hamilton, 4
Cuyamungue Pueblo (*Kuyemuugeh*), 156, 200, 206 (*fig.*), 225

decolonization, 237
depopulation, 22, 101, 108, 125, 132,
Dick, Herbert, 182
Domingo (Tesuque war captain), 156, 157
Domingo Trading Post, 243
Dozier, Thomas, 218
dualism, 97, 172, 173, 209. *See also* moiety
Duwe, Sam, 110

Eagle Hill Place (*Séeshı̨́ı̨nâ*), 66
Eagle Mother (*Séekų̈zée*), 65, 66, 67, 69
Eiselt, Sunday, 177
El Prado marsh, 171, 188
Ellis, Forence Hawley, 104, 105
Embudo, 158
epistemology, 8, 15, 218
Espejo, Antonio de, 232
ethnic shifting, 23, 166, 170; Tiwa-- Apache, 178–84, 186, 187–91
ethnogenesis, 101, 196, 197, 198, 213, 224. *See also* vecino
ethnography, 4, 7, 14, 102, 175, 197, 254
ethnographic: analogy, 4, 5; descriptions, 114, 170, 172, 174, 229; knowledge, 8; research, 60, 80, 87, 88 (*fig.*), 91, 93, 138, 198, 230
ethnohistory, 196, 198

Fabian, Johannes, 7
farming, 16, 49, 54, 91, 128, 195, 201, 202, 204, 207, 227, 243, 244, 249

Index

Ferguson, T. J., 8, 14, 154
Fewkes, Jesse Walter, 4, 140
fingerprints, 45, 46, 52. *See also* metaphor, of sites
Fliedner, Detrich, 71
footprints, 18, 20, 45, 46, 52, 61, 67, 69, 75, 86, 124, 128, 138, 256. *See also* metaphor, of sites
Fort Wingate Depot Activity, 21, 80, 81 (*fig.*), 88 (*fig.*), 90 (*fig.*)
Fowles, Severin, 2
Fox, Robin, 1

Gallina culture, 64
Garcia, Damian, 9, 19, 256, 257
gathering, 15, 49, 51, 54, 61, 65, 91, 200
Geertz, Clifford, 7
gentle teaching: philosophy of, 24, 254
Giusewa (Jemez Historic Site), 67
Git'üt'a Ôplênü (Giant Footprint Place, also known as *Kwǽgíyukwâ*, Bark Beetle Place), 67, 69
Goijiya, 171
Guadalupe Mesa, 154
Gunnerson, Dolores, 176, 178, 183
Gunnerson, James, 183

Habicht-Mauche, Judith A., 184
handprints, 256. *See also* metaphor, of sites
Harrington, John Peabody, 105, 108, 230, 231, 235
Haury, Emil, 5
health and healing, 9, 16, 249, 251
Hemis, *See* Jemez
Hewett, Edgar Lee, 159
Heye, George, 219
Hhó Kįįthelegi (Hole White Place), 65
Hibben, Frank, 111,
Hispanicization, 23, 199
history, 2, 3, 4, 5, 10, 12, 14, 18, 20, 21, 22, 23, 26, 38, 44, 46, 55, 61, 62, 69, 70, 71, 75, 78, 80, 81, 84, 86, 92, 93, 96, 97, 98, 102, 103, 104, 105, 108, 109, 116, 117, 118, 119, 125, 149, 154, 160, 163, 170, 175, 176, 178, 179, 182, 183, 184, 191, 195, 196, 197, 198, 214, 216, 217, 222, 223, 229, 231, 237, 254, 255, 256, 257, 257; archaeological history, 105; culture history, 3, 4, 5, 44; deep history, 23, 168, 178, 182, 256: geologic history, 162; precolonial history, 168, 178, 179
Hodge, Frederick W., 218
Homol'ovi (Be Mounded Up, or Place of the Small Hills), 9, 127, 128, 129, 131, 136, 137 (*fig.*), 138, 139, 140, 141; Homol'ovi I, 129 (*table*), 132, 133 (*fig.*), 134, 135; Homol'ovi II, 129 (*table*), 133 (*fig.*), 135, 136; Homol'ovi III, 129 (*table*), 131, 132; Homol'ovi IV, 129 (*table*), 131; Homol'ovi Settlement Cluster, 22, 124, 125, 126 (*fig.*), 128, 130, 130 (*fig.*), 131, 136, 137
Homolovi State Park, 140
Honyouti, Dwight, 255
Hopi: cultural landscape, 22, 124, 128, 139, 141; emergence, 18, 124; history, 22; identity, 125, 128; katsina, 125, 128, 135, 136, 140, 188; language, 124, 125; people, 15, 16, 18, 68, 124, 127, 140, 188; traditions, 188, 190; tribe, 8, 9, 141; tribal council, 140
Hopi Mesas, 18, 22, 69, 70, 124, 125, 127, 128, 129, 130, 136, 138, 157
hunting, 16, 20, 49, 51, 54, 61, 65, 75, 91, 158, 172, 175, 176, 256

impressions and imprints, 18, 20, 45, 46, 52. *See also* metaphor, of sites
Indian Relocation Program, 236
Indigenous studies, 8
Isleta Pueblo, 100, 152

Jackrabbit Pueblo, 129 (*table*)
Jacona Pueblo (*Sakona*), 156, 200, 233
Jemez Mountains (*Híjmísh P'ëtabu*), 64, 66, 69, 70, 71, 75

Jemez Pueblo (*Wáala Túuwa*), 12, 19, 20, 60–76 *passim*, 61 (*fig.*), 63 (*fig.*), 152, 157

Jemez (*Hį́įmísh*): ancestors, 61, 70, 75; culture, 62, 74, 75, 76; Department of Natural Resources, 71; emergence, 60, 62, 70; history, 20, 61, 62, 69, 70, 71, 75; identity, 20, 61, 70, 75; people, 21, 60, 61, 62, 64, 65, 66, 67, 68, 69, 70, 71, 72, 74, 76, 157, 254; Snake society, 65, 69; traditions, 70, 75; villages, 65, 67, 69, 71, 72, 73, 73 (*fig.*)

Jeançon, Jean, 187

Jironza Petriz de Cruzate, Governor Domingo, 153

Kapo'uinge, 112

Keres: language, 185 (*table*), 252; people, 66, 157; Western Keres Culture Province, 42 (*fig.*), 50; world, 47, 48 (*fig.*), 49, 54

Kessell, John, 160

Kidder, A. V., 4, 11, 178

Killer-of-the-Enemies, 186, 188

kiva, 89, 90, 104, 105, 110, 111, 112, 114, 128, 132, 135, 136, 137, 137 (*table*), 138, 140, 141, 173, 184, 185 (*table*), 216, 232, 244; murals, 213

Koyiyumptewa, Stewart B., 127

Kotyiti, 153, 154, 157, 161

Kowina, 43

Ky'àawäamu, (Largo Canyon, Rock Canyon, or McElmo Canyon), 62, 64, 70

landscape, 2, 5, 6, 14, 15, 16, 17, 20, 22, 41, 43, 44, 49, 50, 53, 61, 67, 69, 71, 74, 81, 82, 87, 98, 105, 116, 117, 124, 125, 128, 138, 141, 150, 157, 158, 161, 163, 171, 188, 189, 197; ancestral, 1, 51; as memory, 44; colonial, 23; cosmological, 158; cultural, 6, 22, 23, 38, 41, 45, 47, 49, 52, 54, 75, 83, 84, 85, 92, 111, 127, 128, 139; ritual, 111; social, 103; storied, 44, 45, 52, 188

language, 7, 69, 116, 117, 170, 184, 186, 245, 249, 251, 253; Esther Martinez Native American Languages Preservation Act, 17, 18; importance of, 75, 140; of pottery, 217; revival programs, 17, 252; shift, 252. *See also* Apache, Hopi, Keres, Tewa, Tiwa, Zuni

Lekson, Stephen, 11

Leo, Juan Jesus (Wa-só-to-yá-min, Small Feathers of the Eagle), 172, 173, 174 (*fig.*)

Liebmann, Matthew, 11, 12, 71, 154

Lugo, Fray Alonso de, 67

Lyons, Patrick, 140

Màasaw, 18, 124

La Madera, 154

Man Mountain (*P'ê Húlése*, Sleeping Ute Mountain), 62

Máape P'êkwâ (Parrot Place, or Macaw Place, Petroglyph National Monument), 66

Martine, Jose, 174

Martinez, Esther, 17

Martinez, Fray Diego, 227

Martinez, Julian, 218

Martinez, Maria, 215

Mendoza, Juan Dominguez de, 152

Mermejo, Richard, 177

Mesa Verde, 5, 6, 43, 62, 64, 96, 100, 101, 102, 108, 110, 178

memory, 6, 18, 21, 22, 44, 110, 127, 135, 138, 218, 238; collective, 84, 93, 231; cultural, 218; historical, 84, 92, 196; living, 195; social, 115, 132, 134, 138, 234. *See also* landscape

metaphor, 18, 21, 101, 110, 189, 195, 207, 217; of movement, 16–19, 26, 37, 52, 96; of sites, 18, 20, 110

metonym, 207–11

Middle Place, 1, 13, 21, 22, 23, 25, 78, 79 (*fig.*), 80, 81, 85, 86, 90, 93, 98, 103, 104, 105, 230, 254. *See also* Center Place

Index

migration, 2, 3–7, 10, 12, 13, 19, 20, 21, 22, 37, 38, 39, 40–46, 47, 48, 50, 52, 53, 54, 55, 60, 61, 62–69, 70, 75, 78, 79 (*fig.*), 81, 84, 85, 86, 96, 101, 102, 104, 108, 110, 115, 116, 124, 127, 130, 131, 132, 138, 139, 178, 184, 187, 189, 190, 195, 196, 217, 222, 233, 245, 254, 255, 256; clan migration, 4, 18, 140; emigration, 22, 98, 125, 138; immigration, 125, 131; in the mind, 242; route, 124, 132, 140, 179, 182. *See also* mobility and movement
Mindeleff, Victor and Cosmos, 4
mission, 67, 68, 69, 152, 203, 225, 226; mission village, 150, 156, 157, 227; missionization, 10, 23, 115, 223. *See also* church
mobility, 1, 23, 71–75, 83, 92, 93, 150, 157–60, 163, 176, 186, 188, 191, 222; as resistance strategy, 150, 162; as survivance, 22; seasonal, 6; small-scale mobility, 78. *See also* migration and movement
moiety, 61, 108, 162, 172, 173, 203, 204, 209, 232; Llanero band, 172; Ollero band, 172; pumpkin people, 16; summer people, 17, 21, 98, 103, 104, 105, 108, 109, 110, 111, 112, 114, 117, 118, 184; turquoise people, 16, 61; winter people, 17, 21, 98, 102, 103, 104, 105, 108, 109, 110, 111, 112, 114, 115, 117, 118, 184, 186. *See also* dualism
Montoya, Florentino, 218
Montoya, Senovia, 235
movement, 1, 2, 3–7, 16–19, 20, 21, 22, 23, 24, 25, 37–55, 60–76, 78–93, 96, 100, 101, 108, 112, 115, 116, 118, 125, 127–28, 138, 139, 149, 150, 158, 168, 170, 177, 183, 185, 195, 196, 214, 215, 216; cultural, 195, 216, 217, 222–38; of ideas, 195, 242; indigenous philosophies of, 187–91; intravillage, 131–36, tradition as, 216; *See also* ethnic shifting, metaphor, migration and mobility
Mt. Taylor, 17, 46, 85, 86

Nake'muu, 155, 157–60, 158 (*fig.*), 162, 163
Nambe Pueblo (*Nanbé*), 102, 103, 104, 109, 156, 225, 226, 227, 230, 231
Naranjo, Tessie, 2, 51, 53, 187
Naranjo, Tito, 53
Native American Graves Protection and Repatriation Act (NAGPRA), 6, 7
Native Science, 150
Navajo, 8, 68, 74, 82, 91, 115, 152, 190, 200, 226, 234
Navawi (Field Gap Village), 155, 158
Nelson, Nels, 4
New Mexico Department of Indian Education, 252
Nuestra Señora de Guadalupe, 225
Nusbaum, Jesse, 218, 219.

obsidian, 6, 21, 61, 71–75, 176; Cerro del Medio, 71–73, 74
Ohkay owingeh, 17, 19, 102, 103, 109, 110, 112, 115, 117, 118, 150, 158, 224, 230. *See* San Juan Pueblo
Olinger, Bart, 183
Oñate, Juan de, 67, 150, 152, 232
ontology, 7, 15, 19, 25, 52, 116, 187, 201, 230
Opler, Edward, 172, 173, 174, 182
oral history, 158, 162, 187, 257.
Ortiz, Alfonso, 14, 154, 189, 199, 216
Ortiz, Simon J., 2, 37, 48
Ortman, Scott, 101, 102, 104, 110, 117, 119
Otermín, Governor Antonio de, 152, 177
Our Lady of Guadalupe (Pojoaque Pueblo), 237

Pajarito Plateau, 22, 85, 101, 103, 110, 114, 155, 160, 163
Palisade ruin, 111, 112
Paquimé, 66, 69, 256
Parsons, Elsie Clews, 174, 175, 191, 231
El Paso del Norte, 66, 152, 153
path, 2, 3, 17, 18, 25, 41, 64, 132, 189, 203, 230, 232, 245, 246. *See also* road, trail
Patkingyam (Water Clan), 140

Patokwa (*Pâ tûukwa*, Flower Shrine), 68, 69, 70, 74, 154, 161
Pecos classification, 11
Pecos clan (*P'ǽækish*), 70
Pecos conference, 11
Pecos Pueblo, 68, 69, 70, 157
Peralta, Pedro de, 152
Pesede'owingeh, 109
petroglyphs, 18, 70, 87, 90, 93, 124, 127
Picuris Pueblo, 19, 23, 100, 105, 168, 170, 171, 173, 175, 177, 182 (*fig.*), 182, 183, 187, 188, 191
pilgrimage, 6, 15, 17, 61, 78, 91, 109, 115, 257
Pino, Pedro, 92
place: center, 189, 223, 227, 228, 229–232, 235, 237; ensouled, 14, 116; Holy, 53, 54; middle place, 1, 13, 21, 22, 23, 25, 78, 79 (*fig.*), 80, 81, 85, 86, 90, 93, 98, 103, 104, 105, 230, 254; power of, 22, 137, 158, 163, stay in, 23, 196, 199
Pojege (Down Where the Water, or Creeks, Meet), 227
Pojoaque Pueblo (*P'osuwaege owingeh*, Water Drinking Place Village), 9, 17, 23, 24, 97, 102, 103, 105, 108, 109, 119, 156, 200, 222–38 *passim*
Pojoaque Grant site, 104
Popé, 199
Posi'owingeh, 103, 108, 109–15, 117, 118
Potsuwi (Village at the Gap Where Water Sinks), 155
pottery, 6, 12, 18, 23, 52, 86, 89, 100, 105, 129, 130 (*fig.*), 140, 173, 181, 195–19, *passim*, 243, 255; as metonym, 207–11
pottery types: Abiquiu Black-on-gray, 108; Biscuitware, 112, 205, 206 (*fig.*); Cuyamungue Black-on-tan, 205; Homolovi Utility Ware, 129; Jeddito Yellow Ware, 129; Jicarilla Micaceous tradition, 182 (*fig.*); Kapo Black, 205; Kwahe'e Black-on-white, 105, 108, 181, 181 (*fig.*); Mogollon Brown Ware, 130; Ocate Micaceous, 183; Ogapoge Polychrome, 23, 203, 205 (*fig.*), 206, 207, 209, 210 (*fig.*), 211–13, 214, 215, 217; Penasco Micaceous, 182, 183; Pindi Black-on-white, 111; Powhoge Polychrome, 211; proto-Apache, 182; Rio Grande Glazeware, 72, 205, 218; Sankawi Black-on-cream, 211; Santa Fe Black-on-white, 110; Taos Incised, 181, 181 (*fig.*), 182, 183, 184; Taos Micaceous, 183; Tewa Polychrome, 206 (*fig.*); Vadito Micaceous, 183; Winslow Orange Ware, 129; Wiyo Black-on-white, 112
practices, 4, 137, 171, 201, 214, 216, 223, 225, 228, 249, 251; acculturation and assimilation, 12; archaeological, 127, 161; closure, 122, 134, 136, 138; collaborative, 7, 9; commemoration, 132; community-based, 230; cultural, 26, 75, 80, 89, 92, 233, 254, 258; daily, 136; depositional, 134, 139; farming, 227; land use, 37, 50; manufacturing, 129; missionizing, 10; representational, 25; residential, 224; ritual, 10, 136, 158; Spanish, 201, 216; subjugation, 152; traditional, 235
prayer, 17, 21, 38, 48, 52, 54, 78, 80, 81, 86, 87, 91, 116, 184, 198, 200, 201, 202, 203, 207, 209, 252, 254, 257, 259; growing corn as, 202; pottery making as, 207, 208 (*fig.*), 210 (*fig.*); song as, 149; visual, 207
El Presidio de Francisco (California), 224
Preucel, Robert W., 153, 154
Promontory Cave, 178
prophesy, 13, 20, 60
Pueblo Revolt: of 1680, 22, 68, 69, 70, 74, 102, 118, 149–63, *passim*, 177, 195, 199, 200, 205, 225, 233, 257; of 1696, 225

Index

raids and raiding, 62, 70, 74, 153, 177, 178, 183, 200, 226
Reed, Erik, 5
Redondo Peak (*Sée Tŏoky'aanu Tûukwâ*, Place of the Eagle, also Wâavêma Ky'ôkwâ, Want for Nothing Peak), 60, 61 (*fig.*), 65, 71, 72, 74, 75, 76, 76, 254
Reneros de Posada, Governor Pedro, 152, 153
repartimiento, 199, 205
resistance, 150, 152, 153, 156, 157, 162, 233,
rest, renewal, and reuse philosophy, 51, 64, 109, 223, 231, 232, 259
revitalization, 1, 6, 20, 24, 102, 212, 222, 223, 235, 236
Riana ruin, 111, 112,
Ribbon Falls, Grand Canyon (*Chimi k'yana k'ya dey'a*), 78, 85
rightful orientation, 41, 47
Rio Chama: region, 109, 110, 111, 112, 114, 115, 117, 119; river, 109, 110, 111; valley, 21, 97, 103, 104, 109, 110, 116
Rio Grande: region, 6, 100, 101, 102, 103, 104, 105, 108, 116, 117, 156, 172, 183, 186, 188, 222, 225, 227, 232, 243; river, 65, 66, 67, 69, 70, 86, 97, 98, 104, 105, 109, 110, 115, 171; valley, 5, 96, 97, 98, 100, 101, 103, 105, 111, 116, 117, 150, 170, 175, 176, 190, 200; villages, 155, 156, 176, 215, 216
Rio Pojoaque, 105
Rio del Oso, 109, 110
Rio Ojo Caliente: river, 109; valley, 114 (*fig.*)
road, 17, 37, 39, 48, 49, 53, 54, 62, 64, 83, 88 (*fig.*), 89, 91, 92, 149, 175, 188, 218, 243, 244, 248. *See also* path, trail
Romero, Governor Tom, 238

Salt Woman, 39, 40, 41
San Cristobal Pueblo, 156
San Diego Exposition, 218
San Diego Museum of Man, 219

San Gabriel del Yungue (*Yungé owinge*, Mockingbird Village), 150, 152, 224
San Geronimo Day, 167, 168
San Ildefonso Mesa, 154. *See* Tunyo
San Ildefonso Pueblo (*Powhoge*), 150, 151 (*fig.*), 154, 156, 163, 255
San Juan Mesa, 154.
San Juan Pueblo, 17, 154, 224. *See* Ohkay Owingeh
San Lazaro Pueblo, 156
San Ysidro, 66
Sandia Mountains, 67
Sandy Place Lake, 98
Sangre de Cristo Mountains, 104, 108, 177, 179, 182
Santa Ana Pueblo (*Tamaya*), 66, 152, 153, 157
Santa Clara Pueblo (*Kha'po*), 2, 7, 51, 53, 149, 156, 226, 230, 233
Santa Fe, Villa Real de, 98, 103, 149, 152, 153, 156, 157, 204, 206 (*fig.*), 210 (*fig.*), 215, 231, 233, 243, 244
Santa Fe Fiesta, 149, 153
Sapa'owingeh, 109
Sauer, Carl, 83
secrecy, 10, 211, 253; privacy, 209, 243, 250, 253, 257
seeking life, 2, 16, 96, 103, 115–18, 216
Sée Shôkwa (Eagle Dwell Place), 65
Séekųzée (Eagle Mother), 65, 66, 67, 69
Sekaquaptewa, Susan, 140, 141
Séeshįįnâ (Eagle Hill Place), 66
Seowtewa, Octavius, 12, 17, 24, 87, 90 (*fig.*)
Setalla, Gwen, 140, 141
Shiny Rock Mountain (*Ky'âagîwe Shį́į*), 71; range (*Ky'âa Gíwē P'êtabu*), 62
Shipap'u, 20, 39, 40, 41, 42, 44, 46, 48
shrine, 15, 16, 17, 18, 60, 64, 68, 69, 75, 80, 84, 85, 86, 87, 90, 91, 93, 114, 140, 154, 155, 188, 255, 256, 257
Silko, Leslie Marmon, 43, 44, 48, 55, 189
Sky City, 1, 47, 50, 52. *See* Acoma Pueblo
slavery, 6, 177, 234

smallpox, 226
sovereignty, 9, 20, 25, 152, 199, 252
Spanish Reconquest, 22, 24, 74, 149, 150, 153, 155, 156, 177, 190, 195, 200, 205, 211, 217.
Spinden, Herbert, 215, 218
Spiritual Beings, 39, 42, 43, 44, 46, 47, 53, 54, 84, 154, 186
spiritual ecology, 42
stakeholders, 8, 9
Stephen, Alexander M., 140
stewardship, 15, 20, 49, 51, 53, 124; principles of, 38, 42–44,
Stevenson, Mathilda Cox, 184, 185 (*table*), 185
Swentzell, Rina, 7, 53, 97, 230
Smith, Linda Tuhiwai, 8
Suina, Joseph, 10, 24, 246 (*fig.*), 258
survival, 1, 18, 26, 43, 150, 156–57, 200, 201, 204, 217, 237, 243
survivance, 22, 25, 26, 222, 225
Suvoyuki Day, 140

T'aitöna (Pot Creek Pueblo), 179, 183
T'owa vi Thaa, Peoples' Day, 237
Tai-faína (Person Red-That), 187
Tapia, Feliciana, 235, 238
Tapia, Jose Antonio, 235
Tapia, Juan Pablo, 233, 234, 235
Taos Pueblo, 1, 10, 19, 23, 64, 68, 100, 105, 152, 166, 167, 168, 170, 171, 172, 173, 174, 175, 177, 179, 180, 182, 183, 184, 185, 185 (*fig.*), 186, 187, 188, 191
Te'ewi'owingeh, 110
Tekhe'owingeh, 102, 103–9 *passim*, 111, 117, 118
Tesuque Pueblo (*Tetsugeh*), 103, 109, 156, 157, 226, 233
Tewa: culture, 108, 117, 195, 197, 207, 209, 217, 218; history, 21, 97, 98, 102, 103, 116, 117, 118, 195, 197, 198, 217; homeland, 21, 100, 101, 102, 117, 195; identity, 24, 116, 222, 223; language, 100, 101, 227, 231; oral tradition, 97, 104, 196; origins, 21, 96–19, *passim*, 230; people, 2, 3, 13, 14, 23, 96, 98, 100, 102, 103, 104, 109, 115, 118, 149, 150, 154, 156, 157, 162, 163, 184, 195, 196, 197, 200, 201, 202, 204, 209, 210, 214, 216, 217, 223, 230, 231; philosophy, 96, 97, 115, 118, 209, 224; pottery, 195–19, *passim*; social organization, 114, 115, 199, 202–4, *passim*; society, 96, 97, 100, 102, 116, 201, 214, 215, 235; tradition, 172, 173; villages, 21, 24, 96, 103, 154, 155, 156, 197, 198, 200, 237; world, 23, 97, 98, 99 (*fig.*), 100, 102, 103, 105, 109, 110, 111, 112, 116, 118, 154, 196, 198, 201, 203, 209, 223, 231
Tiller, Veronica, 171
time, 1, 2, 3, 4, 5, 7, 8, 12, 14, 15, 17, 24, 38, 41, 43, 49, 51, 53, 55, 62, 65, 67, 70, 72, 73, 78, 83, 84, 86, 93, 98, 102, 104, 105, 118, 128, 129, 131, 134, 136, 139, 149, 154, 176, 204, 218, 224, 225, 228, 231, 245, 250, 254; ancient, 15, 76, 216, 230, 256; of emergence, 3, 20, 37, 39, 42, 186; linear, 14; period, 5, 11, 19, 73, 86, 105, 156, 158, 162, 163, 167, 168, 178, 180, 183, 184, 190, 214, 223, 227, 232, 237, 242, 255; timeless, 1, 17
Titiev, Misha, 140
Tiwa: culture, 172; demographic exchange, 190; history, 178, 179, 184, 187; intermarriage, 186; language, 100, 185, 187; oral accounts, 187, 189; people, 64, 104, 166–191, *passim*, 204; society, 175; traditions, 182 (*fig.*); villages, 179, 180 (*fig.*)
Tosa, Francisco, 61
Tosa, Paul, 12, 20, 24, 61, 71
Toya, Chris, 71
traditional cultural properties (TCP), 82, 83
trail, 65, 69, 71, 75, 83, 87–92, 88 (*fig.*), 93, 162, 255. *See also* path, road

Tsama'owingeh, 110
Tsankawi (Prickly-Pear Cactus Gap Village), 155, 205, 206, 211, 213
Tsikumu, 107 (*fig.*), 110, 114 (*fig.*), 118
Tsipin'owingeh, 109, 111
Tsiregeh (Bird Place Village), 155
Tunyo (Spotted Mesa, also Black Mesa), 22, 153, 154, 155 (*fig.*), 156, 157, 160–63
Túuvakwā (Traditional Life-Renewal Place), 65
Turtle dance, 149
Twin War Gods, 154

Ulibarri, Juan de, 177
underworld, 2, 15, 39, 60, 62, 186
unmanned aerial vehicle (UAV), 161
Upham, Stedman, 5
Ute, 200, 226

Valles Caldera, 20, 21, 60, 71, 72, 73, 74, 75, 76
Vargas, Diego de, 22, 149, 150, 153, 156–57, 158, 159, 160, 160, 162, 163, 177, 190, 200, 233
vecino, 200, 224, 227, 228, 229 (*fig.*), 231, 232, 237; Coiota, 228; Comanche, 228; Navajo, 228; Pueblo, 228; ethnogenesis, 224, 225, 231
Villarreal, Jimmy, 236
Viarrial, Cordelia, 235
Viarrial, Feliciana Tapia, 235, 238
Viarrial, Fermin, 235, 238
Viarrial, Governor Jacob, 235
Vierra, Bradley, 160, 163
Voss, Barbara, 225

Wâavēmâ Archaeological Research Project, 71
Walker, Chet, 161, 163
Water Canyon, 158
Westmann, Orloff, 166, 167, 168, 171
Whatley, Bill, 71
wheat, 23, 195, 197, 198, 199–4, *passim*, 208 (*fig.*), 209, 210 (*fig.*), 211, 212 (*fig.*), 215, 216, 217, 218
White House, 43
White Painted Woman, 186
White Shell Woman, 171, 186, 188
Whitley, Catrina, 180
Willis, Mark, 161, 163
Wilshusen, Richard H., 14
Wissler, Clark, 4
Woosley, Ann, 183
Woven Stone, 2

Young, Jane, 84

Zárate Salmerón, Fray Gerónimo, 67
Zia Pueblo, 66, 153, 157
Zuni, 4, 13, 19, 64, 68; ancestors, 78, 86, 87; cultural advisers, 81, 83, 85, 89, 90, 91, 93; culture, 21, 26, 80; Cultural Resource Enterprise (ZCRE), 82; history, 81, 86, 92, 93; origin, 79 (*fig.*), 80, 85; people, 18, 21, 80, 83, 84, 85, 87, 89, 91, 92, 93; reservation, 92; Sword Swallowing Society, 90; traditional cultural properties, 80, 82, 83, 84, 85, 92; tribe, 8, 9, 15, 80, 87, 257; villages, 87, 89, 90
Zuni Pueblo (*Halona:wa*), 21, 70, 78, 81, 85, 86, 90, 254

AMERIND STUDIES IN ANTHROPOLOGY

Series Editor **Christine R. Szuter**

Trincheras Sites in Time, Space, and Society
Edited by Suzanne K. Fish, Paul R. Fish, and M. Elisa Villalpando

Collaborating at the Trowel's Edge: Teaching and Learning in Indigenous Archaeology
Edited by Stephen W. Silliman

Warfare in Cultural Context: Practice, Agency, and the Archaeology of Violence
Edited by Axel E. Nielsen and William H. Walker

Across a Great Divide: Continuity and Change in Native North American Societies, 1400–1900
Edited by Laura L. Scheiber and Mark D. Mitchell

Leaving Mesa Verde: Peril and Change in the Thirteenth-Century Southwest
Edited by Timothy A. Kohler, Mark D. Varien, and Aaron M. Wright

Becoming Villagers: Comparing Early Village Society
Edited by Matthew S. Bandy and Jake R. Fox

Hunter-Gatherer Archaeology as Historical Process
Edited by Kenneth E. Sassaman and Donald H. Holly Jr.

Religious Transformation in the Late Pre-Hispanic Pueblo World
Edited by Donna M. Glowacki and Scott Van Keuren

Crow-Omaha: New Light on a Classic Problem of Kinship Analysis
Edited by Thomas R. Trautmann and Peter M. Whiteley

Native and Spanish New Worlds: Sixteenth-Century Entradas in the American Southwest and Southeast
Edited by Clay Mathers, Jeffrey M. Mitchem, and Charles M. Haecker

Transformation by Fire: The Archaeology of Cremation in Cultural Context
Edited by Ian Kuijt, Colin P. Quinn, and Gabriel Cooney

Chaco Revisited: New Research on the Prehistory of Chaco Canyon
Edited by Carrie C. Heitman and Stephen Plog

Ancient Paquimé and the Casas Grandes World
Edited by Paul E. Minnis and Michael E. Whalen

Beyond Germs: Native Depopulation in North America
Edited by Catherine M. Cameron, Paul Kelton, and Alan C. Swedlund

Knowledge in Motion: Constellations of Learning Across Time and Place
Edited by Andrew P. Roddick and Ann B. Stahl

Rethinking the Aztec Economy
Edited by Deborah L. Nichols, Frances F. Berdan, and Michael E. Smith

Ten Thousand Years of Inequality: The Archaeology of Wealth Differences
Edited by Timothy A. Kohler and Michael E. Smith

The Davis Ranch Site: A Kayenta Immigrant Enclave in the Lower San Pedro River Valley, Southeastern Arizona
Rex E. Gerald, edited by Patrick D. Lyons

The Continuous Path: Pueblo Movement and the Archaeology of Becoming
Edited by Samuel Duwe and Robert W. Preucel